THE MAN WHO WOULD BE KING

ALSO BY KAREN ELLIOTT HOUSE

On Saudi Arabia: Its People, Past, Religion, Fault Lines—and Future

The Man Who
Would Be King

*Mohammed bin Salman and the
Transformation of Saudi Arabia*

KAREN ELLIOTT HOUSE

HARPER

An Imprint of HarperCollins*Publishers*

HarperCollins books may be purchased for educational, business, or sales promotional use. For information, please email the Special Markets Department at SPsales@harpercollins.com.

FIRST EDITION

Designed by Kyle O'Brien

Map by Noah Springer, copyright © 2025 Springer Cartographics LLC.

Library of Congress Cataloging-in-Publication Data has been applied for.

ISBN 978-0-06-339035-5

25 26 27 28 29 LBC 5 4 3 2 1

To the memory of my late brother, Larry Elliott, a world traveler who shared my deep interest in Saudi Arabia.

CONTENTS

Al Saud Rulers

KING ABDUL AZIZ AL-SAUD

Founder, The Third Saudi State, 1932 to present

Died 1953

King Saud

1953–64, Removed

CROWN PRINCE: FAISAL

King Faisal

1964–75, Assassinated

CROWN PRINCE: KHALID

King Khalid

1975–82, Died at 79

CROWN PRINCE: FAHD

King Fahd

1982–2005, Died at 84

CROWN PRINCE: ABDULLAH

King Abdullah

2005–15
Died at 91

Crown Princes

SULTAN	NAYEF	SALMAN
2005–11	2011–12	2012–15
Died age 83	Died age 78	Elevated to king

King Salman

2015–
Age 89 12/31/24

Crown Princes

MUGRIN	MOHAMMED BIN NAYEF	MOHAMMED BIN SALMAN
January–April 2015	April 2015–June 2017	June 2017–present
Removed age 69	Removed age 57	Appointed age 32

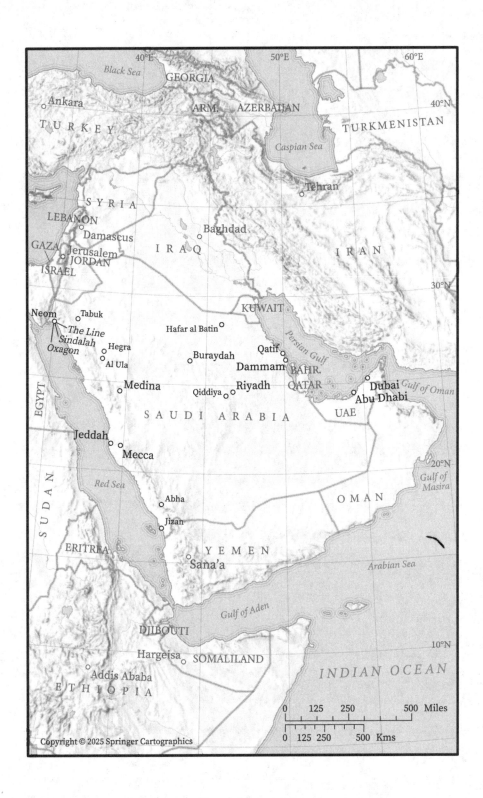

THE MAN WHO WOULD BE KING

The Race to Rule

For nearly half a century, there was almost no change in the stultifying kingdom of Saudi Arabia. One elderly monarch succeeded another. One failed five-year reform plan followed another. And still one more generation of young Saudis grew up wards of government and prisoners of religious restrictions.

But in less than a decade, things have changed dramatically. Today's Saudi Arabia is literally unrecognizable from that of 2016. Ubiquitous black-bearded religious police, who stalked the streets enforcing public piety at the expense of personal privacy, are gone from view. Gone too are the myriad restrictions on women, music, mixing of genders, and entertainment that so constrained the behavior of every Saudi, even those who dared sneak some freedom in the privacy of their homes. In 2024 for the first time, a Saudi woman dared to compete in the Miss Universe contest. A year earlier, a female astronaut was the first Saudi launched to the International Space Station.

Today at my hotel a Saudi man and woman stand side by side at the check-in desk and unquestioningly register a single woman like me, something once forbidden without official approval. Their gender-mixing not long ago would have landed both under arrest by religious police. When I take a helicopter ride at a popular tourist site, the pilot is a slight Saudi woman wearing crisp tan slacks and a white short-sleeved shirt. No black abaya. And her copilot is male.

The CEO of the Saudi stock exchange is a woman. A decade ago men refused even to speak to her when she called their firms as a rare female financial analyst.

And camel racing, Saudi's oldest sport dating from the seventh century, in 2024 for the first time featured female jockeys bouncing atop camels in the Crown Prince's Camel Festival. Some 21,000 riders competed for a $13 million prize. (At my first camel race in 1984, jockeys all were small boys and the winner took home a big water truck for supplying his desert tents.)

Soundstorm, a three-day music festival in Riyadh, draws nearly 700,000 exuberant Saudis dancing in the streets and cheering the music of international stars like Bruno Mars, H.E.R., Shakira, and Wiz Khalifa. Soundstorm is the Middle East's largest music event in a country where music was strictly forbidden before 2016. World-class boxers Tyson Fury and Francis Ngannou compete in "The Battle of the Baddest" before a sellout crowd of 30,000 Saudi men and women. Cristiano Ronaldo, the Portuguese soccer star now playing for a Saudi team, is just one of the global sports heroes I spot in attendance. In 2024 the kingdom hosted its first-ever female boxing match featuring two featherweights, Australia's Skye Nicolson and Britain's Raven Chapman.

Tens of thousands of Saudis old and young who can't afford such concerts or boxing matches nightly fill new Epcot-style theme parks to stroll a dozen pavilions of nations including Morocco, China, and Italy or pose in front of an Egyptian Sphinx. At another park, the very daring can take a spin 160 feet in the air atop "Drop Tower" before falling toward the ground at 70 miles per hour.

Teenage boys and girls sit side by side in Starbucks huddled over computers like their counterparts in the West. Gone is the strict prohibition on gender-mixing and with it the high wooden walls on wheels that restaurants once quickly deployed around tables to segregate families.

Saudi children under age five frequently speak English before Arabic as they are growing up on iPads, TV, and videogames viewing English-language apps and activities. Typical is a nine-year-old boy I met who is in "special Arabic" class at his school. Special Arabic, he explains, is "Arabic for those who don't speak Arabic."

All these changes—and the young change agent who is dramatically reshaping Saudi Arabia and its role in the world—are the subjects of this book. Change was anathema to the kingdom's rigid religious class. They insisted that Saudis pursue lives of virtue seeking to live exactly as their prophet fourteen hundred years ago. The modest beginning of modernization in Saudi Arabia in the 1970s was largely snuffed out when King Faisal, a reformer, was shot by a nephew; that young prince was avenging the death of his brother killed earlier by government police for protesting King Faisal's introduction of television to Saudi Arabia.

The next three kings were plagued by ill health or old age, leading to what Saudis call the "lost decades." By 2015 the kingdom was in crisis. Oil prices had fallen by half from a year earlier and the kingdom's hard currency reserves being used to fund government would be exhausted in five years.

Enter the new king—and his twenty-nine-year-old son. King Salman, then eighty, was well known to Saudis, having ruled Riyadh Province for nearly half a century before becoming crown prince in 2013. But young Prince Mohammed was largely unknown to his countrymen. Yes, he was the sixth of his father's dozen sons. But who was he? In a royal family governed by hierarchy this young man should have amounted to little. Yet he quickly amassed power. The story of what shaped him and how he took power is one purpose of this book. How he uses that power to reshape his nation is another focus. Most importantly, the book will examine the key question for the kingdom: Can his ambitious change agenda succeed? And how will his new Saudi Arabia impact the wider world?

Some of the answers to what shaped MBS lie in half a dozen interviews I've had with the prince since he came to power. Others lie in the stories of his royal cousins, his childhood friends, his ministers who work closely with him, and also the views of Saudi citizens of all walks of life I've spoken with over the years.

In meetings, the prince creates an informal atmosphere. My biggest surprises at our first meeting were the enormous size of his office, the complete absence of any retainers scurrying about, and his big friendly smile and informal dress; he was wearing a loose-fitting brown thobe, an ankle-length robe worn by Muslim men, with no bisht or head covering, revealing his dark hair tightly swept off his face. This is a young man who doesn't need sartorial trappings of power or regal airs because he has the real stuff. His conversational ease is sharply at odds with interviewing some of his powerful, now deceased uncles in the 1980s. Responses to my questions then came back stilted nonanswers as if from a heavenly throne. Retainers milled about, disrupting any opportunity for real engagement with their boss. With MBS, the translator and note taker are the only others in the room and they are barely seen and rarely heard as MBS speaks such good English now.

He does offer Arabic coffee, the first and common gesture of hospitality that opens every encounter with a Saudi. While tradition-ally, the host pours the coffee, the Crown Prince waves to a server holding a brass pot with a long, curved spout. The man pours a stream of translucent brown coffee, spiced with cardamom, into a tiny, gold-rimmed cup with no handle. I gingerly hold the hot cup between thumb and middle finger, and he pours a second one for the Crown Prince. We quickly gulp the hot liquid and decline refills by shaking our cups side to side. Time to get down to business.

The Crown Prince happily (or so it seems) responds to my ques-tions for two hours. In Saudi Arabia, Al Saud royals, even the king, never terminate meetings as seeming to dismiss a guest is impolite. When I end our meeting, the smiling, chatty prince walks me to the door of Iqrah palace, takes time to introduce me to some of his close advisers, and then hops into a golf cart and speeds off alone.

He smiles often and looks one directly in the eye offering fulsome explanations that always seek to persuade; he's a born marketer. He tends to preface answers with historical context but quickly moves to a direct response. In March 2023, he shared the news with me that in a week's time the kingdom would normalize relations with its nemesis, Iran. Shocked, I asked why now? "We have to face reality," he said matter-of-factly. "There isn't a high chance of the U.S. intervening in Iran." Without confidence in U.S. reliability, reducing tensions with Iran was necessary to protect the kingdom's massive investments in modernization.

He is neither condescending nor ingratiating. And he's confident enough to engage on any topic from Saudi foreign and defense policy to how he got an ulcer working for his "super strict" father; or his childhood allowance and favorite videogames. The only thing between an interlocutor and MBS is a pile of documents on the table between us. While a master of all things digital, he still prefers to digest important information the old-fashioned way—on paper.

Once in power, Crown Prince Mohammed bin Salman quickly replaced the kingdom's gerontocracy and chained its theocracy. He fashioned himself as the leader of young Saudis—some 65 percent of Saudis are under thirty years of age. He is promising a modern economy no longer dependent on oil and a life with boundless entertainment so long denied Saudis. Most young Saudis enthusiastically support MBS, as the Crown Prince is widely known. They grew up in a Saudi Arabia where fun was a dirty word according to their religious authorities. As a result, entertainment was forbidden. Yet, thanks to the internet, these young Saudis saw—and sought—lives like youth elsewhere in the world.

MBS is giving them that. A decade ago, the only music permitted was the haunting sound of the muezzin's call to prayer five times a day. Today he has ordered the volume on the call to prayer lowered and made the sound of pop music ubiquitous—in elevators, restaurants, cars, homes, and at sold-out concerts. Thousands of squealing teenage girls stormed the Riyadh airport for the arrival of Korea's popular BTS Boys a few years back.

So far, the Crown Prince is succeeding at bold change where earlier rulers failed even at incrementally confronting the kingdom's challenges. That's partially because the young generation of Saudis provides a supportive constituency for MBS. But it's also because MBS has shown the courage to confront religious authorities and royal relatives to force upon them his vision of a revitalized Saudi Arabia. Some earlier rulers talked of reforms but didn't act. MBS shows no such reluctance. He has a vision of a new, modern kingdom and is driving that with relentless urgency.

His vision, however, leaves little space for political opposition—or even debate. Hundreds of Saudis have been imprisoned, many on imprecise charges, but essentially for offending MBS in some way or another. These include a number of personal friends of mine who have literally disappeared without any official explanation.

Still, most Saudis seem willing to ignore the political repression and enjoy the absence of religious restrictions. Shortly after becoming deputy crown prince in 2015, Mohammed bin Salman banned the religious police from public places. Fear of being arrested by these men had made Saudi women virtually invisible in public during most of my decades visiting the kingdom. A tangle with the religious police could ruin a young woman's reputation and thus her chances of marriage. These days, religious police use megaphones to urge Saudis to go to prayer five times daily but they remain confined to their cars rather than using long sticks to threaten individual Saudis on the streets as in the past.

Today women are visible everywhere. They drive. They work in large numbers in both government offices and private companies. They are CEOs of the stock exchange, a large media company, and their own startups. They are ambassadors, astronauts, and beauty contestants. Visit any government building and women are crowding into elevators with men, seemingly oblivious to earlier strictures. These days, women both young and elderly go out at night in groups to fine restaurants, theme parks, and shopping malls without a male guardian in sight. They are free—even to leave the kingdom without a male relative.

Within two years, Mohammed bin Salman's power increased when he took the title of crown prince. He literally forced his cousin to relinquish the title by holding him captive all night. At dawn, the crown prince resigned his role to MBS. Five months later the new crown prince locked up scores of royal princes, some of his father's ministers, and a host of prominent Saudi businessmen in the Ritz-Carlton hotel in Riyadh to consolidate his hold on power.

The Ritz-Carlton coup was about much more than a dynastic power struggle. Previous Saudi rulers had allowed corruption to grow and spread like kudzu across America's Deep South. A flash flood in Jeddah in 2009 dramatized the costs of corruption to Saudi society. More than one hundred people died and thousands of homes were damaged because public funds intended for constructing drainage and sewage systems had been diverted to corrupt public officials. So pervasive was corruption that some ordinary Saudis I knew at the time took the sheets off their hospital beds. If the elite could steal from the state, so could they. By some reliable estimates, corruption annually was draining 30 percent of the Saudi government's spending into private pockets. Imprisoning the rich and famous was wildly popular with ordinary Saudis.

MBS achieved at least two goals with the Ritz lockup. He disgraced and disposed of the late King Abdullah's sons as potential challengers to his power. One paid the government a reported $1 billion of alleged ill-gotten money and was forced to resign his powerful post as head of the national guard, giving MBS control of all the kingdom's armed forces. Another of King Abdullah's sons remains in prison to this day.

But the Ritz-Carlton lockup was much more than a family affair. It was a terrifying signal to elite Saudis that the way of doing business in the kingdom was changing. MBS would level the playing field so that young Saudis without powerful connections could compete in a revitalized private sector he promised would create jobs the government no longer could afford to provide. Stanching corruption also would save government money needed to help fund MBS's lavish spending to transform the kingdom off oil and on to tourism, entertainment, logistics, manufacturing, and mineral mining.

The big question is whether the Crown Prince can succeed—and at what cost. The kingdom's huge spending on gigaprojects has so far failed to attract big foreign investment, forcing Saudi Arabia to risk its own capital. By early 2024, the government announced, some of its ambitious projects would be delayed due to budget deficits and a reluctance to undertake outsize borrowing. Despite the goal of weaning the kingdom off oil, revenues from energy still account for 62 percent of government revenue.[1] And oil prices have hovered around $82, far below the $96 a barrel price the kingdom needs to balance its budget, according to the International Monetary Fund. It's a flashing yellow light on the road to attaining MBS's vision.

Beyond reforming and revitalizing Saudi Arabia, the Crown Prince also intends to be a powerful voice on the world stage, shaping geopolitics to preserve peace and prosperity for his kingdom. Saudi First. Already he is actively reshaping the kingdom's relations with the United States, long its key ally, by growing closer to Russia and China. He's even trying to reorient Saudi relations with Israel and with Iran, long a Saudi nemesis. And in early 2025 he hosted high-profile talks between the U.S. and Russia to end Russia's war in Ukraine.

If reshaping the kingdom internally has proved difficult, re-shaping the Mideast and global politics is proving far more challenging. Not so long ago, MBS was on the verge of achieving his dream of diplomatic relations with Israel, allowing the two nations to enhance not just Mideast security but also to create a technological power-house in Neom, a $500 billion development in the north of Saudi Arabia, by pairing Israeli technology and Saudi money. This power-ful linkup would also create a key logistics hub connecting Asia to Europe. The Hamas invasion of Gaza blew up this plan.

Indeed, Hamas's invasion of Israel on October 7, 2023, has stunted MBS's race to develop his kingdom and project his power. All this has left Saudi Arabia's international relations in flux. The U.S. is seen as distracted and distrusted. As a result, MBS is actively courting better relations with all other big powers—Russia, China, Europe, and India. The world would be wise to watch this ambitious and determined prince and the assertive game he will play over coming decades to align Saudi Arabia with any power that can ben-efit his kingdom.

During most of my forty-five years visiting Saudi Arabia, see-ing the ruler was of little interest. Meetings with senior princes were royal audiences, not real interviews. But seeing this crown prince is always informative. He is in charge of absolutely every-thing in the kingdom, from policy to play. And nothing seems too small to escape his attention. During a recent visit to his sprawling office, as the Crown Prince pointed me to a seat, he gestured toward my black abaya and said, "You know you don't have to wear that." Having been ordered to my hotel a decade earlier by religious police for failure to cover my hair, this casual comment underscores the dramatic changes he has wrought.

But it also captures the candor, confidence, and capacity for at-tention to detail that are the hallmarks of the leader and the changes we are about to examine in this book.

CHAPTER ONE

Young Man in a Hurry

The tall, bearded young man was in a hurry. He had a government to restructure and a nation to reshape. But first, a royal uncle to bury.

Islam requires quick burial of the dead. Thus there was no surprise in the Kingdom of Saudi Arabia when the late King Abdullah's body was hastily wrapped in a white shroud and buried among his Al Saud predecessors in an unmarked grave in Riyadh's Oud cemetery on January 23, 2015.

But what came next was shocking. On exactly the same day Saudis were observing a day of mourning for the late king, the new king's twenty-nine-year-old son—who was neither crown prince nor deputy crown prince—assembled four individuals to advise him on streamlining his father's new government. At dusk on Saturday, he told them he wanted to eliminate a host of deliberative supreme councils and replace them with two decisive bodies. The older and more experienced ministers told the young prince that such sweeping reorganization would require time. "Take time," he said, "but decide tonight."

By sunrise Sunday, the group had concurred on eliminating a dozen supreme councils on this and that which had become burial grounds for making decisions under the late king, and agreed on only two new councils, one for economic issues and the other for security. In short order Mohammed bin Salman, the largely unknown son of King Salman, was named by his father to chair first one, and later both, powerful councils.

The following afternoon, Prince Mohammed bin Salman again summoned the group to discuss a new cabinet for his father replacing nearly a dozen people. Shortly after, King Salman announced his son's sweeping changes by issuing some thirty royal decrees. As the Pharaoh would say, "So let it be written. So let it be done."

This marked the public rise to power of a young prince most Saudis had never seen or heard. Saudi Arabia's citizens were accustomed to their leaders being elderly and largely inactive. For nearly half a century, kings of Saudi Arabia had been the ever more elderly sons of the kingdom's founder, Abdul Aziz al Saud, who sired forty-five boys by twenty-two wives before his death in 1953. Suddenly here was a twenty-nine-year-old *grandson* of Abdul Aziz. Who was he? How did he get power?

"We don't know him. He just appeared suddenly with no record," said an anguished Saudi conservative summing up a widespread public reaction to the young prince King Salman had named chief of his royal court in 2015.

In just two days Mohammed bin Salman had persuaded his father to create a government that would be far easier for one man to control. And he soon did. Unlike God, who created the world in six days and rested on the seventh, this prince did not pause. Within four months, he was deputy crown prince. A year later, he was crown prince after holding his cousin, Mohammed bin Nayef, captive all night to force his resignation from the role. Five months after that, he locked royal relatives and powerful Saudi businessmen in the Ritz-Carlton accusing them of corruption. He secured $100 billion from his Ritz "guests," freed some to house arrest, and sent others to prison.

Suddenly the largely unknown prince was both famous and infamous. A photo of his youthful face and cryptic *Mona Lisa*–like smile hung in every public building in the kingdom, alongside the stolid visage of his elderly father. The man behind the smile remained an enigma.

"A young man in a hurry," the *Economist* magazine labeled him in January 2016. In that same month, when I asked at my first meeting with him if he was indeed a young man in a hurry, he said, "I am young. And if I am in a hurry I will not miss any opportunity for my country. We've missed so many in the past,"[1] referring to the previous forty years when the kingdom was ruled by a series of infirm and elderly sons of Abdul Aziz, with no vision—and no life span to execute a vision even if they had had one.

One purpose of this book is to unmask what shaped this powerful prince who is relentlessly—and sometimes ruthlessly—reshaping the Kingdom of Saudi Arabia from a rigidly religious and traditionally tribal country into a modern nation he believes will be a top ten global economy by 2050. And without depending on oil revenue for its future prosperity. If so, it will be a total transformation of a country on the brink of crisis in 2015 when his father took power. It's a high-wire act worth watching because what happens in Saudi Arabia impacts the wider world's economic and political future.

Saudi Arabia isn't just another Arab monarchy. It is home to the two holiest sites in Islam. Moreover, the kingdom is home to nearly 20 percent of the world's proven oil reserves. Both these facts give the kingdom outsize influence and impact.

Beyond those long-established verities, new realities also are enhancing the kingdom's centrality to the world. Iran's theocracy, which long has coveted both the holy sites and Saudi oil, continues to pursue nuclear capability despite its surprising 2023 rapprochement with the kingdom. Moreover, the kingdom's traditional protector, the United States, is steadily losing interest and influence in the region as a revolving door of American presidents pledge to "pivot" to Asia.

The Crown Prince has already been in power longer than the last two U.S. presidents. And Mohammed bin Salman, now thirty-nine, could be ruling this critically important country for decades. His determination to play an independent and assertive role on the world stage to put "Saudi first" inevitably will impact America and the economic security of the world for decades to come.

As for his impact on Saudi Arabia, evidence of sweeping change is everywhere, especially to this visitor of forty-five years who traveled every corner of the kingdom, draped in my long black abaya, during its decades of religious rigidity. I vividly recall being ordered to my hotel by the religious police for talking with my Saudi male interpreter in a public coffee shop simply because a man and a woman who aren't related were strictly forbidden to mix. Or not long after being required by an Islamic judge in Qatif to cover my hair and face before he would speak with me on his decision to forcibly divorce a Shia husband from his Sunni wife. To the Wahhabi religious fundamentalists, a man shouldn't be in the presence of an unrelated woman. But if absolutely necessary, the woman must be an invisible black lump. If the sight of a woman arouses a man, the sin lies with the woman for tempting him.

The social and cultural changes MBS has unleashed with his ambitious—even grandiose—Vision 2030 are more visible each year. No country has undergone such dramatic change in so short a time. What was once a somnolent society that resembled a silent movie with infirm old men saying and doing nothing now is an IMAX movie on fast forward. Saudis who once focused only on life in the hereafter now focus on life in the here and now.

In meetings, the Crown Prince is confident, charismatic, and conversational. Speaking with him is easy; getting on his schedule is not. Nor is gaining entry to Irqah Palace, where he works. A palace driver takes me down a dark, desolate road with multiple big barriers that slow his way. After some minutes, we arrive at a small guardhouse where several Saudis with big guns approach our car.

Surprisingly, they don't demand my passport and match my face to the photo. After a short drive on a tree-lined road we enter the palace driveway, swarming with armed men. Inside, scores more men—security, aides, and ministers waiting to see MBS—are milling about now staring at a foreign woman in a black abaya. I am waved around the metal detector and deposited in a waiting room where men serve tiny cups of Arabic coffee. Like all visitors to MBS's large office, I must leave my purse and cell phone with guards. I can take only my notebook and pen. MBS strides quickly toward me, flashes a big smile, and shakes hands. His youthful informality is reinforced by the fact that he's wearing no scarf, thus revealing short, curly black hair tightly pushed straight back from his face.

Others who deal with the Crown Prince also emphasize his confidence and lack of pretention. Jared Kushner, who worked with MBS during the first Trump administration to repair a Qatar-Saudi rift and to push for Saudi-Israeli diplomatic relations, calls him a proud Saudi nationalist. "He takes me to the desert to tents with his crowd of 15 friends."[2] They joke and tease and treat the prince as just one of their group, he says. An Israeli American who spends much time in the Middle East recalls spending an afternoon with young MBS in Abu Dhabi a few years before his father became king. He, too, marveled at the prince's lack of pretention. "He was wearing Saudi national dress and listened intently to others, something royals rarely do," he said. Moreover, many Saudi princes—for instance Alwaleed bin Talal, the billionaire businessman—seek to impress foreigners with their Western sophistication, he noted. But not MBS. "He's very respectful but there's nothing submissive or deferential about it."[3]

MBS is a true son of the desert from prestigious lineage. His paternal grandfather, Abdul Aziz al Saud, founded this latest Saudi kingdom after three decades of tribal fighting. MBS's mother descends from the illustrious Ajman tribe, famous for its persistent opposition to Abdul Aziz. "No surprise, he got the best of the Bedouin values of his father and mother," says commerce minister

Majid al-Qasabi, who has known MBS since his teen years. Those values, the minister explained, are "authenticity, loyalty, and generosity. That is MBS."[4]

MBS is well aware of the enmity between his illustrious ancestors. When I interviewed his father more than a decade ago, the tall, lanky Prince Mohammed observed us silently until Prince Salman explained that tribal tensions make democracy impossible in Saudi Arabia. Each of the kingdom's several hundred tribes would form a party and chaos would ensue. MBS quickly agreed and pointedly underscored his father's conclusion by explaining that his maternal grandfather had killed his paternal grandfather's only full brother.

Indeed, MBS's maternal ancestor Dhaydan al-Hithlain's Ajman troops also wounded Abdul Aziz in a 1915 battle that killed his only full brother.[5] More than a decade later, al-Hithlain was treacherously murdered. Bearing a letter of safe conduct signed by Abdul Aziz, Al-Hithlain and eleven companions met with Abdul Aziz's regional governor's son. When he declined to stay overnight, saying his men would come looking for him if he didn't return, his host refused to allow him to leave. When the Ajman tribesmen did arrive, their chief's throat was slit along with those of his eleven companions.[6] Some Saudis see this treachery as parallel to that of the murder nearly a century later of Jamal Khashoggi, the *Washington Post* columnist invited to the Saudi consulate in Istanbul and then murdered in 2018.

Prince Mohammed is the firstborn of his father's six sons by his third wife. Prince Salman already had five sons (and one daughter) from his first wife. A brief second marriage produced a seventh son a year younger than MBS. In a hierarchical society like Saudi Arabia, the sixth son normally would have little rank or role. Yet somehow, MBS has emerged on top. How?

One answer is his mother. He says she pushed her sons to excel and not be seen as "also-rans" to the first wife's boys. "My mother pushed her children to work hard and excel," he explains in one of our conversations. The emperor Napoleon famously said, "The future destiny of a child is always the work of the mother." And that seems true for MBS.

Despite his mother's pushing, however, he was a shy and insecure boy. He recalls being so shy he couldn't perform in a third-grade play even though he had repeatedly rehearsed at school. On the day of the performance, with his father there to support him, MBS refused to take the stage. His father pleaded. MBS resisted. Speaking in front of an audience of strangers was just too intimidating, he recalls. His resistance is perhaps an early example of his determination to follow his own instincts. That trait has been consistent throughout his life.

Nowhere is that more visible than with his decision early in his father's rule to sideline the religious establishment. Indeed, to really understand the Crown Prince one needs to understand the rigidly religious era in which he came of age. Shortly before his birth in 1985, Saudi King Khalid allowed the religious establishment to impose all sorts of restrictions on Saudi citizens in hopes of preserving Al Saud rule. In November 1979, Islamic insurgents had seized the Grand Mosque in Mecca, leading the Saudi king to fear that the Al Saud monarchy might be toppled by religious clerics like Reza Pahlavi, the Shah of Iran, some eleven months earlier.

Having literally grown from boy to man in the straitjacket of rigid religious rules, MBS's repeated loosening of those bindings in recent years is more than government policy. It's personal. Like all young Saudis his age he grew up with no entertainment options. Movies and music were forbidden. Saudi TV primarily showed grim-faced religious scholars with long beards reading the Quran, or imams leading prayers in Mecca and Medina. So, like other boys his age, MBS's life consisted of soccer and videogames. Nintendo was his first. Then Neo Geo, a gift from his mother when he was six. The Neo Geo console still sits in his childhood bedroom at Al

Shati Palace in Jeddah. To this day, the Crown Prince acknowledges playing a videogame for half an hour each morning when he wakes.

While King Salman has a reputation for being close to the religious establishment, he clearly has allowed his son to curb its power over the kingdom. Interestingly, in a 2010 conversation with Prince Salman, then the governor of Riyadh, on change in the kingdom, I asked how the twenty-five-year-old MBS, seated near him, was different from him. Without explaining how, he seemed to accept differences. He responded by citing a hadith, or saying of the Prophet Mohammed, that admonishes a father not to force his son to be like him. Both father and son seem to have heeded Prophet Mohammed.

By sixth grade the timid prince had turned bold. By his account, he replaced his younger brother, Turki, as the leader of boyhood gatherings among his brothers and their friends. He also became something of a prankster, according to a family tutor. A British tutor of the prince and his brothers described to the BBC how then eleven-year-old MBS enjoyed seizing a walkie-talkie from his guards and disrupting class by making "cheeky remarks" about his teacher and cracking jokes between his brothers and the guards on the other end. "As the oldest of his siblings, he seemed to be allowed to do as he pleased," Rachid Sekkai, the tutor, told the BBC.[7]

As a boy, he seems also to have developed a sense that he "sat below the salt" in the royal family. He recounts to me receiving an allowance of 2,000 Saudi riyal a week (about $500) while in fourth grade. For most of us, that seems quite a generous sum for a young boy. Still, many of his princely cousins, he says, were receiving 20,000 Saudi riyal or $5,000 a week, which seems to have left MBS feeling decidedly underprivileged by comparison.

Moreover, Prince Salman, then the governor of Riyadh, vacationed with his first wife and family at a palace in Marbella, Spain. He visited MBS's mother and their boys at a hotel in Barcelona. "He felt a need to strive for distinction from an early age," says an associate. Indeed, his father spent little time with him as a boy, focusing more on his responsibilities as governor of Riyadh and his older sons, including Prince Sultan bin Salman, the Arab world's first astronaut, sent into space by the U.S. in 1985, the year MBS was born. "With older more accomplished brothers, it must have been hard for MBS to get his father's attention," Jamal Khashoggi mused to me over lunch in Riyadh in 2016. (A year later, frustrated that MBS forbade him to write, Khashoggi left for Washington, D.C.)

Indeed, the Crown Prince insists, and contrary to conventional wisdom among the Saudi populace, that he wasn't his father's favorite. "It's a misconception," he says. "I was not my father's favorite." He matter-of-factly names four of his siblings who he says rated higher in his father's affections. Perhaps such sentiments help explain MBS's constant striving.

One way he stood out in high school was by driving an orange Lamborghini. As a high school senior MBS was old enough to get his first car. His father urged his son to get a car like all the other boys had—luxury but low-key. MBS declined. He had saved money from gifts his uncles had given him on Islamic holidays and he was going to have the car he wanted even though it cost nearly $230,000. The pleasure didn't last long. Driving down Thalia Street, the Champs-Élysées of Riyadh, Prince Mohammed collided with another car and spun several times, leaving his car so damaged he had to call a friend for a rescue ride home.

Knowing that his father, who governed Riyadh at the time, would quickly hear about the accident, MBS rushed home to pre-empt the police report to dad.

Any conversation with MBS yields evidence of his innate competitiveness. For instance, despite his heavy workload and five young children, he describes spending a weekend at his farm challenging the Middle East champion of *Final Fantasy XVI*, a favorite videogame in which the heir to a fictitious throne seeks to retrieve a stolen crystal and discovers he is the "True King" destined to save the world from eternal darkness. The competitive prince acknowledges that his expert guest "won sixty percent of the time," but says he is "pleased" that he won 40 percent.

"If he loses at anything, he will stay up night and day to get better at it," says Prince Abdullah bin Bandar, a childhood friend and videogame partner who is now minister of the Saudi National Guard.

Some of the Crown Prince's close friends believe his boyhood addiction to videogames not only stoked his competitiveness but also fired his imagination. One close associate of the Crown Prince says videogames allowed his imagination and creativity to flow and led him to believe that anything possible in a videogame is possible in life. MBS believes videogames are good for the mind. "Math is training for the brain," he tells me in 2023. "Videogames squeeze the brain to think."

Indeed, his Vision 2030, which seeks to wrench Saudi Arabia's deeply conservative and long-sequestered society into the twenty-first century, is full of his grandiose, videogame futurisms. At the top of a long list is Neom, a $500 billion development nearly the size of Belgium that is located on the northern edge of Saudi Arabia where the Red Sea meets Egypt, Israel, and Jordan. It will feature an AI-driven linear city, "the Line," a high-rise mirrored structure running 110 miles long and standing 1,600 feet high— taller than the Empire State Building. The city will have no cars and no carbon emissions, powered entirely by renewable energy. Residents will travel by high-speed trains and flying taxis while enjoying glow-in-the-dark beaches and a fake moon to light the sky at night. One American businessman who knows MBS well said the prince seeks to avoid "incrementalism," which he believes is demonstrably failing to solve society's problems, and is thus eager to try bold new ideas.

All of this extreme modernity is intended to attract major Western companies to diversify the Saudi economy and reduce its financial dependence on oil. Most important, Neom is designed to create private sector jobs for the young Saudis whom the government can no longer afford to hire.

The Crown Prince also seeks to translate his gaming passion into jobs for young Saudis.

In 2022 he announced creation of a National Gaming and Esports Strategy, with ambitions to make Saudi Arabia the "global hub" for both gaming and esports by 2030. He's confident gaming and esports can create 35,000 jobs by then and generate $13 billion in revenue. His optimism that the kingdom can attract a worldwide audience for gaming events is based on the fact that in 2021 the kingdom's 21 million gamers (an astounding 89 percent of the Saudi population) generated $1 billion in revenue.[8]

If he was shy and insecure as a child, as a man he's supremely confident, driven and decisive, trusting above all his own instincts. Indeed, Crown Prince Mohammed bin Salman can be broadly defined by three qualities. First, a sense of self-confidence bordering on bravado. Second, relentless energy and drive almost unique in the modern history of Saudi Arabia, which slept through much of the twentieth century. Third, quick political instincts that underpin his decisiveness even though sometimes they lead him wrong, yet nonetheless continue to guide him.

Mohammed bin Salman definitely isn't a typical Saudi. Most every Saudi seeks to conform to societal norms and avoid standing out from a group. To be different is potentially to bring shame on your family or tribe. Whereas his late uncles ruled the kingdom through consultation and consensus among the senior sons after the death in 1953 of King Abdul Aziz, this crown prince is determined to act unilaterally and with little regard for tradition. When asked about his willingness—even eagerness—to stand out, he acknowledged the trait. "If you don't stand out you might as well disappear," he said. "If you see something to do, do it." Do it regardless of what others think.

Mohammed bin Salman finally captured his father's attention as a teenager. Prince Salman lost his two eldest sons to heart ailments within one year of each other. The grieving father's other older boys were busy with their families, but seventeen-year-old Prince Mohammed offered his father constant companionship. At that time in 2002, with the late King Fahd near death and his crown prince, the future King Abdullah, running the country, hardly anyone would have forecast power for Prince Salman let alone his sixth son. Two powerful brothers, Prince Sultan, minister of defense, and Prince Nayef, minister of interior, were in line ahead of Salman, who was then approaching forty years as governor of Riyadh, the capital and the most powerful of the kingdom's thirteen provinces. Prince Salman also headed the Al Saud family Descendants' Council, established to reach consensus among the dozens of surviving brothers and to discipline royal family members to deter embarrassing conduct.

Young MBS began to stick to his father, soaking up how to deal with fractious tribal leaders; learning which princes were guilty of which indiscretions; sitting through the many meetings his workaholic father conducted daily. All this learning later was put to use by the Crown Prince as he consolidated power against his royal relatives and subdued religious and tribal forces.

Asked why Prince Salman chose MBS for leadership, the Crown Prince's childhood friend Prince Abdullah bin Bandar offers a uniquely Saudi explanation. "In my opinion, the falcon owner knows the best falcon in his group," he says. Indeed, falcons have been prized by Bedouins for centuries for their courage and speed. A falcon can soar at 200 miles per hour in pursuit of its prey and dive for the kill with equal speed. Once used for hunting, falcons now are mostly a hobby of the rich.[9] MBS's speed and focus surely mimic that of a prize falcon.

"He was always ambitious," says his younger brother, Prince Khalid, a former ambassador to the United States and now defense minister. "He watched and listened to everything our father did."[10]

MBS's formal government career began in 2007, when he graduated second in his class at King Saud University Law School. Top law school graduates are recruited for jobs in the prestigious Bureau of Experts, a center that provides research and legal advice to the agencies of the Saudi Cabinet of Ministers. Issam bin Saeed, who headed the bureau in 2007, recalls interviewing MBS and other top law graduates. "He was smart, not pretentious and flexible, unlike some legal minds that believe one plus one equals two. But for him it could be one plus one equals three," he told me in 2023. "This means he thinks outside the box."[11]

The selection committee unanimously offered the young prince a job at Grade 6 like all the other new hires and a salary of 6,000 Saudi riyal, roughly $1,500 a month, less than his childhood allowance of $500 a week. "He stood out for his eagerness to learn," recalls Issam.[12]

The trouble came when Prince Mohammed was offered an "exceptional promotion" at the Bureau of Experts. King Abdullah barred his nephew from accepting, explaining that the promotion would look like nepotism. It was a somewhat ludicrous claim when at the time, the government was dominated by what surely looked like nepotism, since many ministers and other top officials were Al Saud royals.

The competitive prince was incensed, fearing that others would see the absence of a promotion as evidence he was failing. "It was upsetting that everyone got promoted except me; made me look like a failure," he tells me.[13] His father stepped in to suggest MBS work for him at the Riyadh governor's office, which reported to the Ministry of Interior. Ironically, MBS's boss at the ministry was Mohammed bin Nayef, his older cousin who a decade later would become his chief rival for power.

MBS had insisted in our first interview in 2016 that he wasn't competing with MBN, as Crown Prince Mohammed bin Nayef was known. He said he split his time between serving his father, the king, and his cousin, the crown prince, both more taciturn than he, and thus each favored delivering their messages through him. "Crown Prince Mohammed tells me I am the son he doesn't have," MBS told me then.[14] MBN has two daughters.

At the same time that King Abdullah was barring MBS's promotion, he also was seeking to rein in excessive government spending to distinguish his reign from that of his profligate predecessor, the late King Fahd. As a result, he wasn't nearly as generous with his half brother, Prince Salman, as King Fahd had been. Prince Salman found himself selling land to fund his family. A worried MBS told his full brothers their family was going to be poor if things kept up like this. So, as the eldest of these sons, he sought to help fund the family by starting several businesses. "MBS worked by his own self-reliance" to resolve this family's financial issue, says his brother, Prince Khalid. "It was one of the most significant moments of his life."[15] Prince Khalid indicates this is the origin of MBS's self-reliance mantra espoused to his countrymen in Vision 2030. (A Wall Street Journal investigation found MBS made money the way royals did for decades: He created companies and then used royal influence to steer lucrative government contracts to those businesses. There also were allegations of manipulating stocks on the Saudi exchange and rumors that MBS was briefed by an exchange official that his transactions were improper.)[16]

As MBS grew more confident, he also began to seek alliances with his powerful uncles. Explaining that he felt "isolated" as a young man, he began to build bridges to important members of the larger Al Saud family. Perhaps because of his sense of isolation, MBS was much more ambitious and driven than the average Saudi prince. Friends say that each time he saw an opportunity he captured it and then looked for another opportunity and captured that one too. He told me that in his early twenties he wasn't looking to be crown prince. "At twenty-one I didn't see being crown prince. I saw what I could do at twenty-two. Now I wear a Saudi hat so it's the country, not me, that charges at new opportunities."[17]

One opportunity he seized was to ingratiate himself with King Abdullah, the very royal who had blocked his exceptional promotion at the Bureau of Experts. The king also had angrily warned MBS's father to "keep your son on a short leash" after the prince, piqued at a judge for declining to issue title for a piece of land MBS had been given, allegedly mailed the judge a single bullet in an envelope. It was an early effort at the intimidation he practiced with the Ritz-Carlton lockup a decade later.

With confidence bordering on bravado, MBS set out to win his elderly uncle's approval. As he acknowledged in an interview, King Abdullah eventually decided to use Prince Mohammed to tackle tasks others didn't want to do. One of those was to dislodge the late King Fahd's wife from her palace in Jeddah. The palace, with an estimated value of $350 million, belonged to the Saudi government. King Abdullah's polite requests to the late king's wife to vacate went unheeded as his frustration rose at her persistent appropriation of government property. Enter MBS. He is said to have gone boldly to the widowed princess's palace and told her the king wanted her out. When she sought to dither as before, he pointed to a bus filled with servant women in her driveway and told his aunt, "These women will help you pack. Tonight at eleven p.m. all services to the palace will end." She promptly relocated to Paris.

MBS finally won King Abdullah's trust after he resolved a complex issue at the Ministry of Defense involving miscommunication between his father, then minister of defense, and the king. As usual, MBS studied the details. Then he offered a face-saving solution that led a grateful King Abdullah to name MBS to head Crown Prince Salman's defense office, something he had earlier refused to allow the crown prince to do. MBS already was heading the office of the crown prince. A year later, in addition to these two ministerial jobs, King Abdullah named MBS a minister of state.

The twenty-eight-year-old prince now held three ministerial rank positions, more than anyone in King Abdullah's government. "Without my work for King Abdullah, I wouldn't be in this position now," he told me in 2016 as deputy crown prince. "King Abdullah made me."

Indeed, there is a video from that time of a slim-faced, serious Prince Mohammed, formally dressed in a black and gold bisht, his head covered under a red and white checkered scarf, standing stiffly in front of the elderly King Abdullah, who is seated. The new minister of state is swearing his allegiance to the king. "I swear by almighty God to be faithful to my religion and my king . . . and to perform my duties with honesty and sincerity," intones Prince Mohammed.

The king responds, "May God help you to serve your religion, your country, and your Arab and Islamic nations." Then, pointing his right hand toward the prince, he adds, "God willing you will rule your land."

Some Saudis thought the elderly king was just being nice. Regardless of his intentions, he proved prophetic. In less than a year MBS was ruling the kingdom without yet being named king.

CHAPTER TWO

Kinder, Gentler Islam

For centuries, religion and the Al Saud have been inseparable partners in Arabia. The Al Saud have used religion to legitimize their rule and the Wahhabi religious establishment has used the Al Saud to preserve and promote its version of the one true Islam.

MBS has a very different idea on this ruling partnership. He has pushed to the background puritanical Islam and its laser focus on life in the hereafter in order to focus Saudis on resolving long-festering challenges confronting the kingdom right now. He and his generation have seen firsthand religious excess tolerated by his father's generation since a fateful day in 1979.

November 20, 1979, dawned like any other. A sea of humanity from all over the world knelt about the Kaaba in the Grand Mosque in Mecca, Islam's holiest site, as the imam concluded his blessing on the worshippers. But as he was offering final wishes for peace, gunshots rang out. Frightened worshippers spotted a young man brandishing a rifle surrounded by three other militants pushing their way toward the imam. The militants grabbed the imam's microphone. When he protested, one held a dagger to his neck with a bloodcurdling scream. Panicked worshippers fled for the exits of this stadium-sized mosque. But all fifty-one doors were chained closed. The huge crowd of men, women, and children were trapped.[1]

Dislodging the militants took the Saudi regime nearly two weeks and the assistance of French commandos deploying a deadly gas to immobilize the religious rebels. Some 170 militants were captured and sixty-three of them were beheaded in eight cities across the kingdom.[2] At least 1,000 soldiers, militants, and worshippers died in the two-week standoff at the Grand Mosque, according to independent observers.[3]

The nightmare at the Grand Mosque was over. But the nightmare of rigid religiosity that followed gripped Saudi Arabia for nearly four decades. It is still being dismantled by King Salman and his son, Crown Prince Mohammed, thirty-nine, who grew up chafing under the domination of religious rules and restrictions. The royal family, fearful of being overthrown like the Shah of Iran, had quickly agreed to impose all sorts of religious restrictions on society to preserve their rule, a pact made with Islam's senior Wahhabi clerics.

MBS isn't a tool of the Saudi religious establishment. Yes, the Quran remains the kingdom's constitution, but religion is between Allah and the worshipper. Government isn't Allah's judge and enforcer on earth.

The tight grip of religion that followed the Grand Mosque incident and its loosening today is simply the latest chapter in a centuries-old tale of partnership between the Al Saud and conservative Islam. Understanding this long partnership is essential to understanding the historical and royal constraints MBS seeks to escape as he reshapes Saudi Arabian society and economy.

From the founding of the first Saudi state nearly three centuries ago, the Al Saud have used religion to help them win and then maintain control of Arabia. Fighting in the name of Allah has more than once proved successful in subduing other tribes to the Al Saud. Over the centuries, the Al Saud have sometimes pulled religion close, as after the Grand Mosque incident, and at other times sought to distance their rule from Wahhabism, as now. But at all times, priority number one for the regime is its survival. That remains MBS's priority too. Right now he believes young Saudis seek freedom from the harsh hand of religious rigidity. So, to preserve Al Saud rule, he is pushing religious fundamentalism into the background and replacing it with Saudi nationalism as the new glue binding Saudis to their ruler.

Ironically, it was excessive religious fervor that helped destroy the first Saudi state. The Al Saud rulers in the grip of Wahhabism criticized their Ottoman neighbors for failing to sufficiently enforce sharia law and sacked the Iraqi town of Karbala, destroying the tomb of the Prophet's grandson. The Ottoman ruler had had enough. He sent an army against the Al Saud, destroying its capital at Diriyah, near today's Riyadh, and carrying its leader to Constantinople, where he was beheaded. His body, gruesomely holding his severed head, was displayed for three days, then ignominiously tossed into the Bosphorus.[4]

The decision to again pull religion close on that November morning in 1979 also proved costly to Saudi Arabia. While it preserved Al Saud rule, it helped spawn more radical Islamists in Saudi Arabia. While Al Qaeda was dominated by Egyptian Muslim Brothers, not Saudis, it was fifteen Saudi hijackers who led the dramatic attack on September 11, 2001, on the World Trade Center and the Pentagon, and possibly on the U.S. Capitol until United Airlines flight 93 was brought down by passengers in Pennsylvania, killing all onboard. All that complicated Saudi relations with Americans to this day and cost the U.S. between $4 trillion and $6 trillion in failed wars against terrorism in Iraq and Afghanistan.[5]

On that November morning in 1979, Saudi religious clerics actually felt sympathy for the militants occupying the mosque. The imam's sermon that very morning lamented the kingdom's moral decay. And the revolt's leader had studied with the imam he now held captive. His goal was to end what he saw as the Al Saud's tolerance of infidel innovations like women working and mixing with men or the government's tolerance of Shias, a sect of Islam that he and his fanatics saw as heretics, not Muslims.

Regardless, the kingdom's most respected religious scholar, Sheikh Abdul Aziz bin Baz, concluded the regime must be preserved to avoid chaos in Saudi Arabia. So the other senior religious scholars signed a fatwa, or religious ruling, reaffirming the Al Saud's Islamic legitimacy. But now, they insisted, the Saudi rulers must live up to those religious obligations. No more movies. No more alcohol. No more women on television. No more gender-mixing anywhere. No more soccer to distract youth from studying Allah's holy Quran. And the regime must spend its growing petrodollars to spread the true Wahhabi Islam worldwide.

Almost overnight, everything changed in Saudi Arabia. During my first visit in 1978, I attended a dinner at Oil Minister Ahmed "Zaki" Yamani's home in Jeddah where men and women mixed, alcohol was plentiful, and after dinner the minister and his guests watched a cable feed of the 1978 World Cup soccer final between Argentina and the Netherlands. Just the sort of evening deplored by religious clerics.

A year after the attack, when I visited Najran Province on the Yemen border, I was asked by the governor's wife to trade my knee-length skirt for a long one she provided before meeting with her husband and his men. A year after that, I was permitted to meet the head of Saudi intelligence in Riyadh wearing a knee-length skirt. But when I rose to depart, his assistant handed me a long black silk abaya and scarf to cover my body and hair. "You must wear these or I can't drive you to your hotel in the front seat of my car," he said. I've worn an abaya while in the kingdom ever since.

By the time Crown Prince Mohammed was born in 1985, the

religious grip had tightened further. Videogames like Pokémon were banned for promoting blasphemy and laziness. Importing dolls was banned because creating any human image is forbidden in Wahhabi Islam as idolatry. The religious police closed mixed beaches, began to smash windows of photographic studios, and sought to prevent any Christian celebrations. The ulama protested the photographs of royal rulers who hung in every building in the kingdom. Such images were forbidden, as no one but Allah should be worshipped. Some religious officials even blacked out the face of the Saudi king on paper currency to protest images.

As noted, the marriage of the Al Saud and religious fanatics is centuries old. Nearly three hundred years ago, when Arabia was nothing but harsh desert inhabited by wild and warring tribes, Mohammed al-Saud, leader of one such tribe, discovered something as potent as Aladdin's magic lamp. That "magic" was a fanatical preacher, Mohammed ibn Abd al-Wahhab, who was determined to return Arabia to the pure Islam of Prophet Mohammed a millennium earlier. The sheikh preached an austere Islam stripped of any innovations since the Prophet's time. Alcohol, tobacco, and shaving were strictly forbidden. Prayer five times daily was strictly enforced. Even marking the grave of a dead loved one was forbidden as veneration of someone other than Allah. In short, he demanded strict monotheism and rejected any practice not supported by the Quran or Islamic Hadith. Back to the Islam of the Prophet, was Sheikh Abd al-Wahhab's demand.

By the time Mohammed al-Saud met Sheikh Abd al-Wahhab in 1744, the sheikh was fleeing for his life, having destroyed the tomb of one of the Prophet's companions and stoned to death a woman accused of adultery. This religious excess didn't bother Mohammed al-Saud. He heard the preacher's call for Islamic jihad as a golden opportunity to use religion to trump his tribal enemies and conquer Arabia. The two teamed up. Sure enough, the Al Saud sword, wielded in the name of religion rather than mere tribal conquest, proved triumphant. Their cooperation led to the founding of the first Saudi state in 1745.

Despite the subsequent destruction of that first Saudi state by the Ottomans in 1819, another Al Saud prince escaped capture and founded a second Saudi state in 1824. To preserve his rule, Turki bin Abdullah al-Saud carefully avoided provoking the Ottomans with any acts of religious intolerance. But he was ambushed and assassinated by a sword-wielding cousin. If religious excess doomed the first Saudi state, family infighting destroyed the second in 1891. That year the Al Rashid tribe defeated the divided Al Saud, ending its rule until the return of Abdul Aziz al-Saud, MBS's grandfather, in 1902.

Aware of this family history, MBS moved quickly upon taking power to tackle both threats: he curbed fundamentalism by containing the religious police and he deposed and put under house arrest powerful princes who might challenge his rule.

Seeking to revive Al Saud rule and with the boldness that would mark his grandson MBS, Abdul Aziz sneaked into Arabia from exile in Kuwait in 1902 and launched a predawn raid at Masmak, a mud fort still standing in Riyadh today. (MBS has made Masmak a historic tourist site, with displays inside detailing the history of Al Saud control of Riyadh.) Abdul Aziz's men successfully murdered the Al Rashid governor and reconquered Riyadh.

Once again he used religion just as his ancestors had to help the Al Saud reconquer Arabia. He convinced the Bedouin to congregate in agricultural villages and adopt a sedentary life focused on puritanical Islam promoted by Mohammed ibn Abd al-Wahhab. The imam taught that belonging to the umma, or community of believers, took precedence over all other social bonds, including tribe. Anyone who made a judgment based on anything other than the Quran was a nonbeliever.[6] Still, it took Abdul Aziz thirty years to subdue and unite warring tribes under his rule. In 1932, he announced the creation of the Kingdom of Saudi Arabia.

This third Saudi state has been by far the most successful. Abdul Aziz established the combination of cruelty and cunning that marks his grandson's current rule. Moreover, he brought his kingdom from abject poverty to oil wealth in the late 1930s and established in 1945 an essential security relationship with the U.S. Abdul Aziz, seeking security for Saudi Arabia, met President Franklin Roosevelt, who was seeking reliable oil supplies to undergird America's new global leadership role after World War II. The two leaders laid the foundation for decades of U.S.-Saudi cooperation on oil for security.

Abdul Aziz was a shrewd man who knew how to use religion to build his kingdom but also, like his grandson, how to stand up to the religious when their zealotry threatened his rule. When his Ikhwan warriors sought to spread fundamentalist Wahhabism by invading Iraq against the wishes of the British, Abdul Aziz crushed them in 1929. He depended on Britain for cash to fund his rule in the days before oil revenue. Using force to keep followers in line is an Al Saud practice repeated by his grandson. As noted, Crown Prince Mohammed early in his rule harshly confronted both religious policemen and powerful cousins to tighten his grip on power.

If religion is the first source of Saudi survival, the second is money. Abdul Aziz understood this well even in the pre-oil era, when he had very little of it. Until the discovery of oil in 1938, his only sources of modest income were a tax on pilgrims making the annual hajj to Mecca; the *zakat*, an annual tax paid by Muslims on their wealth and assets as required by the Quran; and his small subsidy from the British.

"Neither I nor my ancestors have kept a chest in which to hoard money," he told one of his ministers. "In peace I give all, even this cloak, to anyone who may need it. In war I ask and my people give all they have to me."[7]

By the 1930s the cost of government salaries, an army, and payments to tribal leaders to maintain loyalty, plus small expenditures for nation-building such as installing radio and telegraph stations and creating a water supply for townspeople, had left Abdul Aziz essentially broke. So desperate was he that in 1933, for only 50,000 pounds (about $250,000), he sold Standard Oil of California, which had struck oil in Bahrain a year earlier, a concession to drill in Saudi Arabia. "Put your faith in God and sign," he instructed his finance minister.

In 1938, Standard Oil found billions of barrels of oil beneath the kingdom's Eastern Province. The king's first royalty check was $1.5 million. He was so delighted he led a caravan of two thousand people in five hundred cars from Riyadh to the oilfields to turn the tap and allow the first Saudi oil to flow for export.[8]

Succeeding Al Saud monarchs have lived luxurious lifestyles funded by oil. That flood of oil revenue quadrupled after the kingdom embargoed oil sales to the U.S. and other Western supporters of Israel in its October 1973 war with Egypt. By January 1974, oil prices had jumped from $3 a barrel to $12.[9]

As oil prices rose, Saudi Arabia decided to take full control of Aramco, its national oil company, and in 1980 bought out its U.S. owners. Saudi Aramco now is the most profitable company in the world, posting $159 billion profit in 2022.[10] In that year, Aramco also overtook Apple as the most valuable company, with a valuation of $2.43 trillion.[11] MBS shocked his countrymen by selling 1.5 percent of Saudi Aramco on the Saudi stock exchange in 2019 to secure $29.4 billion for the Public Investment Fund (PIF) to invest in the Saudi economy.[12]

As the kingdom's riches grew in the 1980s and '90s, its rulers began to stray from the bargain struck in 1979 with their religious partners to protect and promote fundamentalist Islam. Religious conservatives felt betrayed.

They saw an opportunity to act in 1990. That year, Iraqi dictator Saddam Hussein's troops invaded Kuwait and the frightened Saudi regime of King Fahd welcomed 500,000 U.S. troops to protect the kingdom and its oil installations from potential attack. The decision was approved by the religious establishment of senior ulama.

But foreign troops on Saudi soil outraged religious fundamentalists. Allah forbids infidels in the sacred land of the two holy mosques, they insisted. This group of political Islamists saw an opportunity to build their influence around an issue that was deeply troubling to many Saudi Muslims: American troops in Saudi Arabia, and worse yet, male and female U.S. soldiers working together in a land where religious authorities strictly forbade gender-mixing. The religious authorities were preaching one thing and practicing another in approving U.S. troops in Saudi Arabia, the conservative Islamists asserted.

They boldly dared to advise King Fahd of his alleged religious errors in a "Memorandum of Exhortation." Clearly, they sought not just control of public piety but a political role as well. Finally, King Fahd had enough. To curtail the Islamist movement, in 1994 he jailed two prominent leaders—Safar al-Hawali and Salman al-Awdah. (Both were freed five years later, in 1999.)

Given that recent history with political Islamists, it's not surprising that MBS today sees Islamists such as the Muslim Brotherhood as his major internal threat. In a bit of déjà vu, he has ordered both these same men rearrested (along with several other religious scholars) and Salman al-Awdah faces the death penalty.

Over the years as Saudi transitioned from abject poverty to abundant petrodollars, the kingdom became a welfare state. Though Saudis paid no taxes, the government provided widespread, if often poor-quality, services, from free education and health care to water and electricity and, of course, cheap energy. Increasingly, Saudis, who once worked in menial jobs at the national oil company, Aramco, or as day laborers in Palestine or Iraq to earn a living, began to refuse manual labor, preferring to work for the ever-expanding government sector, where hours were short and job security guaranteed for life. As a result, development of the kingdom fell to highly skilled and highly paid foreign workers while menial labor was left to unskilled, low-paid foreigners imported from Pakistan, Bangladesh, or Yemen. By the 1980s Saudi Arabia was like a first-class hotel: Saudis checked in at birth and were served by others for life, with government paying the tab.

"By the 1990s we became a society of two maids and one driver," says Dr. Ibrahim Babelli, deputy minister of planning and economy. Children no longer had chores. School became a place to have fun and escape the boredom of home, not to learn, he continued. "The generation under thirty-five feels entitled to support. They don't want responsibility. Just a comfortable life."[13]

But by the beginning of King Salman's reign, Saudis of all ages were dispirited and fearful of their future. Decades of economic stagnation and religious suppression had left society more sullen than rebellious. Islam teaches that all Muslims must obey Allah and their earthly ruler whose legitimacy comes from enforcement of Islamic law. So, obedience is almost instinctive. Therefore, most Saudis don't long for democracy but merely for transparency and accountability from their government. They weren't accustomed to much of either for decades.

After King Abdul Aziz's death in 1953, a succession of his sons has lacked their father's vision and cunning; they have been spenders, not builders.

King Saud, his first successor, literally bankrupted the kingdom during his eleven-year rule. Finally, his brothers banded together to remove him. His successor, King Faisal, fifty-eight, is widely seen as the most admired Saudi monarch, launching the kingdom's first modernization effort in the early 1970s. His reforms were cut short when a nephew shot him in 1975 to avenge the killing of his brother protesting King Faisal's introduction of television to the kingdom.

Then came a succession of ill and infirm rulers. King Khalid, sixty-two, a reluctant monarch, gave authority to his crown prince,

Fahd, who succeeded him in 1982. King Fahd, who enjoyed his yacht and palace in Marbella, suffered a debilitating stroke in 1995, leaving rule essentially in the hands of his crown prince and half brother, Abdullah. By the time Abdullah became king in 2005, he was eighty years old. Beloved as a kindly man, his timid efforts to curb the influence of the religious establishment and to expand opportunity for women were largely unsuccessful. During his decade of rule, a growing number of Saudis were fed up with the hypocrisy of royal rulers using religion to cage Saudis while flaunting profligate lives themselves.

Religion, once a pillar of stability, became a source of division. Both modernists and religious conservatives grew offended by the Al Saud's exploitation of religion to support its political prerogatives, and the accommodating flexibility of the religious establishment eroded its credibility. The establishment scholars decried infidels in the land of the two holy mosques yet had supported American troops in the kingdom in 1990 to save royal rule. Similarly, the scholars condemned mixing of men and women and deployed religious police to enforce the prohibition on ordinary Saudis, yet acquiesced in 2009 when the late King Abdullah opened a richly endowed university near Jeddah where Saudi men and women mixed with each other and with foreign infidels. And, of course, the religious authorities had long accepted all sorts of heresies, including movie theaters and women driving at the large and largely isolated compound of Saudi Aramco, the national oil company, which almost alone funds the Saudi government. Sin in the company that funds the kingdom—including privileges for the religious establishment—apparently was permissible.

As a result, during the decade 2005 to 2015, even the balm of money wasn't enough to blind Saudis to the decay rotting the very foundations of their society and threatening their future and that of their children. Islam as preached was not practiced. Jobs were promised but not delivered. Corruption was rampant, entrapping almost every Saudi in a web of favors and bribes large and small, leaving even recipients feeling soiled and resentful. If, for example, a female teacher sought reassignment to a different school, rather than wait months for the bureaucracy to decide, she could bribe an Education Ministry official. A satellite dish bringing foreign influences was illegal but nearly every Saudi home had one. Powerful and powerless alike were seeking to grab whatever they could get, turning a society governed by supposedly strict sharia law into an increasingly lawless one, where law was whatever the king or one of his judges said it was—or whatever people felt they could get away with.

Corruption was prolonged, pervasive, and publicly known. Saudi princes, who received government stipends ranging from $250,000 for a grandson of the founder down to $100,000 for a great-grandson,[14] used their contacts to procure lucrative contracts; some sons of Abdul Aziz, like Prince Sultan, the defense minister, were alleged to fence off big tracts of government land for personal use and sale. On a visit to Hail, a poor province in the kingdom's northeast struggling to find public land to build new schools, King Abdullah, by prearrangement with one of his nephews, asked who owned all the vast vista of land before him. Prince Sultan, sitting next to the king, was on the spot. The land is "all yours," the defense minister said. The king accepted, and gave the governor of Hail land to build new schools.

All this was widely known to Saudis. For the first time, the internet allowed the young generation—65 percent of Saudis are under thirty—to view what was going on at home and abroad. These young people were aware of government inefficiency and of princely corruption and of the fact that 40 percent of Saudis lived in poverty[15] and at least 60 percent couldn't afford a home.[16] They also knew that 40 percent of Saudi youth between twenty and twenty-four were unemployed[17] at the age most men would like to marry if they could afford the "bride price," or dowry. And they knew that

90 percent of all workers in the private sector were foreigners[18] whom business owners, often including Al Saud princes, exploited for low wages. All these things they communicated with each other on the internet.

Moreover, almost all Saudis lived dual lives. Outside the kingdom, those who traveled saw and lived normal lives only to return to a life of restriction and duplicity in their homeland; one standard preached, another practiced by their religious authorities.

Saudis, undereducated and indolent, sat idly by rather than work for what they regarded as slave wages for menial jobs. If all too many Saudi men wouldn't work, educated women often couldn't work because gender-mixing was forbidden and strictly enforced by the religious police. One Saudi mother whose daughter wanted to work in interior design in 2010 said she just couldn't allow it. While there were religiously mandated separate office areas for men and women, she feared that the two groups at some point would mix to discuss work. Should a religious policeman see them, her daughter's reputation would be ruined, destroying any chance of a marriage, she told me.

These young, internet-savvy Saudis were breaching the walls that had been so carefully constructed over decades by the regime to ensure their near total dependence on Al Saud protection and largesse. Thanks to the internet, these young Saudis now knew they were living medieval lives compared to their contemporaries in the Arab Gulf and in the West.

Mohammed bin Salman knew it too. One of the first acts of MBS and his father in 2016 was to tether the religious police.

"I don't want to waste my time," Prince Mohammed told *Time* magazine in 2018. "I am young. I don't want 70% of the Saudi population to waste their lives trying to get rid of this. We want to do it now," he said, explaining the abrupt end to conservative religious domination in the kingdom.

So let it be written. So let it be done.

CHAPTER THREE

The Path to Power

Prince Miteb bin Abdullah, head of the powerful Saudi National Guard and son of the late King Abdullah, was summoned to King Salman's palace in Riyadh late one November night in 2017. Upon arrival, he was summarily stripped of his military command, accused of corruption, and detained in the Ritz-Carlton hotel, the most luxurious accommodation in the capital and soon its most infamous. He was only the first. His younger brother, a former governor of Riyadh, was also forcibly dispatched to the Ritz.

Throughout the night a succession of other prominent royals, cabinet ministers, and wealthy businessmen were similarly summoned, charged with corruption, and ensconced at the Ritz. The detainees included the kingdom's richest and most famous royal, Prince Alwaleed bin Talal, chairman of Kingdom Holdings with stakes in prominent international companies like Citigroup, Twitter, Lyft, and the Four Seasons Hotels & Resorts.

Before the night was over, another young prince, the deputy governor of Asir Province, died in a mysterious helicopter crash along the Yemen border. Significantly, Prince Mansour bin Mugrin was a son of Prince Mugrin, whom King Salman deposed as crown prince soon after taking power. While government explained that the prince was inspecting the border when his chopper went down, some skeptical Saudis surmised he might have been trying to flee.

While Al Saud infighting is centuries old, this roundup of royals shocked the Saudi populace. The government explained the arrests as a campaign to root out corruption. Before the arrests, King Salman issued a royal decree forming a new committee chaired by Crown Prince Mohammed to combat corruption "by some weak souls who have put their own interests above the public interest in order to illicitly accrue money." He granted the new committee extraordinary powers of arrest, travel bans, blocking money transfers, and any precautionary measures necessary to seize and retrieve illicit holdings procured through corruption.

The big winner of the night was MBS. Stripping Prince Miteb of his command of the National Guard removed the last major obstacle to MBS's ascension. Guard forces were the only military in the kingdom not already under the king and Crown Prince Mohammed's control. He was defense minister from the outset of his father's reign and had removed and replaced Crown Prince Mohammed bin Nayef, who controlled the Interior Ministry's troops, six months ahead of this royal roundup.

Mr. Everything, as Saudis called MBS, was now Mr. Impregnable.

The night also brought revenge for King Salman. As the designated disciplinarian of Al Saud princes for decades, Salman saw firsthand the transgressions of his brothers and their sons. He inherited the task of family disciplinarian upon the passing of his half brother, Mohammed bin Abdul Aziz, famous for ordering the death of his own granddaughter in 1980 for sneaking out of the kingdom for a tryst with her boyfriend. The incident was immortalized in the British documentary *Death of a Princess*.

King Salman's Ritz-Carlton punishment of prominent princes was mild compared to that of his brother, though far more massive in the numbers punished. Salman had been humiliated by the late King Abdullah and his chief of the royal court. King Abdullah had slashed the income provided Prince Salman. The chief, Khalid al-Tuwaijri, had in the late king's name routinely humiliated Prince Salman by such indignities as denying him use of government aircraft and maneuvering to block MBS's rise to power. Now both Khalid al-Tuwaijri and the late king's sons were in the Ritz, charged with corruption.

Needless to say, the news that the kingdom's most prominent elite were in prison—and in such a luxurious prison at that—was sensational at home and abroad. At home, most Saudis were delighted to see corruption countered from the very top of power. "We show them all the files that we have, and as soon as they see those, about 95 percent agree to a settlement," MBS said, adding that 1 percent establish innocence and are freed while some 4 percent insist on going to court to fight the charge of corruption.[1]

MBS seemed to be imitating the sage advice of Singapore's Lee Kuan Yew, famous for running a squeaky-clean country among rampantly corrupt Southeast Asian neighbors like Malaysia and the Philippines. "To clean the stairs, start at the top," Lee once quipped. Starting at the top allowed MBS to intimidate royals who might oppose him and to insulate himself from future threats to his power.

"MBS killed so many birds with this one stone," said a Saudi who worked with a prince of the Ritz roundup. "He is sending a message to the royal family, 'Don't raise your head.' And he is signaling the public, 'I am Robin Hood, cleaning the country. Your future investments here will be pure.'" If so, that signal was garbled: In reality, his actions frightened investors both foreign and domestic. Foreign direct investment in Saudi Arabia hit a record low of $264 million in the fourth quarter of 2017 after the lockup.[2] Capital flight by Saudis totaled $80 billion in 2017 and another $64 billion in 2018.[3]

At the start of King Salman's reign, most Saudis had been eager for some change. But the pace and scope of actions by MBS was wrenching. Evolution might be welcome but rapid revolution was frightening. By the close of 2017, both proponents and opponents of MBS felt they were spinning on an out-of-control merry-go-round. Unable to get off, some were squealing with delight, but most with fright.

The Ritz-Carlton arrests pretty much ended any talk of royal revolt against MBS. In 2016, Prince Miteb had complained to me that his younger, inexperienced cousin had invaded Yemen without even alerting him—let alone consulting him—even though his National Guard troops would inevitably be drawn into patrolling the Saudi-Yemen border. Similarly, the late Prince Talal bin Abdul Aziz, MBS's uncle, had told me that the surviving sons of Abdul Aziz intended to go talk to King Salman to seek justice. "Is this the country of MBS only?" he had asked rhetorically. "We need Salman to open his eyes and his heart to his brothers and take us out of the current quagmire."[4]

A group of family members are reported to have written the king a letter outlining their concerns with his son delivered by the king's sister. King Salman is said to have replied that MBS is his choice. When the king dies, the family will have an opportunity for a new choice. The right of a Saudi king to name his crown prince is something Salman had defended before in 1991, when his brother Sultan, then minister of defense, called all of his full brothers, the so-called Sudairi Seven (all sons of Abdul Aziz by one mother), and their older sister together in Italy to urge their brother, King Fahd, to remove Crown Prince Abdullah. Their elder sister supported the move. Prince Salman is said to have insisted that this decision rested with King Fahd alone. King Fahd then told his brothers and sister, "Abdullah is a good man. Don't play with fire."

Royal infighting accelerated in the waning days of King Abdullah's reign. Some of his brothers insist he sought to control succession from the grave by naming Prince Mugrin, the first-ever deputy crown prince. His intention, they say, was to block the future king, Salman, from being able to name his son, Mohammed, as crown prince. When

Salman ascended to rule, Prince Mugrin would rise from deputy crown prince to crown prince.

Sure enough, when Salman became king, Prince Mugrin became crown prince. Upon Abdullah's death, King Salman was handed a letter said to contain the late king's dying wish that his brothers agree to name Muhammed bin Nayef as the new deputy crown prince, replacing Mugrin. According to aides, at least one of the late King Abdullah's sons believes this letter was forged by his chief of the royal court, Khalid al-Tuwaijri, who felt MBN would be more likely to protect him from the corruption charges he feared would come in a post-Abdullah reign, having used his role at the royal court to fabulously enrich himself. That wish, whether genuine or forged, was honored by King Salman.

If King Abdullah had hoped to block MBS from power, paradoxically his creation of the deputy crown prince job merely provided an on-ramp for him. The new king fired Crown Prince Mugrin, promoted MBN to the role, and, taking advantage of the late king's creation of the deputy crown prince position, named MBS to that spot. While no deputy crown prince has yet become king, no deputy crown prince has had the power vested in him that King Salman gave MBS. Nor was either Prince Mugrin or MBN the son of a serving king as is MBS. Soon King Salman dumped Crown Prince Mohammed bin Nayef and elevated MBS to become crown prince and king in waiting.

The country King Salman and his son inherited on January 24, 2015, was in crisis. Oil prices had crashed to $44 a barrel from $108 six months earlier. A whopping half of the government's budget went simply to pay salaries to a population almost exclusively dependent on government largess. The late King Abdullah, seeking to forestall unrest in Saudi Arabia during the Arab Spring uprisings across the Mideast in 2011, had slathered on another $130 billion of annual government handouts to Saudis. The government budget was unsustainable. Faced with inadequate oil revenues,

King Salman's regime was tapping the country's foreign currency reserves to cover current spending obligations. But sustaining the Saudi welfare state would exhaust those reserves in five years, the World Bank projected, leaving the kingdom broke and endangering the social contract between the rulers and Saudi citizens.

Having eliminated—or intimidated—all royal opponents with his anticorruption roundup at the Ritz, MBS now had a firm lock on power. Those who would remove him had themselves been removed to prison or house arrest and banned from flying lest they seek to escape.

But the powerful MBS also had a problem. All these myriad, long-festering financial, social, and geopolitical headaches needed both swift yet sustainable solutions. Nearly five decades of five-year plans pledging to wean the kingdom off oil had failed utterly. Instead of diminishing reliance on oil, the government had addicted Saudis to oil-funded handouts it could no longer afford.

What's more, the prince had earlier faced Saudi Arabia and the world at an internationally televised press conference to lay out his ambitious plans to reform and redeem the kingdom. What he described was a long journey as ambitious as Moses leading the Israelites from captivity to their promised land, though he didn't use that analogy. And, like the Israelites, the Saudis would have to learn to obediently follow their new leader yet at the same time learn to be self-reliant. That was a very tall order for a nation long accustomed to living off government handouts, not individual enterprise.

Prince Mohammed's Vision 2030 envisioned a completely new Saudi Arabia, one eager to join the world, not isolate itself from it; one where citizens would support themselves, not lean on government; one where women would be full participants, not suppressed shadows; one where foreigners would be welcome visitors, not intruding infidels. He talked of a "vibrant society, a thriving economy, and an ambitious nation," consultant-speak for transforming a suppressed society, a moribund economy, and a lazy nation.

Now MBS was like the proverbial frog seeking to carry the scorpion across the river without getting stung. He had nearly 20 million somnolent, spoiled Saudi citizens on his back to carry to a new promised land that he had described in his Vision 2030. That plan called for transforming Saudi Arabia and its citizens over the coming fifteen years from dependence on oil to dependence on themselves.

"He has launched unprecedented revolutionary transformation," says Minister of Commerce Majid al-Qasabi, "not reform but trans- formation," he stresses.[5]

Truly transforming Saudi Arabia's economy is a task every bit as challenging as Deng Xiaoping's effort in 1978 to lead China from a Marxist, centrally planned economy to a market-oriented one. China would "cross the river by feeling the stones," Deng said. Steady and cautious.

Not MBS. Rather than cautious, careful, consensual steps, he has chosen bold, brutal, high-risk actions, always opting to act quickly because mistakes can be rectified. Dallying is destructive. So, nothing is sacred or off-limits. Centuries of Saudi tradition—the Al Saud partnership with Wahhabism, royal family consensus, seniority—all are ruthlessly jettisoned. Since his teenage years, MBS had believed that his elderly uncles, infirm and inactive, were dissipating Al Saud power, prestige, and prosperity, potentially leaving his generation bereft at best, or out of power at worst. Now, with the opportunity to save his country—and Al Saud rule for his line of the family—he wasn't going to bother with baby steps.

If his overnight reorganization of government had surprised the kingdom, his rapid and brutal consolidation of power stunned Saudis. First, in 2016 he defanged the religious establishment by banning its *mutawa*, or religious police, from pursuing, detaining, or questioning Saudi citizens on the streets. For decades thousands of these men, often self-appointed members of the Committee to Promote Virtue and Prevent Vice, or Haia, had roamed Saudi streets carrying a long, slim stick forcing women to cover their heads, herding Saudis to the mosque at prayer time, ensuring that all shops and stores locked their door for half an hour at prayer time and that Western influence like Barbie dolls or Pokémon cards didn't pollute Saudi youth. They were easily recognized by their trademarks of public piety—long, untrimmed beards, shorter-than-average thobes hitting above the ankle to reveal several inches of hairy leg, and headscarves devoid of the black agal or double circle of twisted yarn that most men wear to anchor their scarf.

In the waning years of the late King Abdullah's rule, the Haia had gotten completely out of control. Hearing music inside one family's car, the religious police chased the car until it rolled off an overpass, killing the driver and injuring his wife and two young children.[6] A few months later, two young Saudis died when Haia members, suspecting alcohol, chased the young men's car, bumping it at high speed causing the car to roll off a bridge. The religious police fled the scene. Still, six members of the Haia were later acquitted of all charges.[7] Saudis tweeted their anger on social media: "The Haia are blood thirsty," @Talal tweeted. @Nejer wrote, "The Haia's situation is similar to many government entities in Saudi; they all need restructuring and fixing."[8]

Indeed, many Saudis, tired of constant harassment at the hands of these meddlesome men, cheered their banishment from Saudi streets. Regardless, it was a shock to society on a par with what Americans would feel if the U.S. Supreme Court suddenly ruled that the Second Amendment right to bear arms was unconstitutional and void. Something immutable had vanished.

Years earlier, Crown Prince Abdullah had sought in vain to curb excesses of the *mutawa* after they were accused of causing the death of fifteen teenage girls at a Mecca school in 2002. Despite the visible flames high above the walls encircling the school, the *mutawa* refused to allow Civil Defense officers to enter or the screaming girls to flee because they weren't wearing abayas and scarves, observers said. A Ministry of Interior inquiry conveniently blamed the deaths on panic and overcrowding of the school, but nonetheless the cleric in charge of the school was fired and girls' education was moved from the control of religious clerics to the Ministry of Education. King Abdullah had used the tragedy to allow girls the same education as boys even if still in separate buildings. Vehement religious opposition to schooling girls at all had been assuaged by an earlier king also with a compromise: girls' schools would open in 1956 but religious clerics, not the Ministry of Education, would control those schools. Girls would not be required to attend but welcome to do so. Any changes involving women in Saudi Arabia always are a tug-of-war between the regime and the religious establishment.

More recently, King Abdullah had sought to allow women to sell lingerie in department stores where all salesclerks were men, mostly foreigners, as Saudi men refused such jobs. This was the king's toe in the water to begin expanding job opportunities for women. The religious police balked, blocking the idea for six years. For a woman to stand behind the counter and sell bras might mean mixing with a male seeking to buy lingerie. Apparently, Allah isn't troubled by a woman standing in front of the counter to buy a bra from a Pakistani salesclerk, but she is headed for hell if she stands behind the counter and sells a bra to the same unrelated man. For six years the late king tolerated the suppression of this tiny step to create opportunities for women.

MBS didn't have time to negotiate with such nonsense. By showing the courage simply to assert Al Saud primacy over their religious partners, he prevailed where Abdullah had prevaricated.

Banning the *mutawa* was only the beginning of reining in religious influence on the kingdom but it was by far the most visible and vivid action.

"King Salman and MBS know the religious aren't that popular with citizens," a Saudi pollster explained in 2018.[9]

Over the decades since Sheikh Abdul-Aziz bin Baz, a revered religious scholar and grand mufti, died in 1999, the religious leadership had lost much of its legitimacy. It wasn't just incidents like letting schoolgirls burn to death in school. Increasingly, the top scholars gained a reputation with the populace for selling their interpretation of Allah's word for Al Saud cash. Small wonder that religious authority had dissipated by 2015. In a 2017 poll asking Saudis whether they choose to listen to government, religion, or themselves, only 15 percent responded religion.[10]

MBS's strategy for taming religious extremism centered on getting clerics to debate each other, not the government. By his estimate, nearly 50 percent of the country's ulama, or senior Islamic scholars, held extremist views. Dialogue and government intimidation have cut that number by more than half, he tells associates. Some were removed from the Council of Senior Scholars, the highest religious body that advises the king on religious matters. Others were jailed. Still others, like Sheikh Ayed al-Qarni, a popular preacher who appeared often on Qatar's Al Jazeera television, recanted, accusing Qatar of "conspiring" against Saudi Arabia. The sheikh apologized on Saudi television for extremist views he and others held. "I am today supportive of the moderate Islam, open to the world, which has been called for by Crown Prince Mohammed bin Salman."[11]

After tethering the religious, next came the ruthless removal of all competing centers of royal authority and the concentration of all power in the hands of King Salman and his son. "No longer will we have 'mini' kings," predicted a prescient academic in the first year of King Salman's reign, but "one king who controls everything."[12]

During the two decades preceding King Salman, the kingdom

had been run by three senior princes. Each had what amounted to his own armed forces and easy access to drain the Saudi treasury for pet projects and loyal retainers. Each operated separate hospitals and housing projects just for his ministerial employees. The late King Abdullah ran the Saudi National Guard for nearly half a century. His half brother, Sultan, headed the Defense Ministry for a similar period. Their brother Nayef was minister of interior for some thirty-five years, controlling 30,000 security forces responsible for protecting key government installations, including the Saudi oil facilities and more recently for fighting terrorist threats to the kingdom. These multiple centers of power, seeking consensus, most often wound up producing paralysis. First Prince Sultan then Prince Nayef served as crown prince to the late King Abdullah.

The deaths of these three powerful Al Saud princes in quick succession over four short years suddenly cleared the way for Salman, the twenty-fifth son of Abdul Aziz, to become king. King Salman is only the sixth of Abdul Aziz's sons to rule—but almost surely the last. His younger brother, Ahmed, who opposed MBS's elevation to crown prince, is under house arrest.

King Salman and his son are indisputably the strongest rulers in the history of Saudi Arabia. No longer are there any competing centers of power. All institutional power bases are under their control. All the Saudi military—defense, National Guard, and interior—report to King Salman and in reality to his son. And, if things go as they plan, MBS will succeed his father and pass rule to his son, launching a new Salman dynasty.

Even MBS's powerful grandfather, Abdul Aziz, was forced to consult with his tribal leaders and accommodate religious sheikhs. Indeed, there are uncanny similarities to the rule of MBS and his grandfather a century apart. Abdul Aziz was under thirty when he conquered Riyadh in 1902, beginning the reestablishment of Al Saud rule in Arabia after more than a decade-long gap. Squabbling among his father's brothers over who should rule had resulted in their defeat by another tribe in 1891. Abdul Aziz fled to Kuwait, sneaking back eleven years later through the desolate deserts of Arabia's Empty Quarter to Riyadh, where he boldly hid overnight in the home of the governor, who had sought safety in a nearby fort after rumors Abdul Aziz was near. At dawn Abdul Aziz's men murdered the governor, recapturing Riyadh and launching a thirty-year civil war to subdue all of Arabia once again to Al Saud rule.[13]

It was something of a precursor to MBS's overnight lockup of Saudi Crown Prince Mohammed bin Nayef (MBN) and his stoic surrender at dawn of his power to MBS. MBS displayed his grandfather's cunning, daring, and determination to secure his royal power.

That fateful evening of June 21, 2017, MBN was called to a palace in Mecca. Once there, his guards were forbidden to accompany him inside. All phones also were surrendered to palace guards. MBN was taken to a room where Turki Alalshikh, a contemporary and friend of MBS and now minister of the General Entertainment Authority, and others began bullying him to resign. Denied contact with his men and the painkillers to which he was said to be addicted, he finally succumbed early the next morning after Prince Khalid al-Faisal, the governor of Mecca, urged him to obey the king.

Prince Khalid, a contemporary of his uncle, King Salman, pointed out that at eighty-three he was twenty years MBN's senior, the son of a king, and had been a provincial governor or minister for forty-five years. Without question, Prince Khalid, an Oxford University graduate and poet, is by far the most experienced of Abdul Aziz's grandsons. He reminded the crown prince that he hadn't protested when the king passed over him to name the younger MBN crown prince. "In this family, we obey the king and that is what you are going to do now."[14] It worked. MBN signed his resignation letter.

MBS promptly became crown prince. While MBS didn't crown

himself as Napoleon had done in 1804 when he made himself emperor of France, MBS, like the French general was essentially a self-made man. His own ingenuity had brought him from sixth son of King Salman to king in waiting. Indeed, he was for all practical purposes ruling Saudi Arabia with his father's blessing if not his title.

Video of MBN meeting the victorious MBS was released by Al Arabiya. An exhausted MBN tells his cousin, "I pledge my allegiance to you." An obsequiously humble MBS kisses MBN's left hand, then bowing before his cousin, rises to say, "May God reward you and prolong your life." MBN slaps his younger cousin on the back as if the two are sharing a joke. "I am relieved now. May God help you."[15]

In 2009 while running a program to rehabilitate terrorists, a "reformed" terrorist had sought to meet him allegedly to facilitate the surrender of a group of Saudi terrorists in Yemen. The prince, who regularly met with terrorists he hoped to convert, agreed. An aide to the prince recounts to me what happened next as we stand on the very site in MBN's home where the prince received his guest.

The "reformed" terrorist guest cleverly arrived at the prince's home on a weekend, avoiding the Interior Ministry's extensive security. While Prince Mohammed's guards patted down the visitor they failed to discover plastic explosives hidden in his rectum. Seated beside the prince, the terrorist dialed his friends in Yemen on a cell phone and handed it to the prince to arrange their supposed surrender. Instantly the prince's guest exploded, his body blown into seventy-three pieces, according to the aide. The largest, a bloody arm, fell in front of the prince, who, miraculously, was barely scratched.[16] His mind wasn't so lucky. Trauma leading to addiction was rumored and the prince nodded off frequently in meetings, something visible to all. In the end, the hero of Saudi antiterrorism efforts succumbed quietly to his removal from power. He now is under house arrest.

Arrests for corruption continue well beyond the Ritz roundup of princes and businessmen. In January 2024, the government arrested the high-profile CEO of the Royal Commission of Al Ula, the organization charged with transforming the historic region of Al Ula into a major tourist site and global arts center. He was accused of "abuse of power and money laundering." Less prominent individuals are arrested regularly on corruption charges.

Prince Miteb was freed from the Ritz after being completely stripped of all power and agreeing to surrender $1 billion of his assets. Once a contender to power, he now is forbidden to leave the country or to access his own plane to fly within the kingdom lest he seek to escape. Yet, as with the deposed MBN, a smiling MBS is shown in an official palace photo standing alongside a dejected and unsmiling Prince Miteb at the annual horse race ceremony in Riyadh only a month later as if nothing had happened.

The horse race had once been Prince Miteb's princely and proud domain. An avid horseman, his horse won the race in January 2016 on a beautiful track bedecked with flowers and fountains of spouting water outside Riyadh. Prince Miteb had invited me to attend this race to see firsthand the emerging social changes in the kingdom, including women being allowed to attend this race. Indeed, there were women strolling the grounds and sitting in the stands. And when a beaming Prince Miteb held aloft the winner's gold trophy, the photographer who captured his satisfied smile was a Saudi woman.

Similarly, Prince Alwaleed bin Talal, the kingdom's most prominent businessman, was freed after eighty-three days of confinement at the Ritz-Carlton and an agreement to pay $6 billion.[17]

The prince, who owns investments in many international companies, insisted his retention wasn't an arrest but rather a "misunderstanding" and said he holds no grudges. "I've forgotten and forgiven the whole process," he told Bloomberg News in a 2018 interview. "It's behind me." He acknowledged a "confirmed understanding with the government going forward" but insisted, "We're all one party here. The ruling family of Saudi Arabia."[18]

The Ritz-Carlton scene was intended to humiliate royal competitors and intimidate the whole Saudi populace with its shockingly brutal tactics. All this echoes King Abdul Aziz. To demonstrate his willingness to use power when persuasion failed, Abdul Aziz razed the villages of some of his own cousins who dared mass an army to threaten his hold on Riyadh. He forced the surrender of one village, Laila, and condemned to death nineteen of its leaders.

Demonstrating a flair for dramatic brutality, he granted the leaders a twenty-four-hour stay of execution while a platform was built outside the village's main gate. At dawn he took his seat before the assembly of men summoned from the countryside. In pairs the condemned men were led before him, and each, upon his command, was beheaded by a black slave wielding a sword. With eighteen men dead, Abdul Aziz abruptly pardoned the nineteenth and told him to go tell all men what he had seen of the just vengeance of Abdul Aziz.[19]

It was classic Al Saud—offering people a choice between brutality and submission.

CHAPTER FOUR

Early Omens

T he young Crown Prince had power and he had a plan. But first there would be pain before any gain for his countrymen.

Despite promises in spring of a bright new future under Vision 2030, the fall of 2016 turned distinctly dark. The government was hemorrhaging money. Oil revenues, which accounted for 80 percent of its budgeted spending, had fallen in half. To sustain its spending, King Salman's government had tapped into its foreign currency reserves at a rate the World Bank estimated would deplete them in four years. Worse yet, the treasury faced a deficit of $100 billion and growing.[1] Abroad, the kingdom's war with Yemen was consuming an estimated $500 million a month and rising as the engagement intensified.

Confronted with a fiscal crisis, MBS sharply reduced salaries, bonuses, and financial "benefits" for all government employees and the Saudi military. The "benefit" cuts alone reduced the average Saudi's income by 50 percent. Because 65 percent of Saudis work for government, this was a huge hit to income for a majority of Saudis. Despite warnings from some of his ministers that economic growth would grind to a halt, MBS proceeded. To add insult to injury, the Saudi civil service minister took to television to accuse government employees of working "only an hour a day."[2]

MBS's handling of this fiscal crisis reveals much about how he operates. Study the data—if any exists—but act boldly. If you make a mistake, you can fix it. Told by his ministers there was no hard data on "benefits" and that gathering it from archives could take years, he opted to act. He would tackle the clear and present danger of the kingdom's deteriorating fiscal situation—a huge budget deficit and shrinking Central Bank reserves—rather than delay for fear of an unquantified risk to economic growth.[3] Seven months later he reversed himself.

For decades, these "benefits" had been a clever way for government to provide additional income to workers without adding to the salaries of these lifetime employees. The benefits had been layered on year after year. While theoretically temporary, none was ever trimmed or terminated. By now there were some 260 different "benefits"—one for typing, for using a computer, for inputting data, and so on. While these "skills" might have deserved extra pay for a time, clearly by 2016 they were minimal talents required for government employment—or should have been. By 2017 these "benefits" constituted anywhere from 10 to 150 percent of a worker's income.[4]

Most paradoxical was a so-called novel benefit for academic departments with fewer than 50 percent Saudis. Ironically, this benefit led departments to refuse to hire Saudis to protect their income despite government demands for Saudization of all jobs. The left hand contradicting the right hand. Saudi government was riddled with such contradictions.

Given the longevity and generosity of these benefits, their sudden removal amounted to a 50 percent earnings cut for the average Saudi.[5] Such a sharp income contraction for the majority of the populace quickly crashed consumer spending. Coupled with already declining oil prices, these austerity measures helped reduce economic growth in 2016 to 1.6 percent, the lowest since a

2009 recession. Three months later at the end of the first quarter of 2017, economic growth turned negative at –0.4 percent.[6]

All this came on top of earlier cuts in government subsidies for gasoline, water, and electricity. While gasoline prices rose 50 percent, horrifying Saudis, gas was still only 96 cents a gallon. But Saudis regarded cheap energy as a national birthright. (The average price in the U.S. at that time was $2.64; Europe was double that.)

"We had Christmas every day and Grinch has stolen it," is how one Saudi economist, who supports government reforms, described the national mood. Social media buzzed with bitter Saudis stoking each other's fury. "It is government's job to balance the budget, not ours," said a Saudi citizen, reflecting a popularly held view in the kingdom that government should miraculously cut spending without touching citizens' livelihoods. By April 2017, a Twitter hashtag "April 21 movement" was calling for protests in four major Saudi cities.

Prince Mohammed bin Salman, firmly focused on shrinking the kingdom's $100 billion budget deficit, had boldly forced these austerity measures on a population addicted to generous government handouts. Now the resulting negative economic growth coupled with public anger forced government to reverse. On April 22, 2017, King Salman issued a royal decree restoring "all allowances, financial benefits, and bonuses." He also fired the offending civil service minister for insulting Saudi workers.[7] He didn't, of course, fire his deputy crown prince.

After at least four decades of truly gargantuan Saudi oil revenue, it is understandable why the Saudi populace felt little or no responsibility for curbing spending and reacted angrily when government forced it upon them. After all, oil revenues had soared since the kingdom embargoed oil sales to the U.S. in 1973 for supporting Israel in a war with Egypt. Over the years, the Al Saud family has become one of the richest on earth, with a net worth estimated at $1.4 trillion.[8] That is sixteen times the wealth of the British royal family.[9] The House of Saud now comprises more than ten thousand sons, grandsons, and great-grandsons of the founder but most of the wealth is believed to be controlled by a few thousand princes.

The Al Saud net worth is larger than the annual gross domestic product of all but nineteen nations.[10] Indeed, the country of Saudi Arabia only joined the trillion-dollar club in 2022, finally reaching a GDP of $1.11 trillion.[11] This abundant revenue seems likely to continue for at least several decades. The kingdom has the second-largest oil reserves in the world, 297 billion barrels, a tick behind Venezuela's 300 billion barrels of reserves.[12] Despite those large reserves, Venezuela isn't a threat to Saudi Arabia's continued dominance of global oil markets since corruption of its state-owned oil company has left production declining for decades. While climate activists hope to force an end to fossil fuel use, green energy almost surely will take far longer than they hope, giving Saudi Arabia many decades more of oil wealth. So abundant are Saudi oil reserves that should exports dry up, the kingdom can meet its own energy needs for an estimated 221 years.[13]

King Salman's restoration of benefits produced some gratitude but also more grumbling. For some Saudis the reversal was a sign that the reform plans were poorly thought through and thus should be shelved; for others it was a sign that government listens to people—and thus can be pushed further. If the king could roll back cuts in benefits and bonuses, why not push him to restore citizen subsidies for energy and electricity?

Like the Greek hero Odysseus, confronting the choice of sailing between a deadly whirlpool or a six-headed monster, MBS would face many more Scylla-and-Charybdis choices. But this very public reversal dented Saudis' confidence in him. "The government should use less 'shock and reverse' and more moving slow-and-steady," a seasoned economist told me. Saudi citizens I spoke with expressed relief at the reversal but anxiety about what might come next.

"It's like being in the back seat of a speeding car," explained one Saudi. "You can't see where you are going. You just pray the driver won't crash."

A few months after the policy reversal on benefits, MBS became Crown Prince with the overnight removal of Crown Prince Mohammed bin Nayef. Now Crown Prince Mohammed bin Salman was in charge of the economy, defense, and Saudi Aramco, the national oil company that funds the government. "Mr. Everything," Saudis dubbed him.

Sure enough, as the new year 2018 dawned, the government imposed an 80 percent hike in gasoline prices, tripled electricity prices, and imposed a 5 percent value added tax or VAT, a consumption tax on almost all goods and services. It was the first tax in Saudi Arabia, where Saudis long have defended their tax free life by jokingly repeating American colonists' slogan, "No taxation without representation." Prince Mohammed and his father certainly weren't offering Saudis representation. Not surprisingly, the VAT was as unpopular as the tax on tea that a heavily indebted Britain imposed on the American colonies in 1773. That one sparked a revolution. This one produced only malcontent.

"Saudis are angry about all three," said a Saudi pollster when asked to explain the public reaction. "Low income and high costs are their number one concern." Still, he said, "People hesitate to oppose government. They do not want to lose their job security."[14]

This time, however, government did seek to sweeten the bitter pill of abrupt price hikes by creating a new handout, the Citizen's Account, to offset the higher costs of economic reforms for low-income Saudis. Higher prices for gas and electricity were intended to curb wasteful domestic consumption, thus reshaping public habits and giving the kingdom more oil to sell on the world market.

Like almost all government programs in modern Saudi history, this one ballooned into an entitlement. The precise payments to families would vary by family size and income, the government said, with a family of six earning $2,320 receiving a monthly payment of roughly $400.[15] These payments were intended to bridge Saudis to paying world market prices for energy by 2020. Yet by 2023 some 10.9 million Saudis, half the native population, were receiving payments averaging $500 per family.[16] In January that year, the government announced that King Salman, on the advice of his son, had extended the Citizen's Account to April; then in April the king extended this subsidy to July, and then August. The extensions are continuing. Already the Citizen's Account program has cost the Saudi treasury some $32 billion since its launch.[17] And rising.

If MBS surprised the Saudi people, he could be equally abrupt and shocking with his ministers. The government rotated through four health ministers in a two-year period. One learned he had been fired by watching an announcement on Saudi television.

When Salman became king, MBS called Mohammed al-Jadaan, a prominent Saudi lawyer, to ask him to head the Capital Markets Authority, which regulates the Saudi stock market. al-Jadaan politely declined, saying he had just started his own law firm and was enjoying some time with family. "You guys gossip at night about what's wrong with government but how is it going to get better if you won't help?" he recalls an annoyed MBS asking.

"I was taken aback," al-Jadaan recalls.[18] He agreed to serve and was sworn in as head of CMA in January 2015 as the reign of King Salman began. A year later, he was named minister of finance.

While MBS's ministers acknowledge he is demanding, sometimes even harsh, they claim to appreciate his decisiveness. Relentless in demanding higher performance, MBS pushed his new minister of communication and information technology in 2017 to speed his plans to digitize the kingdom. Saudi Arabia ranked 105 in the world in internet speed and the minister promised top-twenty status in three years. What do you need to cut that to two years? Abdullah Swaha recalls MBS asking him. MBS had recruited Swaha, a Saudi engineer at Cisco Systems, in 2016 as his personal adviser when they met during MBS's tour of the U.S. A year later, MBS named him minister. The minister responded to MBS with two requests: that government provide a digital stimulus package and that the Crown Prince help him with another minister who controlled spectrum.

Who is that minister? MBS asked. "Your Royal Highness, don't be upset, but that minister is you," Swaha responded.

The Crown Prince was also minister of defense, and for decades the Defense Ministry under the late, powerful Prince Sultan had controlled spectrum allocation.

"On the spot, he created a committee to gather the facts," recalls Swaha in an interview. "Three days later, we all assemble and made a decision." The minister received the spectrum he needed to advance digitization rapidly. Today Saudi Arabia is the second-ranked nation in the G-20 in spectrum behind Japan.[19] In 2023 the kingdom ranked second among G-20 nations and fourth globally for its digital readiness, according to the United Nations International Telecommunication Union.[20]

Saudis now can do almost anything online—secure a marriage contract, pay bills, check the validity of a mortgage, secure telemedical services, and much more. Foreigners too can use all these services plus secure quick e-visas to visit the kingdom for tourism or for hajj. Visiting Saudi Arabia these days is like visiting Seoul, where everything is digital, especially paying for services. The kingdom, once a place where huge wads of cash bulged from the large pockets on men's thobes, now is essentially cashless. This digitization allows government close monitoring of citizens and makes it easier to collect its VAT on all spending. But for a foreigner accustomed to tipping with cash, it is virtually impossible to get change for large bills from any individual or a hotel reception. Most simply don't keep much cash.

The minister of communication isn't the only place where MBS has made big demands but also stepped in to assist.

In 2015, King Salman named Princess Reema bint Bandar, now the kingdom's ambassador to the United States, as the first head of a new department of women's sports, working under her cousin Prince Abdullah bin Musa'id at the Ministry of Sports. Princess Reema, forty-seven, grew up in Washington, where her father served as ambassador for nearly a quarter century. Returning to a religiously rigid kingdom in the early 2000s, she dared open a beauty salon and spa, both forbidden by the religious police, who charged that women might use such female places to sneak off and meet men. The facility had no public signage, was hidden behind high walls, and was posted with a guard so the meddlesome religious police wouldn't know and interfere with the Saudi ladies who discreetly came and went.

Her new government job in women's sports didn't escape the eyes—and enmity—of the religious police. Though a princess and the granddaughter of late King Faisal, revered for his religious rectitude, she wasn't spared. Princess Reema recalls that on her first day at work, some twenty to forty bearded men told her to go home and then protested to her boss about the presence of a woman in his domain. To avoid confrontation, she did.

The next day she came to her office through a back entrance. On her third day at work, bearded men met her in the hall and escorted her out. A Ministry of Sports official suggested she use the private entrance of her boss, Prince Abdullah bin Musa'id, but she refused, since she didn't want the men protesting her presence at the ministry seeing her sneaking in and out through his private entrance. So she worked from home to finalize a sports plan for ladies.[21]

Once the sports plan was ready, the princess and prince sat down side by side to present the plan to multiple government entities from the Foreign Ministry to the Council of Religious

Scholars. Princess Reema began by stressing that competitive sports would build female confidence as well as improve women's health in a country where more than a quarter of all females have diabetes largely due to inactivity. Her thorough presentation showed every Islamic country, which sports its women participated in, and what the female athletes wore. She concluded by asking, "What would this look like if Saudi women participated?"

One of the clerics looked across the table at her and inquired if she were happy with the way Muslim women were engaging in sports. She judiciously responded that Saudis can't criticize other nations' female athletes if the kingdom doesn't participate and set an example. The cleric bluntly responded, "If we continue down this path, we will be laying the first stones on the pathway to hell for our girls." The speechless princess was excused by her colleague. Prince Abdullah thanked the princess for her presentation and said, "I'll take it from here."

Yet more obstacles remained for Princess Reema. To create a sports economy around professional and amateur sports as well as mass-participation exercise opportunities for women, Princess Reema needed many bureaucratic permissions from many government ministries. She needed approvals to open gyms; to organize transportation for women who then weren't allowed to drive; to institute physical education for girls in public schools; to get a sports business plan approved. Approvals were repeatedly withheld by disapproving bureaucrats.

MBS summoned Princess Reema to his office to inquire why she hadn't accomplished the goals laid out in her plan. "I want to see women running in the streets," he said. "Why don't I see that?"[22]

She explained that beyond religious roadblocks, many ministries weren't providing the multiple bureaucratic licenses needed. Come back in one week and show me your obstacles and plans to overcome them, he ordered. When she returned to review her list of impediments, MBS asked his then minister of sports, Turki

Alalshikh, to engage myriad ministries to clear all obstacles. Moreover, the Crown Prince arranged a royal decree in September 2018 mandating physical education in all girls' schools. No exceptions. The only way a girl could opt out would be to leave the school for homeschooling.

So let it be written. So let it be done.

Interestingly, earlier the kingdom's Shura Council, whose members all are appointed by the king, had recommended physical education for girls as part of King Abdullah's efforts to loosen religious restrictions. That recommendation was ignored because religious officials opposed exercise for girls.[23] MBS doesn't tolerate such religious defiance of his decisions.

Soon after, a few courageous Saudi women began running on public streets clad in long black abayas and sneakers. A bit later, they donned baggy sweatpants and soon some dared run publicly in formfitting tights. Such public display of active women was shockingly at odds with my first sighting of female athletes in the kingdom in 2009. Then, the kingdom's first-ever female soccer team, funded by billionaire Prince Alwaleed bin Talal, invited me to their practice behind high walls in Jeddah. Each chauffeured woman arrived shrouded in a black abaya and scarf to hide her sports clothes underneath. Some of the women prayed before throwing off their abayas and organizing into two teams for a spirited practice in T-shirts and shorts or tights. Observing such illicit dress and activity seemed daring to me then. For decades, religious clerics had forbidden females to exercise, insisting it would damage their reproductive capability, the one true role of a Saudi woman.

But these days, MBS's Vision 2030 reforms call for not just economic reforms but also for a "vibrant society." Specifically, he wants 40 percent of Saudis doing weekly exercise by 2030, up from a mere 13 percent in 2015. Clearly, many women are eager to comply. A government survey found that in 2021, the most active Saudi women are those between twenty and twenty-nine where roughly 43 percent engage in at least thirty minutes of exercise weekly.[24]

Because the Crown Prince is related to many of those with whom he works most closely, they say he keeps a strict line between work and private friendships. One of those closest to him is Culture Minister Prince Badr bin Abdullah bin Farhan. Their fast friendship dates back to a third-grade encounter on a soccer field. They sometimes played for hours, the prince recalls, "as we had no activities in Riyadh in those days." Still, he says the Crown Prince keeps a strict wall between their friendship and work. "When he finishes the daily work, he is a normal guy. But he never mixes friendship with work."

The minister insists that despite his royal birth, his boss is humble. He illustrates that humility by telling a story of the prince returning alone in his own car from an outing with friends. A tire blows out. Prince Mohammed calls a tow truck, which loads his car, and he hops into the cab with the Syrian driver, never indicating who he is. During their ninety-minute ride to Riyadh, the driver seeks assurance he'll be paid. Only when the two pull up to MBS's palace does the shocked driver realize his passenger is a prince. "He never called his security or his father's security," says Prince Badr. "He just handled it." Clearly, Prince Badr is an unabashed friend and admirer. He tears up when asked to describe MBS's legacy. "I would never have the words to describe. . . . I love him so I want to help deliver his vision."

Faisal al-Ibrahim, the kingdom's astute and impressive minister of economy and planning, responsible for helping the Crown Prince drive economic diversification, says after six years in the ministry, "Every day feels like day one. It's a once-in-a-lifetime opportunity" to contribute to helping build the kingdom. A University of Pennsylvania graduate with an MBA from the Massachusetts Institute of Technology, al-Ibrahim typifies today's Saudi cabinet ministers. In sharp contrast to earlier, more elderly cabinet ministers who worked short days, these men are young—midforties to midfifties—and well educated. They are vigorous enough to withstand all-night cabinet sessions with MBS and are seemingly genuinely devoted to the opportunity to help him reform the kingdom. This very large minister tears up recalling Saudi Arabia's soccer team's victory over Argentina in the 2022 World Cup in Qatar. "We believed in ourselves and we achieved," he said.[25]

Whether one man's determination is enough to truly make believers of 20 million Saudi citizens remains unanswered. "This is a marathon, not a one-hundred-yard sprint," Mohammed al-Sheikh told me in 2018.[26] Indeed, the Crown Prince seemed to agree. He insisted in 2018 that he was relying more on his ministers and driving himself less relentlessly. According to MBS, he rarely had a weekend off in his early days in government.

In 2018, he says, he eased his workload. He began to see his young children for two hours a day, work out for an hour, spend thirty minutes playing videogames, and also an hour each day with his mother and father. Weekends he devotes to relaxing with family and friends. He summers at the Red Sea and spends winters in Al Ula, the spectacular historic tourist site on the ancient incense route that linked India to the Levant and Europe. All around Al Ula are rock dwellings from Nabatean times some two thousand years ago. The Crown Prince is building a home in Al Ula, a region many fundamentalist Muslims believe is cursed by Allah, who they insist punished earlier dwellers for their idolatry by sending an earthquake and lightning to destroy them. This crown prince is unafraid of such omens.

CHAPTER FIVE

Heavy Lies the Head

E ven before his sensational murder made Jamal Khashoggi an international name, he was one of the kingdom's best-known nonroyals. A journalist in a kingdom where Al Saud royals were largely inaccessible, Khashoggi readily explained his country to visiting foreigners.

In my last of many meals with him over a decade, he expressed pleasure at the generational change in leadership represented by MBS and supported his war in Yemen against Iranian proxies. Still MBS had forbidden him to write, alleging he was a member of the Muslim Brotherhood. He handled that frustration with his characteristic humor. He expressed his desire for more personal liberty by poking mild fun at MBS's habit of measuring his ministers' performances by tracking their KPIs on an iPad.

"Key Performance Indicators are as close to accountability as we are going to get," he said. "I'd prefer democracy but at least we have KPIs."[1]

Saudi nepotism, he observed, was nothing new. What was new with King Salman and MBS was that no longer were powerful uncles alive to curb MBS, as they had with previous kings' empowered sons.

Shortly after that conversation in a Riyadh hotel over lunch,

Khashoggi left Saudi Arabia for Washington, D.C., to once again be free to write. His columns in the *Washington Post*, which grew ever more critical of MBS, led to his shocking death in October 2018 in the Saudi consulate in Istanbul. Khashoggi's body was sawed into pieces and hauled out in suitcases.

That brutal murder was sensational news worldwide. Overnight, MBS, the Saudi savior, was now widely viewed as a savage. Suddenly MBS stood for "Mr. Bone Saw" to his critics.

The smiling, vibrant prince who had charmed America's elite as he hopped across the U.S. visiting universities, government officials, and business VIPs in April 2018 was, only six months later, shunned. While the Crown Prince denied any prior knowledge of or involvement in the murder, many Saudis and certainly most in the West believed that his near-total control of the kingdom meant no one would have dared carry out such a brutal murder without his knowledge.

Khashoggi had been a lifelong retainer of the Al Saud family but most closely associated with the late King Abdullah's family. He had served as a journalist at *Arab News* and *Al Watan*, two Saudi newspapers. He also had been posted to London and Washington with Prince Turki al-Faisal while he served as ambassador in both cities. But he had run afoul of Prince Mohammed, who ordered him to stop writing, suspecting him of being a member of the Muslim Brotherhood and on the payroll of Qatar, a small Gulf nation with which Saudi broke diplomatic relations in 2017. Khashoggi was close to Osama bin Laden, a Saudi who fought against the Russian occupation of Afghanistan with U.S. support but later declared jihad against the U.S., orchestrating the 9/11 attacks before President Barack Obama ordered his successful murder in a predawn raid by U.S. Navy SEALs in Pakistan in 2011.

Khashoggi, a large, charismatic man who smiled often and displayed a confident candor absent in most Saudis' conversation, had a career in and out of newspapers and government. His confidence almost surely confirmed that he was at least as much government operative as journalist.

Backlash against the Crown Prince for Khashoggi's death was swift and savage abroad. The man everyone had wanted to meet became the man no one wanted to be seen with. Richard Branson, the British business magnate who founded the Virgin Group, swiftly pulled out of two tourism projects in Saudi Arabia and suspended discussion with the government over a possible $1 billion investment in Virgin's space companies. Hollywood entrepreneur Ari Emanuel, CEO of Endeavor, an entertainment and media agency, quickly returned a $400 million investment in Endeavor by Crown Prince Mohammed.

World leaders at the G-20 summit some seven weeks after Khashoggi's death shunned the Saudi Crown Prince publicly. At the official "family photo" of leaders, he stood awkwardly alone on the far right wrapping his long white bisht around him and folding his arms defensively across his chest as leader after leader walked by without even nodding to him. French president Emmanuel Macron was caught criticizing the Crown Prince for not listening to him. Donald Trump spoke to Saudi officials away from the cameras. The Saudis labeled his encounter with MBS a "friendly meeting." The White House called it a "quick greeting." Only Vladimir Putin, always eager to exploit tension between Saudi Arabia and the U.S., greeted MBS warmly. The two exchanged an infamous high-five as the Crown Prince took a seat alongside the Russian president.

Inside Saudi Arabia, reactions were mixed. Even many of those distraught by the killing were offended by the vehemence of U.S. outrage, especially at President Joe Biden labeling their country a "pariah." "Saudi Arabia, not MBS, was targeted by the West," one angry Saudi man said. "He's more popular now than before." A young Saudi professional woman told me, "We know he is involved in the Khashoggi matter. But we don't want to think about it because he has done so much other good."

Some devoutly religious Saudis saw Khashoggi's death as treachery, a forbidden sin against Allah. These individuals point out he was lured to the Saudi consulate on the promise of receiving a paper permitting him to marry his Turkish fiancée. Instead he was murdered. "Allah does not love him who is treacherous," one Saudi quoted me from the Quran.[2] He reinforced his point by noting that Caliph Umar, quoting Prophet Mohammed, said that on Judgment Day, "Allah will raise a banner for every betrayer,"[3] and the greater the betrayal, the higher the banner.

Sifting through the circumstances of this murder, it's hard not to conclude it was a rendition gone wrong. Like dictators through the centuries, Crown Prince Mohammed certainly would have no qualms about eliminating anyone he deems a threat. But doing so in his nation's consulate on foreign soil seems too stupid and inept. Indeed, kidnapping critics—even princes—is an established practice of Al Saud rulers. Once in the kingdom, their "disappearance" through whatever means never makes headlines in the government-controlled press and rarely abroad.

Belated discovery of their disappearance may lead to mention by human rights groups, but rarely any international outcry. For instance, Mohammed al-Qahtani, one of the kingdom's few true democracy activists, was jailed in 2013 by the late King Abdullah, for a ten-year sentence. A jovial Indiana University graduate, he met often with foreigners like me, but hardly seemed a threat to government. Indeed, Arab Spring protests in Saudi Arabia fizzled in 2011. Yet he was sentenced to ten years in prison. On his release date in 2023, he simply disappeared from the prison when his family went to bring him home. That cruel tale has received little Western press attention though human rights groups have issued statements of protest.

A 2016 kidnapping of a Saudi prince seems the clear model for what was intended for Khashoggi. Prince Sultan bin Turki II, a grandson of Abdul Aziz, had been crippled for life when King

Abdullah's government drugged and dragged him aboard a plane to Riyadh in 2004 after he criticized the Saudi government as corrupt.[4] After nearly a decade of incarceration and when he was near death, the government allowed him to go to Massachusetts for medical care. With no money, he petitioned MBS for compensation for his injuries. MBS said no. So Prince Sultan wrote letters to two of his uncles alleging that King Salman was a prisoner of MBS, who was corrupt and had diverted $2 billion of government funds to a private account. The letters leaked to the *Guardian* newspaper in London.

Prince Sultan soon found $2 million in his bank account and an invitation from his father in Cairo to visit courtesy of the Saudi government. A 737 was dispatched to Paris to pick up Prince Sultan. The captain of the plane was named Saud; also, the plane had a crew of nineteen, double the normal complement, and these crew members were muscular men, not leggy blondes. Despite his staff warning Prince Sultan against boarding, when Captain Saud pledged to leave ten crew members behind to prove the flight wasn't a kidnapping, the prince boarded.

Not surprisingly, the flight landed not in Cairo but Riyadh. The prince was dragged down the jetway and never seen again. His staff were kept for several days in a hotel, then summoned to a large conference room with a table. At the head was Captain Saud, now dressed in a white thobe. "I am Saud Al Qahtani," he said. "I work at the royal court."[5]

Saud Qahtani is the same man believed to have orchestrated Jamal Khashoggi's capture and ultimate death in the Saudi consulate. Though nominally the Crown Prince's media adviser, Qahtani was effectively his right-hand man charged with enforcing the zero-tolerance campaign against critics of the Crown Prince's ambitious social reforms. Qahtani was fired days after the murder of Khashoggi by King Salman and put under investigation by Saudi authorities. His closeness to the Crown Prince implicates MBS.

Qahtani had famously declared a year earlier that his ruthless actions in jailing government critics were taken with royal approval.

"Do you think I make decisions without guidance?" he tweeted. "I am an employee and a faithful executor of the orders of my lord the king and my lord the faithful crown prince." Yet it is clearly possible that a planned rendition collapsed once Khashoggi realized he was dealing with kidnappers, not friendly consulate staff. At that point, an overzealous Qahtani, who managed the operation from Riyadh, may have simply decided to dispatch Khashoggi on the spot. Or possibly he died when his captors injected him with drugs. Regardless, the Crown Prince ultimately is responsible even at a distance.

While denying any prior knowledge, he has acknowledged his responsibility. "It happened on my watch," he told PBS documentarian Martin Smith one year after the murder. "I get all the responsibility because it happened under my watch." Asked how he couldn't know of such a plan, he said, "I have officials, ministers to follow things and they're responsible."[6]

Despots deal in death. They say—or sincerely believe—they are protecting themselves or their country. Peter the Great, the czar who forcefully wrenched Russia from backwardness to European modernization—like MBS a reformer on a grand scale—brutally ordered his eldest son beaten with a knout in 1718 until he died for allegedly conspiring against his father.[7]

Nearly a century later, Napoleon Bonaparte ordered the kidnapping of a royalist opponent, Duke d'Enghein, who he believed was plotting against him. Napoleon's henchmen secretly crossed the Rhine River to seize their prey at his home in Baden. He was brought back to a chateau near Paris where he was hastily tried and a week later shot in a nearby ditch. Charles-Maurice Talleyrand, the famous French diplomat whose career spanned nearly four decades, remarked that the murder "was worse than a crime . . . it was a blunder." Napoleon wrote in his will that he had ordered the murder "for the safety, interest, and honor of the French people," adding that "in similar circumstances I would act the same way again."[8] In the case of Khashoggi, his death was both a crime and a blunder.

Closer to home, MBS's grandfather brutally destroyed his so-called Ikhwan (Arabic for brothers) fighters, whose religious zealotry had helped him conquer Arabia. But when they threatened Britain's support for him by raiding Iraq, Abdul Aziz destroyed the men who helped make him. "The Frankenstein of his own creation surely would have destroyed him if he had not taken the initiative to destroy it himself," St. John Philby, a British civil servant who defected to work for Abdul Aziz, wrote admiringly of the Ikhwans' 1929 defeat.[9]

Eleven Saudis went on secret trial for the murder of Khashoggi. Three were said to be acquitted, three sentenced to prison, and five sentenced to death. Saud Qahtani was fired in 2018 and banned by the U.S. from entering the country. A Saudi court cleared Qahtani of wrongdoing in 2021 and in June 2023 he was seen publicly at a social gathering at his uncle's home in Jeddah, using a walking stick but otherwise appearing unchanged from posts on social media. Progovernment Saudis called him "beloved"; a Saudi journalist critic called him the "dirty hand" of Mohammed bin Salman.[10]

These days, of course, no one defends murder signed off on by heads of state like Vladimir Putin, who continues to eliminate opponents with regularity. Some are in foreign lands when they are murdered. Others, like Alexei Navalny, an opposition leader, die in Russian prisons.

Some political realists point out that autocratic countries like China, Russia, and Iran routinely murder more political opponents than does Saudi Arabia, yet the U.S. utters barely a word of public admonition while repeatedly labeling Saudi Arabia a "pariah." Even U.S. presidents murder citizens they see as a threat. President Obama in 2011 ordered a drone strike in Yemen to kill Anwar Awlaki, a New Mexico native, after intelligence operatives labeled him a threat to U.S. security.[11] Following similar threat warnings, President Trump ordered the murder of Qasem Soleimani, an Iranian commander of the Quds Force.

The Crown Prince handled the Khashoggi problem as he does all others—by going on offense. He asked G-20 leaders to help Turkey investigate the journalist's murder. Then, early in 2019, to project business as usual, he went on a five-nation tour of friendly Asian countries: Pakistan, Malaysia, Indonesia, India, and China. In Beijing he was warmly greeted by President Xi Jinping, who, of course, never mentioned human rights. China holds at least one million Muslim Uyghurs in "reeducation camps" subjected to torture, forced labor, and forced abortions, according to Human Rights Watch. The Crown Prince essentially gave the kingdom's blessing to China's so-called antiterrorism activities against Uyghurs. "We respect and support China's rights to take counterterrorism and de-extremism measures to safeguard national security," he said. The Crown Prince also announced that Saudi Aramco would invest $10 billion in a joint venture to build a new refinery in China, already Saudi Arabia's largest oil buyer and trading partner.

Fortunately for the Crown Prince, Covid-19 pretty much ended head-of-state travel worldwide in 2020 and 2021. Thus his isolation by nervous world leaders was masked and the scandal largely faded. In October 2021, at Saudi Arabia's Future Investment Initiative in Riyadh, prominent U.S. investors once again were visible after boycotting the 2018 session to protest the killing of Jamal Khashoggi. While Crown Prince Mohammed was personally absent, his message was delivered loud and clear at the opening ceremony when 1970s disco queen Gloria Gaynor belted out her signature song including the lines, "You think I'd crumble? You think I'd lay down and die? Oh no not I, I will survive."

MBS has survived the black mark of the Khashoggi murder. By 2023 oil prices had rebounded. Saudi GDP grew at a record 8.7

percent in 2022, the highest of any G-20 nation. Non-oil revenue grew at 5.4 percent, well ahead of the 1.9 percent in 2016 before the launch of Vision 2030 reforms to wean the kingdom off oil. Female participation in the labor force rose to 37 percent, surpassing the government goal of 30 percent by 2030. Unemployment, which peaked at 14.9 percent in 2020, fell to 7.1 percent in late 2024. Abroad, the Crown Prince is pursuing an independent and prominent role on the world stage. The prince, whom President Biden labeled a "pariah" and pledged to punish, instead turned the tables on him. When the U.S. president flew to Jeddah ahead of the 2022 midterm elections to ask for more oil to reduce gasoline prices for U.S. voters, the prince just said "no." To further underscore that Saudi Arabia isn't a U.S. puppet, MBS deepened cooperation with China, which Biden called America's biggest threat, and Russia, which Washington confronts in a hot war in Ukraine.

The years of shunning by Western leaders seem to have made the prince more independent but less impulsive. "Learning is experience," Einstein famously said. "Everything else is just information." The disastrous Khashoggi experience seems to have brought learning. The man once famous for rapid decisions is said to have learned the importance of governance systems. "He learned the need for systems of governance, not whim," says a close Saudi associate. "He has learned to sit, think, reflect, and then react," says this official. One of his ministers recounts that MBS has on more than one occasion in recent years even agreed to accept a decision by the majority of his ministers though it contradicted his own view.

"MBS is more thoughtful and less brash," says a foreign intelligence official. "He's learned it's not smart to tick off everybody at one time." Perhaps it's cunning more than conscious but since the Khashoggi death, the Crown Prince has actively sought to reduce tensions with opponents in the region—reopening the kingdom's consulate in Iraq, patching up his rift with Qatar, welcoming Syria's Bashar al-Assad back into the Arab fold a year before Islamic insurgents drove him into exile in Moscow. And he even restored diplomatic relations with Iran. In short, offering more carrot and less stick. At home the regime continues to lock up critics and suspected political opponents. But there has been no repetition of the brutal and clumsy dispatch of Jamal Khashoggi. Once was enough.

CHAPTER SIX

Women Win

Of all the reforms promised by Prince Mohammed, none was more swift or successful than the liberation of Saudi women. And almost surely none will leave a more indelible imprint on the future of Saudi society. Regardless of whether he can end the kingdom's economic dependence on oil, MBS has significantly ended female dependence on men.

For much of history, to be born a woman in Saudi Arabia was at best to endure a lifelong sentence of surveillance by a male relative and to take no action outside the household without male approval and, most often, male accompaniment. A father controlled every aspect of a Saudi girl's life until she was passed to a new dominant male—her husband. At worst a woman's life was one of not just subjugation but virtual slavery in which wives and daughters could be physically, psychologically, and sexually abused at the whim of male family members who were protected by a criminal system and judiciary in the rare cases where a woman dared appeal to authorities. Small wonder. The supplication to Allah that a groom offers on his wedding night is the same he is instructed to offer when buying a camel: "Oh Allah, I ask you for the goodness that You have made her inclined toward and I take refuge with You from the evil within her and the evil that You have made her inclined toward."[1]

MBS's Vision 2030 pledged to change all that. Instead of being chained by men, women would be liberated to help build a new, more equal, and more prosperous Saudi Arabia. After all, some 60 percent of university graduates are women. Women not only are better educated than men but far more motivated after decades of being denied an opportunity to use their talents. Calling women a "great asset," MBS pledged to invest in enhancing their "productive capabilities and enable them to strengthen their future."[2] Women were—and still are—eager to stampede through this suddenly open door.

Within a year, a woman was named to chair the Saudi stock exchange. Another woman led a major bank; yet another served on the board of the new General Entertainment Authority, created to bring once-forbidden entertainment to Saudi Arabia. (Conservative Saudis labeled the GEA the General Evil Authority.) And Princess Reema bint Bandar was named to lead women's sports, an activity previously forbidden by religious authorities as "following in the devil's footsteps."[3]

These weren't affirmative action appointments. Sara al-Suhaimi, the CEO of the Saudi stock exchange, Tadawul, in February 2017, had been working in the financial industry for more than a dozen years enduring daily the restrictions imposed on women in the workplace. In an interview a few months after her appointment, she recalled how much had changed for women since she began working in 2004 as a research analyst at Samba, a Saudi bank. Not only was she segregated from her male colleagues, but the men she telephoned as an analyst seeking information on their companies hung up on her. "I had to write my questions and get my male colleagues to ask them for me," she recalls. Undeterred, she moved to Jadwa Investment, a Saudi investment company, where she soon became chief investment officer. She recalls organizing a large client event at a public hall in Riyadh only to be banned from entering because no one from her company had secured permission from the Riyadh city government for a mixed event. Without that permission, the religious police forbade her to mix with male clients.[4]

Now, she said, as social changes led by women's new freedoms began to accelerate in the kingdom, society was becoming more tolerant. Fathers, familiar with the rude treatment endured by their daughters, are becoming more cooperative with young female employees. Recalling how men had hung up on her fourteen years earlier, she said, generally young females these days are welcomed by the companies they study. "Fathers in those companies are proud to meet with women like their daughters," she said.

A general counsel of a leading financial institution described her own father's changing attitudes in 2017. A few years before, when she was invited to do a television interview, her father agreed with trepidation at the prospect of his daughter appearing unveiled and thus so publicly inviting criticism. This year when she was invited to be among a group of accomplished Saudi women meeting a prominent Western female political leader, her father again asked if she would be seen on television. But this time with pride, not concern. "He wanted to be sure not to miss me," she told me.

Of all the goals laid out in Vision 2030, meeting the target of growing the percentage of females who work to 30 percent from 22 percent by 2030 proved the easiest. In only six years, female participation in the labor force hit 37 percent in 2022, a more than 70 percent increase.

Prince Mohammed has always presented change for women as an economic opportunity, not a feminist luxury. This approach makes it harder for the religious conservatives to object and mobilize public opposition. He also moved cautiously, announcing women would be allowed to drive some nine months before they actually took the wheel in June 2018. While hardly the most significant change for Saudi women, driving was the most symbolic of their liberation. A woman could determine where she was going and get there without a male.

For nearly two decades some activist women had pushed for the right to drive. In 1990 after Saddam Hussein's invasion of Kuwait, they had watched Kuwaiti women driving their families to safety in Saudi Arabia and insisted they too must have the right to drive. Some dozens with valid international driver's licenses dared assemble and drive in Riyadh. Religious police quickly stopped them. Because there was no legal restriction they were violating, the women were all released. But they didn't escape punishment. Religious officials angrily denounced the women in sermons at mosques and distributed leaflets on the street titled "Names of the Promoters of Vice and Lasciviousness," the sort of spontaneous backlash that had long made even Al Saud rulers cautious about pushing reform too fast. Now, at last, Saudi women could get behind the wheel of a car to go where they pleased.

One young Western-educated career woman recalled her joy at attending one of the kingdom's first entertainment events—a three-day electric car race paired with nightly concerts featuring international celebrities like the Black Eyed Peas and French DJ and songwriter David Guetta.

"I drove there with my girlfriends and we danced until one thirty a.m.," she tells me. "It was unreal to have boys and girls mixing so close in Saudi Arabia." Indeed, six months earlier she wouldn't have been permitted to drive and only a few years ago such mixing would have landed her in the headquarters of the religious police.

These bearded *mutawa* had confronted me a decade earlier in the food court of the Faisaliah Tower, one of Riyadh's first high-rise buildings. I was seated with my Saudi male translator in the so-called "family section" where married couples and single women sit isolated from the "male" section. "Cover your head. You're in Saudi Arabia," the *mutawa* ordered in good English. Single men violating their own rules by invading the sanctity of the family section.

I raised the black scarf I always keep around my neck as insurance in such encounters to cover my offending hair. That wasn't good enough. The *mutawa* demanded my passport and the identity card of my Saudi companion, an employee of the Ministry of Information who had been assigned to help me. I was ordered to return immediately to my nearby hotel. My companion was taken to the headquarters of the Committee for the Promotion of Virtue and Prevention of Vice for simply doing his job. Again, the paradox of one government entity canceling the orders of another.

These days once-strictly segregated sexes are mixing everywhere without prohibition—or inhibition. Whether in workplaces or restaurants or newly opened cinemas, men and women can be seen side by side. And teenage boys and girls, like their American counterparts, huddle over computer screens and Pepsis in McDonald's. In the space of only a few years, such mixing has gone from nonexistent to nonchalant.

When the signs designating segregated seating for single men and families first began to disappear, groups of men and groups of women could be seen dining in the same room, surreptitiously exchanging glances across the room at the sheer daring of their proximity. Now in all restaurants and cafes young men and women share a table chatting casually, oblivious to others around them. It's as natural as if they were in Paris or New York. And even more shocking, once-forbidden music permeates virtually every restaurant, from casual to elegant. Songs like "Look of Love," with the lyrics "I can hardly wait to feel my arms around you . . ." shock me one evening dining with a Saudi family at the Cipriani restaurant in Riyadh. Knowing how horrifying music, especially with such lyrics, is to religious conservatives, just listening sends a shiver through me. But neither the family I'm dining with nor any other

Saudi in the restaurant seems to notice the music or lyrics. These days some upscale restaurants have gone beyond piped music to live bands and singers entertaining their mixed-gender diners. Il Baretto, an Italian restaurant in the King Abdullah Financial District, features a blond Ukrainian singer in a slim black dress performing nightly.

Indeed, the integration of sexes has been as sudden and significant as racial desegregation of the American South in the 1960s. And in the case of Saudi Arabia, with no visible protest, albeit with unhappy conservatives biting their tongues. "Before, government forced people to be conservative. Now it has completely flipped. This change isn't from the people. It can't last," one conservative told me in 2017, perhaps reflecting more a preference than a prediction.

For generations of Saudis, social life consisted for men of visits to the mosque to pray and sipping tea with groups of relatives or friends in each other's homes or rented guesthouses. For women, social life was limited to female-only gatherings of family members in homes or rented guesthouses. Now groups of single Saudi women frequent expensive restaurants dining with friends and smoking hookah. In Islam, a woman's earnings—or inheritance—belong to her only. So Saudi working women can easily indulge these days enjoying the fruits of their new labors. While most women still wear an abaya, increasingly they are a stylish fashion statement, not just a way to modestly mask a woman's figure. Upper-class women often wear expensive pastel abayas flowing open to expose expensive clothes underneath or to conceal tight, revealing sportswear.

Unlike women's liberation in the U.S., in Saudi Arabia there was no bra-burning and no feminist icon like Gloria Steinem. If confrontation was the predominant tactic for American women, co-option was the strategy for their Saudi sisters. Faced with religious leaders using Islam as a sword against women, Saudi ladies long used the holy book as their shield—and occasionally as a sword—

against religious officials. When the grand mufti forbade driving, stating it would lead to adultery, Saudi women pointed out that females, including the Prophet Mohammed's wives, rode camels. Indeed, they noted, his favorite wife, Aisha, rode a camel into battle against the Prophet's son-in-law.

They also pointed out that the Prophet's first wife, Kadijah bint Khuwailid, was a prominent businesswoman. Having lost two husbands to raids, she hired her distant cousin Muhammed to lead her caravan to Syria. She was so pleased with his performance that *she* asked him to marry her. "Son of my uncle," she said, "I love thee for thy kinship with me and for that thou art ever in the center, not being a partisan among the people for this or that. I love thee for the beauty of thy trustworthiness and for the beauty of thy character and the truth of thy speech."[5] Muhammed accepted her proposal and informed her uncle of their marriage desire. Islamic historians believe she was ten to fifteen years older than her new husband.

One of the ironies of strict Wahhabi Islam, which encourages Muslims to return to the original teachings and practices of the Prophet, is that the practices of the Prophet were, as Prince Mohammed is fond of underscoring today, far from what Wahhabism seeks to impose. Women in Prophet Muhammed's day attended mosque, listened to his discourses, and even participated in war. Nusaybah, a woman of Medina, joined other women providing water to Muslim soldiers at the seventh-century Battle of Uhud. When the Prophet came under attack, she defended him with her shield and sword,[6] something Wahhabi scholars never mention. He allowed his wives to speak freely to him and laughed when one of them literally told his companion, Umar, to mind his own business. Umar was at the Prophet's home encouraging him to demand that his wives show him more respect. Prophet Mohammed enjoyed running races with young Aisha, whom he married at age six, though he is said to have consummated the marriage only when she was nine.

The Saudi government in 2019 finally banned marriage for Saudis under age fifteen and it now requires court approval for those under eighteen to marry. This decision, approved by two-thirds of the Shura Council, the kingdom's advisory parliament to the king, came only after a decade of discussion. A Saudi father sparked a public outcry in 2009 by marrying his twelve-year-old daughter to an eighty-year-old man in exchange for a $20,000 bride payment or dowry. The specter of a father selling his young daughter to such an elderly man horrified even quiescent Saudis. Responding to public anger, then King Abdullah named a religious scholar to advise him on the issue—Sheikh Abdullah al-Mutlag.

Senior ulama are usually stern and inaccessible to foreign females, but Sheikh Mutlag agreed to meet me to explain the role of religious scholars in the lives of Saudis. When I asked about child marriage, he declined to share his advice to the king but explained, "If there is harm to the girl, it is forbidden. This is what Prophet Muhammed said." When I noted that the Prophet was betrothed to a six-year-old, the sheikh waved off any comparison saying, "Aisha was not like a nine-year-old today. The Prophet consulted her on all issues."[7]

All these sweeping changes for women have led today's young Saudi girls to dream big. One of MBS's close aides, Mohammed al-Sheikh, proudly reported to me in 2018 that his sixteen-year-old daughter, Joharah, told him, "I am going to be more successful than you."[8] Some months later, over a family dinner at a Riyadh restaurant, she spoke for herself: "I want to be the first female government minister in Saudi Arabia."[9] Her father and mother, one of the kingdom's prominent professional women, who is Chief Transformation Officer at Riyadh Bank, beamed with pride. Even five years ago, almost any Saudi father would have been chagrined at a daughter voicing ambition so beyond the borders of acceptable conduct for a Saudi woman.

Indeed, during a visit in 1982 to Najran, a poor province near the Yemen border, the eighteen-year-old daughter of that provincial governor told me she hoped to follow in her father's footsteps and be governor one day. I wrote about her ambition in a series of stories for the *Wall Street Journal* detailing the small roots of change still surviving the increasingly heavy hand of religion. In a chance encounter more than a decade later, her mother repeatedly condemned me for humiliating her daughter and their whole family. "My daughter would never say such a thing," she insisted over and over.

A woman's ambition is no longer deplorable but laudable. While there isn't yet a female governor of one of the kingdom's thirteen provinces, one seems inevitable in coming years given women's capabilities and the government's willingness to tap them.

"I support Saudi Arabia and half of Saudi Arabia is women so I support women,"[10] Prince Mohammed told *Atlantic* writer Jeffrey Goldberg. "In our religion there is no difference between men and women," he said, stressing that they are paid equally in Saudi.

The Quran in surah 3:195 indicates Allah's view on equality. "I suffer not the good deeds of any to go to waste be he man or woman: the one of you is of the other."

In another surah, the Quran indicates that righteousness, not gender, determines Allah's true preferences. "O mankind, indeed We have created you from male and female and made you peoples and tribes that you may know one another. Indeed, the most noble of you in the sight of Allah is the most righteous of you."

Women in the workplace clearly are one of the reasons for the kingdom's burst of economic success. Many of them studied to be teachers of math, science, and literature at a time when teaching girls was about the only career open to women under the heavy hand of religion. But at least they learned something useful even if many couldn't find jobs in that overcrowded field. Their male colleagues grew up studying Islam in school and at after-school programs and all too often also majored in Islamic studies at university. With no marketable skills, most took jobs in government guaranteeing lifetime employment and few expectations beyond showing up.

On the other hand, women possessed marketable skills. When given a chance to work in recent years, they have flocked with their education and energy not just to government jobs but also to the private sector. Almost any minister or Saudi CEO expresses a preference for hiring women.

Walid Abukhaled, CEO of Saudi Arabian Military Industries (SAMI), is typical. "I had rather employ women as they are willing to take any training you ask and they are educated and eager to prove themselves," he says. SAMI's corporate executive female hires have grown from zero in 2018 to 22 percent five years later, he says.

One young Saudi female lawyer says she's happy to see so many women getting job opportunities but frets about any hint of affirmative action. This outspoken lady remonstrated with her boss from Dubai when he visited the Riyadh office and met with female associates. He must meet with all associates, she says, just as he met with all the firm's partners, who happen to be men. "We are workers, not women," she says. She has just joined the firm, doubling her salary at an earlier law firm. She says she negotiated hard, saying no to the job three times before securing the salary she sought. "I know my worth and I asked for it."[11]

The large number of working women has not only provided needed skills for the long-term task of transforming the economy from oil, but also fueled near-term economic growth. For instance, auto dealers in Riyadh reported an influx of women buying their first car even before they were allowed to drive in June 2018. "Women used to come and sit in the back seat," a Hyundai dealer on Kharis Road, a popular street for car dealerships in Riyadh, told me in 2017 when the government announced women would drive in 2018. "But now they try out the front seat." He said women who visit his dealership want bright-colored automobiles, like red and blue, not the gray and white many have ridden in with their drivers. And safety features are their top concern. "They ask how many air bags," the salesman said. Sure enough, a Saudi female friend took me to lunch soon after she got her Saudi driver's permit in a bright turquoise BMW.

At dinner with sixteen professional Saudi women in June 2018, a week after women were permitted to drive, only one of the ladies had driven herself to the dinner. The others had come with drivers in part because only six had yet obtained a driver's license. The government required driver training to get a license in order to control and slow increase of female drivers on the road. For MBS, always in a hurry, gradual and more cautious was the strategy where women were involved, given the religious and societal sensitivities. For instance he announced women would drive in 2017, nine months before they were permitted to do so in June 2018.

"The point of driving isn't so much getting in a car as getting freedom of choice," explained Amal al-Shaman, a member of the kingdom's consultative assembly, the Majlis Ash-Shura.[12] The dinner, organized by Tadawul CEO Sara al-Suhaimi and Hanadi al-Sheikh, then head of strategy and development at the stock exchange, was much like a gathering of American women discussing their work and balancing family. All but two of the women were married and most had children. Of course, unlike American women, each of these ladies wore a scarf covering her hair though none covered her face.

All were grateful for the pace of liberalization in the kingdom. "Females now can go to dinner with foreign guests and male colleagues," they explained. "We used to have to invite men to our homes as we couldn't risk taking a male guest to dinner in Riyadh and being dismissed from our guest by the religious police," said Deema al-Yahya, executive manager of innovation at MISK, Prince

Mohammed's foundation, which focuses on education, culture, and media. She serves on the board of Microsoft and is one of the kingdom's most expert technologists. Visiting Saudi schools to discuss technology and computer programing with young pupils, she finds them far advanced over her generation. "They say, 'We know all about programming, tell us about cryptocurrencies,'" she says.

Another woman tells of a man in her place of work who refused to deal with her. She continued to politely persist by talking to him. Finally, he acknowledged she was the first woman other than his wife and mother he had ever encountered and he simply didn't know how to treat her.

"We were told forever women can't drive," says Shihana Alazzaz, then general counsel of the prestigious Public Investment Fund (PIF) and now a royal court adviser. "Suddenly we can. So now we know there are no limits."

For Saudi women, the word *haram*, or forbidden, is now like the story of the boy who cried wolf in Aesop's Fables, repeatedly giving a false alarm. Saudi women no longer run when someone cries "forbidden." Indeed, four years after Alazzaz's assertion of no more limits she was appointed deputy secretary general of the Saudi Cabinet of Ministers, the first woman to hold the post.

None of these women hesitated to ignore the restaurant's closing for prayer when our dinner ended. With the front door locked for prayer time, traditionally Saudis were confined inside for the half-hour duration for prayer. But by 2018, upscale restaurants like the one we were in dared to leave their back door unlocked. These women casually exited through the unlocked rear door scattering to their cars, something unthinkable a few years earlier. What was daring in 2018 is normal now. Restrictions continue to ease in virtually all walks of Saudi life. Shops and restaurants increasingly don't bother to close for prayer time.

Shortly after this all-female dinner, I attended a mixed dinner in Riyadh where the conversation was much like one might have heard in the U.S. in the 1970s, when women first entered the American workforce in significant numbers. The Saudi men are explaining to their female counterparts that they must "wait" for leadership roles because they lack experience. One Saudi lady responds, as I might have in 1970, that women haven't been given opportunities. She describes being interviewed by the minister of finance for a job. He concluded by asking her, "Can you do all these things?" She boldly responded, "I could be minister today." Fearing she had been too forceful, she acknowledges relief when she is offered a job. "Women have got to seize opportunity," she insists.

With the emerging seniority of women in the Saudi labor force, some now are encountering the delicate issue of how to deal with other women reporting to them. One senior woman at a private company recalls her assistant disclosing her engagement. "My first thought was, 'Oh, she'll quit.'" Later at home she reflected on her lackluster congratulations to her colleague and reproached herself. "How sexist of you." She resolves to encourage the young assistant to combine marriage and high performance at work by pledging to support her in achieving that goal.

One of the most prominent female CEOs is Jomana Alrashid, who leads the Saudi Research and Media Group (SRMG), a publicly listed company. Founded in 1987 around two respected titles, *Asharq al-Awsat* and *Arab News*, the company now owns thirty-five titles, has a new TV station in partnership with Bloomberg, and is actively pursuing partnerships with international media brands. Under Jomana's leadership, SRMG revenues totaled nearly $1 billion in 2023, a 66 percent increase from 2020's $603 million annual revenue. "When I joined SRMG it was clear we need an overhaul," she says. "With everyone scrolling through the news on their smartphones we knew we had to double down on digital and social media." She is producing content on a wide range of interests—travel, health, crime, cooking, reality—even producing a true-crime docuseries that SRMG sold to Netflix. The company has expanded its portfolio to include new platforms with new digital content, podcasts, and radio reaching 195 million people worldwide. SRMG under her leadership typifies MBS's goal of engaging the kingdom with the world. And she typifies the large group of Saudi women who studied and prepared long before Vision 2030 posted its welcome sign for women in the workplace.

"This progress didn't happen overnight," she says. "Women prepared for over a decade for change." Indeed, the late King Abdullah began sending hundreds of thousands of Saudis abroad for study in 2005 and, surprisingly, allowed women too to receive scholarships plus a stipend to pay for a male relative to accompany them, since religious rules required a woman always to be in the charge of a male guardian. Jomana was one of those King Abdullah scholars.

She grew up in Lebanon, the daughter of a prominent Saudi journalist who moved his family there to secure better education for his children than the kingdom's religiously bound curriculum provided. In 2007 she moved to London to pursue a degree in political science at the School of Oriental and African Studies despite her father questioning her devotion to higher education at a time when Saudi women were limited largely to roles as teachers, health care workers, or personal assistants. Despite those limited opportunities, she was determined to proceed. When jobs proved elusive, she earned a master's in journalism to pursue a writing career. When employment continued to elude her, she began freelancing. Ever determined, she bravely approached the Saudi embassy in London dressed very unconventionally—no abaya, no headscarf, and no niqab to conceal her face. She pounded on the door until someone answered. "What do you want?" he asked. "I'm a reporter with a Riyadh newspaper," she confidently responded. She was taken to see the Saudi ambassador.

Soon she was working on the communication staff, the first female employee in the kingdom's London embassy. She met with a wide range of foreign media to answer their questions and arrange interviews with visiting Saudi dignitaries. By the time serious opportunities opened for women under MBS, she had the experience to qualify for more senior roles. In 2019 she returned to the kingdom working as a media adviser to the royal court. One year later she was approached by the Saudi Research and Media Group to interview for the CEO role. At the end of the interview, the board asked her, "When can you start?" Ironically, she had finally won a job at SRMG, a company that over the years had repeatedly rejected her applications.

"I applied for various roles—from researcher to reporter—but I was always turned down," she says, smiling at the irony of now running the company that refused to hire her.

One of the most famous women in Saudi Arabia today is Rayyanah Barnawi, thirty-four, an astronaut who spent ten days in space in 2023. This lovely woman with engaging green eyes is soft-spoken but exudes confidence and poise. When we meet at the Saudi Space Center some six months after her flight, she stresses her gratitude to a government that made possible her dream to study biomedical research, a field that enabled her as an astronaut to conduct experiments at the International Space Station. Biomedical research was unavailable in Saudi but thanks to a government scholarship, she studied in New Zealand. After graduation, she landed a job at the King Faisal Specialist Hospital in Riyadh, where she worked for a decade before being nominated to compete to be the kingdom's first female astronaut. The grueling selection process took sixty days during which the contestants were interviewed repeatedly and given IQ tests, psychological testing, critical thinking tests, and a test to measure their ability to withstand G forces.

The news of her selection came while she was driving to work. "You are now one step closer to your dream," she recalls being told. I ask how she reacted to that news. "I cried," she says. She took the day off to share the news with her family before entering training.[13]

Barnawi's voyage to space is the starkest example of change in the kingdom. Not long ago, women were forbidden to be in the presence of an unrelated man. In 2023, Barnawi spent ten days in a small space station with two unrelated men—a Saudi and an American—and an American woman. She says she was honored to be "trusted to do experiments in the most expensive lab in the world." Her feat was followed by the whole of Saudi Arabia, fascinated by their first female astronaut. (The first Saudi male astronaut was MBS's older half brother, Prince Sultan bin Salman, who orbited the Earth in a U.S. space capsule in 1985.)

The Saudi Space Commission was established in December 2018, another effort by Crown Prince Mohammed to put Saudi Arabia at the cutting edge of achievement. The Saudi Space Agency plans its first lunar orbit in two to three years to deploy a rover to the moon's south pole, where water is believed to exist.[14] Asked what is her new goal, Barnawi replies instantly, "I hope to go on a lunar mission."

For women whose every action once was controlled by a man, the list of freedoms beyond driving in 2018 seems boundless. Without male permission, women can get medical care, attend college, rent a hotel room or apartment, establish a business, buy real estate, file a case in court, deal with a government ministry, and get personal identification. Within a year King Salman issued a decree granting women the right to get passports and travel abroad without a male guardian.

Still, a Saudi woman, regardless of her age, needs guardian approval to marry according to a new Personal Status Law passed in March 2023.[15] If the woman's guardian prevents a marriage, however, she can apply to the court and the judge can appoint a new guardian or act on her behalf. The kingdom still regards homosexuality, same-sex marriage, and LGBTQ as taboo. But human rights groups say it's hard to determine if such restrictions are enforced. And in 2023, the kingdom's tourist website updated its FAQ page to answer the question of whether LGBTQ visitors are welcome in the kingdom, with this response: "Everyone is welcome to visit Saudi Arabia and visitors are not asked to disclose such personal details."[16]

These days it's not just high-profile positions women are filling but all kinds of private sector jobs, from helicopter pilot to hostess, hotel receptionist to tour guide. These young women say they will create future opportunities through hard work and high performance in whatever job they hold.

During a visit to the Red Sea, a young female pilot dressed in a white shirt and khaki pants, her hair cut short, is at the end of her workday. But asked to fly several of us to Al Wahj, the small northern Arabia town made famous in 1917 when Lawrence of Arabia launched the Arab army's attack on Aqaba from there, she doesn't hesitate. The round trip extends her day by at least three hours.

This tiny twenty-eight-year-old says she decided to be a pilot well before Vision 2030 boosted opportunity for women. Because Saudi forbade women pilots, she trained in Florida to earn her pilot's license. Back home, with new opportunities opening for women, she took a job piloting a helicopter. Her employer owns one hundred of them since demand for transport by helicopter is especially high at the Red Sea, which is seeking to become a major tourist destination.

She hops in her seat and starts the engine with her male co-pilot seated on her right. Quickly she jumps out and rapidly checks that passengers are properly buckled. Then she slams the big chopper's heavy door with one swift swoosh, hops into her seat, and lifts off. Like other Saudi women working in jobs created by Vision 2030, she says she is grateful for the changes in her country and the opportunities they are creating for her.

At Six Senses, a five-star hotel in the sand dunes near the Red Sea, another young Saudi woman is hostess for the hotel's dining room. A poised Nayar Ajieani, twenty-six, greets customers with a

smile and confidently leads them to a table. Saudis, who once refused service jobs, now proudly take them. She studied public relations at King Abdul Aziz University in Jeddah and says she intended
to seek a public relations job in some corporation in Jeddah. "But
after I saw the Vision I wanted to be among the first women to help
build the vision," she says. So she left her family and moved to the
Red Sea to work in the hospitality industry. Given the importance of
family in Saudi Arabia, this willingness to separate from life with a
large extended family is new. But the necessity to earn a living, not
depend on government, is creating many new trends in the kingdom.

In Al Ula, the guide to Dedan's seventh-century BC tombs is
swathed head to toe in black. A local resident, Shahad al-Bedair
says she was planning to go to New York to study until she read
about Vision 2030. "We have opportunities we never had before,"
she says. Another local guide agrees. Raneem Obaid was a medical
chemist before becoming a guide. "All I could talk about were hor-
mones and enzymes," she says, imitating a look of boredom. "Now
I talk to people from all over the world and I know my local history.
I'm grateful to his royal highness for this opportunity."

All these young women are part of the reason private sector
employment has grown in Saudi Arabia. Shifting Saudis off government dependence and into private sector jobs is the core goal
of the Crown Prince's plan to remake the economy. The fact that
women aren't just working as teachers, or in the financial sector
in banks or the stock exchange, but in less glamorous and lower-
paying jobs at all levels of the economy is a hopeful sign that Saudis
will step up and work to transform their national economy—and
secure their own livelihood.

Still, there is a long way to go. Saudis account for only 21 percent of total employment in the private sector, up from 16 percent
in 2016. There now are 2.3 million Saudis employed in the private
sector compared with 8.87 million foreigners.[17] The overwhelming
majority of private sector workers continue to be foreigners despite

prolonged efforts since 1985 by the Ministry of Labor to incentivize companies to hire Saudis.

Another 3.5 million foreigners, mostly women, work as domestic helpers in the kingdom.[18] Saudis working in the public and private sector include 2.27 million men and 1.42 million women, with female employment rising more rapidly than that of males.[19] The Crown Prince's goal is to cut unemployment from 11.6 percent in 2016 to 7 percent by 2030. By the fourth quarter of 2023, it had fallen to 7.7 percent,[20] clear progress, and by late 2024 it stood at 7.1 percent.

The longer-term impact on Saudi society of more and more women working rather than staying home to breed children and serve men isn't clear. But already women in the workplace are changing traditional marriage mores. Once families arranged marriages for their children to assure a "suitable" match in terms of tribal affiliation or keeping wealth within their extended family. These days more young Saudis, especially women, are selecting their own mates from those they work alongside.

One accomplished young Saudi woman recounted, in 2023, how she had chosen her husband. He had commented on LinkedIn about her work in a manner she found overly familiar and offensive. She didn't respond. But within months, the two wound up working together and their personal interactions convinced her they had much in common. Both work on defense issues. Now they are married and each is planning to pursue a PhD. Finding the best opportunity for both isn't easy, she says, but they are pursuing their ambitions together. A very modern solution.

Saudi men increasingly find they aren't needed to help locate a match for Saudi women. A Saudi friend tells me he offered to help a female colleague find a husband for her daughter. "No," the mother replied. "I'm sure she'll find someone at work."[21]

Interestingly, the Crown Prince too found his own wife, friends say. The data-driven prince studied various of his royal cousins and in 2006 asked his mother to arrange a lunch in a restaurant with one of those cousins and her sister. As always, Prince Mohammed was in a hurry. After only half an hour of polite conversation, MBS asked Princess Sara bint Mashour if she wanted to proceed to a formal engagement announcement by their parents. She agreed. Two years later, the couple married. They are children of half brothers born to the kingdom's founder, Abdul Aziz.

While most Saudi women these days are highly visible, the females closest to the Crown Prince are almost invisible—at least outside their royal palaces. As noted earlier, MBS's mother, Fahda, was a powerful influence on him and his brothers, instilling relentless ambition and determination mostly from behind the scenes. The Crown Prince's wife is even more private. Friends say she has guarded her privacy so completely that she can go out in public without ever being recognized. Like her mother-in-law, she is the primary influence on her children. The Crown Prince acknowledges that his busy schedule often keeps him from his young children just as his father's devotion to duty as governor of Riyadh largely extracted him from MBS's childhood years.

Though the royal women around MBS aren't seen, that doesn't mean they aren't heard. Those close to the Crown Prince say he is comfortable with strong women because his childhood included constant interaction with the outspoken women in his father's home. While King Salman was a conservative traditionalist in his public life, at home his wives, his daughter, and the wives of his older sons all were accustomed to candid conversation where women's views were not only expressed but respected. "He's not afraid of women," says a cousin. "He's accustomed to candor between the sexes." Those who know his family say he respects his wife's decisions and is careful never to contradict her in front of their five children, ages fifteen to four years. And he's rearing his two young daughters to be equal to his sons, enjoying scuba diving and other more traditionally masculine pursuits. Still, only their eldest son, Prince Salman, is occasionally photographed in public. His younger sisters and brothers remain out of sight like their mother.

From conversations with the Crown Prince and his brother, Prince Khalid, and others close to their family it's easy to believe that his mother was surely one of the greatest influences on her son. When I quoted Napoleon's assertion, "The future destiny of the child is always the work of the mother," the Crown Prince outlined his mother's efforts to instill a drive to excel into her children. Indeed, Saudis say MBS's mother fought hard for her family. When her husband wanted to divorce her and offered a large payment, Princess Fahda said, "I don't want money; I want Salman." Prince Salman was so touched by her devotion that Fahda and her children remained part of his royal household. But, as MBS began his climb to power in 2016, U.S. officials say he kept his mother a palace prisoner. According to these officials, when his concerned father sought access to his wife, MBS explained she was receiving medical treatment in New York, which U.S. officials knew wasn't true. "The story was so widespread but not any details," says a U.S. intelligence official. "If it happened it was some sort of family turmoil, families are families." And the Al Saud family knows how to keep its secrets. MBS's parents remain together after four decades of marriage. Their son has inherited the strong will of his mother and the royal power of his father.

CHAPTER SEVEN

Castles in the Sand

Most of the world brags about its megaprojects. Saudi Arabia boasts of its *giga*projects.

Whoever heard of a North Pole in the desert? Saudi Arabia's North Pole, a sprawling new urban area near Riyadh, won't feature flying reindeer but flying taxis, vertical living, and the world's tallest building, a slim, shiny toothpick rising more than half a mile, topping Dubai's Burj Khalifa tower, now the world's tallest building.

Even Medina, Islam's second-holiest site, where Prophet Mohammed is buried, will transform into a fun park with e-karting, a state-of-the-art cinema with IMAX and VIP screens, and a ten-lane bowling alley.[1] Pray and play.

The most expensive gigaproject is Neom, a $500 billion futuristic development the size of Massachusetts in the kingdom's northwest near Jordan, grandly said to be "of this earth but not of this world." Neom features "The Line," a smart city built completely from scratch in the desert. It consists of two unbroken rows of mirrored skyscrapers standing taller than the Empire State Building and running for 105 miles—more than the distance from New York City to Philadelphia—connected by a high-speed train and no cars. It will be a zero-carbon environment. The Line's 9 million residents will occupy only 2 percent of the land area used by London's 9 million residents.[2] All this will provide more sustainable living for humans and their climate, says the Crown Prince.

Nearby, Trojena, a mountain village, will offer the Middle East's first outdoor snow skiing and host the 2029 Asian Winter Games. Sindalah, a group of islands in the Red Sea, opened in 2024 offering a year-round yachting hub for the rich in the lush marine life of the Red Sea.

In the capital city of Riyadh is gargantuan King Salman Park, five times the size of New York's Central Park and seven times as big as London's Hyde Park. Nearby, the "Mukaab," a 1,300-foot cube structure large enough to encase twenty Empire State Buildings, will offer eighty entertainment venues, including the world's first "immersive" destination where planners claim "you enter a new reality transported to Mars one day and magical worlds the next."[3]

Not far from Riyadh is Qiddiya, an amusement park planned to be three times the size of Walt Disney World. Beyond these grandiose structures, the kingdom also has a ten-year lock on Formula 1 racing and a five-year lock on hosting men's tennis "next-generation" finals as well as women's tennis finals for three years, owns professional golf, and has snagged the world's highest-paid soccer player, Cristiano Ronaldo. And it has been awarded the 2034 World Cup.

In short, MBS plans to make Saudi Arabia home to the biggest and best that a vivid imagination, vaunting ambition, and boundless billions can buy.

These grandiose projects, most yet to be built, are fundamentally marketing hype for the new Saudi Arabia MBS hopes to create by 2030. Periodically unveiling a dazzling gigaproject helps mesmerize Saudi Arabia's young people with the prospect of promised modernity and prosperity. The projects also help mask the daily drudgery requiring decades to truly transform the Saudi economy off dependence on oil revenue. That oil transition is only inching along. Napoleon famously said, "The men who have changed the world never succeed by winning the powerful but always by stirring the masses." MBS seems to agree. He has jailed the elite and courted the young.

The gigaprojects, of course, aren't *just* marketing. They are the core of a $1 trillion plan by Saudi Arabia to attract global tourists with deep pockets whose spending can create jobs and help sustain Saudi Arabia's economy beyond oil. Worldwide tourism revenues in 2022 totaled around $2 trillion[4] and the Saudi government believes its pristine landscape and novel new tourist attractions will appeal to both the young and the superwealthy who seek unique adventures in places their friends haven't been.

So far there is early evidence of success. The kingdom drew 109 million tourist visits in 2023, ahead of its 100 million target for 2030. So the goal has been upped to 150 million by 2030, growing the tourism sector's contribution to Saudi gross domestic product to 10 percent from 3 percent in 2019, according to the kingdom's tourism minister. The 2023 tourist visits included some 27 million foreigners and 77 million local visits. Saudi international tourism grew faster than that of any other G-20 country in 2023, according to United Nations Tourism. But Mideast tensions seemed to put a lid on growth in 2024 as the kingdom was on track to match or only slightly boost its number of foreign visitors.

MBS's ambition for Saudi Arabia is literally limitless. His Vision 2030 calls for the tourism sector to contribute at least 10 percent of Saudi GDP by 2030, triple its 2022 contribution of 3.2 percent.[5] Part of that will come from enticing Saudis to vacation in their own country, not abroad. But the plan calling for 150 million annual visits by 2030 envisions nearly half, some 70 million, would be international tourists.[6] A host of luxury gigaprojects are part of the plan for luring international visitors. Another is a full calendar of sports events.

Surprisingly, Saudis who once couldn't wait to flee their

homeland to relax now are vacationing in the kingdom. "Saudi Arabia is a work camp," a disgruntled young Saudi man told me in 2009. "We work hard all year just so we can escape and relax for one month a year." A year later, Prince Sultan bin Salman, a half brother of MBS and the kingdom's first director of tourism, acknowledged that sentiment. "We can't continue to live in Saudi Arabia and feel alive only somewhere else," he told me in 2010. "People need to be able to live in their country and have fun, to love it and enjoy it." Fifteen years later, MBS has freed Saudis from religious strictures to do just that—have fun and enjoy their country.

Despite all the marketing hype devoted to the kingdom's gigaprojects, they aren't without controversy. The staggering cost of Neom, the $500 billion project to build bountiful tourist attractions along with a business and industrial zone in northwest Saudi Arabia, has raised doubts in the minds of many Saudis. The scale of it also may scare as many potential investors as it seduces. Moreover, the fact that the area was the ancestral homeland of Howeitat tribesmen forcibly removed to make way for Neom raised an outcry from human rights activists abroad. The United Nations Human Rights Council called on all international companies doing business in Neom to ensure they aren't contributing to human rights abuses.[7]

Foreign investors have been reluctant to support projects in Neom, perhaps partly for fear of human rights backlash.

More recently, the government has been forced to admit it will slow spending on some of its ambitious projects, including Neom, as oil revenue stagnates, budget deficits persist, foreign direct investment remains elusive, and heavy government borrowing risks overheating the Saudi economy. "The delay or rather the extension of some projects will serve the economy," Saudi finance minister Mohammed al-Jadaan diplomatically explained in 2024. That year in an effort to quiet critics and entice foreign investors, the government unveiled two million photos of Neom on a website and will maintain 563 cameras and 300 drones to document its progress continuously.

The name Neom is derived from the Greek *neo*, meaning new, and *m* for the Arabic word *mustaqbal*, meaning future. The ambitions for Neom are gargantuan. The Crown Prince first announced the project in Riyadh at the inaugural Future Investment Initiative in October 2017. Four years later, he announced the beginning of construction of Neom's centerpiece, the Line. "Why should seven million people every year die because of pollution?" he asked rhetorically. "Why should we lose one million people every year due to traffic accidents? And why should we accept wasting years of our lives commuting?" His answer: "We need to transform the concept of a conventional city into that of a futuristic one." The Line is his futuristic, carless city.

While many critics regard Neom and other Saudi projects as outlandish, those close to the prince say he believes the world's construction concepts all are far too incremental; what the world needs is innovative, futuristic concepts.

Neom's ambition is to be precisely that—a futuristic city that attracts companies involved in cutting-edge research and manufacturing; the world's new Silicon Valley offering a vast array of entertainment and tourism attractions even if no alcohol. Alcoholic drinks will be available a short drive away over a bridge connecting Neom to nearby Sharm el-Sheikh in Egypt. "I see Neom as wonderful alchemy, taking a raw and ancient land and melding it with ideas that will shape the future," gushes Neom Tourism's marketing director.

My first visit to Neom in 2019 with a group of Saudi high school students found more "raw ancient land" than futuristic development. Neom, planned to occupy an area thirty-three times the size of New York City, was mainly bare sand and sandstone mountains. The promised ski village, glow-in-the-dark sand on beaches, an artificial moon, the linear wonder city, the "Line": none yet existed.

Indeed, we land at Tabuk Airport, some 160 miles by car to Sharma, one of the few villages in the Neom region. Sharma boasts a small hotel with a conference room where the two best students from each of the kingdom's forty-seven towns assemble for what Neom's manager of communications, Wael Hussein, describes as a "diverse student dialogue." Each school selects its best student in Arabic and its best student in English and assigns the boys a topic to research; Neom is this year's topic. Hussein extols the "exceptional livability" of Neom, with thriving businesses and protected environment; residents will not drive cars but live close to work, utilize electric flying taxis, and supply their food needs from organic farming. Neom, according to its planners, will be the world's most self-sufficient city in food production, utilizing innovative vertical farming and greenhouses.

The precocious teenage boys are full of pointed questions and comments. You are just re-creating Dubai, says one. Will robots replace jobs for students like us? Why announce it if the plans aren't yet complete? Why spend $500 billion in one province of Saudi Arabia? Why not spread that money around the country? How can Neom protect nature? Why not use proven nuclear power, not nascent sun and wind technology? Will Neom be a new fourteenth province in Saudi Arabia since you say it will have its own laws, not governed by those of the kingdom? Hussein responds to most of these questions by underscoring that Neom will be a twenty-year project, a living lab for the world on how to control climate change and keep the planet clean. In short, lifelong learning.

None ask the obvious question: How will Neom get water to its projects and people? Like much of Saudi Arabia, Neom will rely on desalinized water from the nearby Red Sea. A massive desalination plant is under construction that will produce 50,000 cubic meters of clean water daily from renewable energy sources. The water will be stored in six reservoirs yet to be built. Wastewater will be reclaimed and recycled to minimize water loss.

Our next stop is a newly constructed housing site for 350 workers at Neom. This is about the only new structure at Neom other than a royal palace for the king finished in 2018 and an airport largely used for private VIP flights, though more recently opened to commercial flights of tourists to Al Ula. Hussein seeks to proselytize visiting officials from the Saudi Ministry of Education and the Shura Council, the kingdom's handpicked parliament. These men are more restrained in their questions and comments than the high school students. "This is a lot of money to spend on one project in this part of the country," says one. "Please convince me it will bring benefits to our country."

"This is a difficult development project," acknowledges Hussein. "By 2023 we want people living in Neom. We want one million living there by 2030 and five million visitors by 2030."

Yet in 2023, Neom remained largely illusive. Its CEO, Nadhmi al-Nasr, announced that year that Neom's infrastructure is 20 percent complete and that Sindalah Island, the luxury resort and yacht club, will open on schedule in 2024. It did. But al-Nasr was replaced as CEO that year as costs and delays mounted. Drone photos show work beginning on the Line, the 105-mile-long linear city, and on the underground railroad that will connect its residents. In June 2023, Neom hosted the first test flight of the Volocopter, an electric-powered air taxi, after eighteen months of collaboration between Saudi civil aviation and Volocopter GmbH, a German company. The company expects to get certification to make its VoloCity air taxi in 2024 and produce some fifty aircraft a year at its plant in Germany.[8]

All the futuristic plans with little to see in the present made some Saudis doubt that these projects were a wise use of the kingdom's money. And the foreign press often wrote about the many gigaprojects with a dubious slant.

Finally, MBS has had enough of doubters. He stars in a Discovery documentary with project designers to insist that the Line can and will be built. "They say a lot of projects in Saudi Arabia can't be done, they're too ambitious," he says. "They can keep saying that and we can keep proving them wrong."[9]

The documentary features an exuberantly confident MBS interspersed with half a dozen designers who talk eloquently about the need for new concepts yet seem to draw a collective sigh of anxiety at the project they're discussing. The Line is "intriguing to many people, troubling to many people, and troubling in some ways to those who are designing it," says Sir Peter Cook, an elderly English designer who is the godfather of the Line's design team, which was assembled from several firms. "You can't look at this for the first time and not ask yourself: What are they thinking?" says Houston-based designer Roger Soto.

MBS was thinking, "Why can't we build a circle?" But after brainstorming with the world's best designers he had assembled, one proposed turning the circle into a line. That concept fit the vast open geography of Neom. "The northwest of Saudi Arabia is untouched; almost empty with mixed typography—mountains, valleys, oases, dunes, beaches, islands, coral everything from skiing to diving," the Crown Prince says. Prince and designers all agree that this new Saudi city must not wreck the magnificent landscape in the way the beauty of California has been marred by sprawling suburbs and clogged highways.

To assure that the Line's design includes wildly imaginative thinking, the group added one of Hollywood's most prominent creative art directors, Olivier Pron, who worked on sci-fi and fantasy films like *Guardians of the Galaxy*, Harry Potter, and *Doctor Strange*. "Is it really sci-fi or is it really the world?" asks Michael Bischoff, one of the designers. "That's what's at the heart of this whether you want to believe it or not."

To actually construct this massive project, the city will be divided into 140 modules, each 800 meters long and housing 80,000 people. Exactly how many modules will be constructed by 2030 isn't yet clear. But constructing the entirety of the Line will go on for decades, giving designers time to learn from early mistakes.

Even MBS acknowledges he doesn't know the outcome of his project. "We are bringing all the pieces of the puzzle together; I don't know what's the outcome of it," he says. "I can promise you that there's going to be something new and creative but what it is, I don't know. We are going to see."[10]

But, he insists, the Line is all about ambition, about showing what Saudi Arabia can do and can be. "We have the cash, we have the land, we have the stability; we have the good infrastructure; we are a G-20 country," he says. "We want to create the new civilization for tomorrow."[11]

The Line is literally the largest infrastructure project in history. Can such a massive structure running 105 miles long and taller than the Empire State Building really be constructed as a viable city for 9 million people?

I ask the chairman of Tishman Speyer, a New York company that has built large projects all over the world, including in 1988 Europe's tallest building, in Frankfurt. Is such a structure even possible? Jerry Speyer, with more than forty years experience, says, "It's eminently doable if you have the money and the courage to do it." His firm isn't involved in the Line or any of the other planned cities in Neom. When he read about the building projects in Neom, "I thought, 'Wow, what a gutsy thing to do,'" he says. Will the $500 billion investment in Neom ever produce a return? "MBS's return isn't in cash," Speyer says. "It's in changing the culture of a country. He's going to change the face of Saudi Arabia."[12] That's in the future.

Right now, all that is visible of the Line is a huge gouge in the earth as excavators remove massive amounts of dirt to prepare the building site. What is visible today in Neom is its breathtaking scenery and its ancient history.

At Al Bada, Neom's largest town with 3,000 residents, one can see Jebel Lawz, the "mountain of almonds," rising 8,400 feet. Many evangelical Christians believe Jebel Lawz is the real Mount Sinai where Moses received the Ten Commandments. This is disputed by mainstream religious scholars. But evangelicals continue to flock here, especially since MBS met with Joel Rosenberg, an evangelical Christian living in Israel, to personally encourage Christians and Israelis to visit Saudi Arabia. Ironically, when I asked in 2009 to visit Jebel Lawz, mentioning that I had heard it was Mount Sinai, I was quickly shushed. "We don't want Christians going there," a Saudi diplomat then told me in a near whisper as if even the very topic was dangerously haram.

While the Line will be a city for permanent residents, the kingdom is planning numerous tourist destinations throughout Neom where tourists can not only enjoy the natural beauty of the region but also vacation in style. Amaala, a luxury resort on the Red Sea, makes a virtue of the Islamic ban on alcohol by marketing itself as a health and wellness destination.

Early surveys by consultants on the Saudi payroll found 90 percent of Europeans and Asians eager to vacation on the Red Sea, but only 30 percent were positive about vacationing at a resort with no alcohol.[13] Therefore Amaala, located in the Prince Mohammed Nature Reserve, promises "transformative personal journeys inspired by art, wellness, and the purity of the Red Sea." Amaala promises also to be the "globally recognized hub for arts and culture," with a focus on contemporary art.[14] Like all projects owned by development company Red Sea Global, Amaala will be powered day and night by renewable energy. The project boasts 740,000 solar panels, creating the largest solar farm in the world.[15] Looking down on these solar panels from a helicopter in 2023, they resemble a vast gray blot on the brown sand and beautiful aqua water.

Red Sea Global's project also features the world's largest nursery. At some 185,000 hectares, it is larger than 400,000 football fields! The plants growing here will be transplanted at the multiple hotels being built by the Red Sea projects. Already the nursery is home to plants from eighty-five nations accumulated here at the enormous cost of $178 million and rising. The most expensive plants are olive trees from Spain said to be 2,500 years old. Each one cost Saudi Arabia about $530,000, according to my guide, Muteb al-Osaimi, an agriculture engineer from King Saud University.

The giant nursery, like everything else at the Red Sea projects, focuses on sustainability. To avoid depleting ground water, its 4.5 million plants are watered with recycled wastewater from nearby Turtle Bay Island, home to a hotel and housing for workers building the Red Sea projects. As the number of Red Sea tourist hotels grows, so will the wastewater they produce. With more recycled wastewater the nursery will add more plants, seeking to reach its goal of 35 million by 2030. So far some one million plants have been dispersed to Red Sea hotels like the new Ritz-Carlton, St. Regis, and the Six Senses to transform the brown-dirt surroundings into attractive gardens and pathways.

Among his other projects, al-Osaimi also is tending a greenhouse packed with mangrove plants. These plants are part of the effort to reduce greenhouse gases produced in Saudi Arabia. He is transitioning the mangroves from using fresh water to surviving on seawater. Once they thrive on seawater in the nursery, they will be planted in the saltwater reefs of the Red Sea to help reduce carbon dioxide and enhance survivability of coral reefs. Mangroves capture carbon dioxide emissions and other greenhouse gases, thus improving the environment.

All these grandiose gigaprojects in Neom undeniably bear the imprint of Crown Prince Mohammed. Imagination. Innovation. Initiative. These he believes will save his kingdom. These will launch it to a top spot in the G-20. Doubters, he believes, simply lack his vision. Indeed, in 2024, Saudi ranked 16 among G-20 countries, up from 19 when Vision 2030 was announced.

Yet doubt hangs over these grandiose projects. Will they really transform Saudi Arabia's economy off oil and on to a bright future? Or will they prove white elephants that bankrupt the nation and leave its people poor?

In the Crown Prince's rush to get things done quickly, he has allowed his megaprojects to become magnets for misbehaving Western executives paid enormous salaries to relentlessly drive a diverse workforce of 100,000 white- and blue-collar construction workers who live in temporary trailer parks a hundred miles from any city.[16] A *Wall Street Journal* investigation found numerous incidents of senior Neom executives awarding expensive contracts to firms that included their relatives or friends. The executive in charge of building the Line, Antoni Vives, pleaded guilty to public-malfeasance charges that he gave a friend a no-show job worth around $165,000 over four years. Despite that, the Crown Prince wanted him retained at Neom. Vives has again been charged by Spanish prosecutors with criminal conspiracy, fraud, and perversion of justice.[17] By late 2024 as problems mounted and cost overruns skyrocketed, Vives was removed along with CEO Nadhmi al-Nasr. When the Crown Prince announced the Line, construction costs were estimated at $500 billion. Those costs are now estimated by former executives at $2 trillion, far more than the kingdom has to spend on a development project.[18]

"We're not allowed to debate these huge expenditures to learn will they bankrupt the country or leave it wealthy," says one Al Saud prince. "It will be one or the other. No middle. He [MBS] is mortgaging future generations so these projects better work."[19]

Saudi Arabia's recent history with big projects isn't encouraging. True, its first massive projects, Jubail and Yanbu, launched in the mid-1970s to create new industrial centers, were a success. These projects focused on oil refineries and petrochemicals, industries based on plentiful Saudi oil. So each has proved successful at creating jobs and attracting foreign investment. Yanbu is the kingdom's second-largest port and an important oil-shipping terminal as well as home to three refineries.

But more recent efforts to diversify beyond oil have proved stunningly unsuccessful. In 2005, under the late King Abdullah, the government announced ambitious plans to build a half-dozen "economic cities" around Saudi Arabia to diversify the economy, create jobs, generate vast foreign investment, and enrich the living standards of the Saudi people. In words eerily similar to today's pronouncements about Neom, the government promised "twenty-first-century urban living" and "ubiquitous connectivity" for residents of these new cities. Yet nearly twenty years later, only one survived the planning stage and it is a monument to inflated cost and failed promises. The King Abdullah Economic City near Jeddah promised to create 1 million jobs and host 2 million residents. Today this $100 billion city has 7,000 residents and still won't be completed before 2035.[20]

"We are aware that the economic cities of the last decade did not realize their potential," MBS acknowledged in Vision 2030.

Sure enough, the King Abdullah Financial District in Riyadh, another gargantuan development project, was a failure literally from its inception. MBS's government has criticized it for being built without consideration of its economic feasibility. The original concept was to prepare land for business and financial firms to purchase and build offices, creating a financial center in Riyadh. When that concept proved unsuccessful—businesses didn't buy land and build office towers—the government doubled down and began erecting business towers, some fifty-nine in all[21] according to the Bin Laden Group, which constructed eighteen of them. As oil prices plummeted in 2014, building cranes stood inert.

When MBS became crown prince, the Public Investment Fund assumed control of salvaging the $10 billion King Abdullah Financial

District as part of Vision 2030's economic and social reforms.[22] The kingdom's first movie theater in thirty-five years opened in a converted section of a sprawling conference center there in 2018. The PIF has moved its headquarters to a seventy-six-story tower there, Riyadh's tallest building, and is repurposing the King Abdullah Financial District as a special economic zone where businessmen can come and go from Riyadh's King Khalid International Airport on a high-speed train without having to get a visa.

As the kingdom knows from half a century of experience, grand plans don't always equal financial progress. The big projects the government favors and funds almost invariably suffer from long delays and large cost overruns. A survey in 2011 of three hundred project managers and supervisors found that 97 percent of government projects aren't completed on time and a staggering 80 percent exceed budget. Also, it found that the government officials in charge don't fret about either the delays or the enormity of such national waste.[23]

In 2011, at the height of big construction projects in the kingdom, an angry Saudi prince told me that "cartels, collusion, and corruption are making the rich richer and foreclosing any opportunity for the poor to get richer." He complained that constant cost overruns on big projects also led to low quality as "each company subcontracts to someone else to do the work which becomes ever shoddier." Why doesn't the government end this? "When the king and crown prince ask questions, they get answers from a culprit official at the Finance Ministry, not someone independent," the prince explained.

No doubt some corruption still occurs, but MBS's crackdown that began with imprisoning prominent royals and businessmen in the Ritz hotel has created new transparency that is reducing waste and cost overruns in government projects. Moreover, MBS has established Key Performance Indicators (KPIs) for each minister that function as something of a stopwatch to hasten progress without sacrificing quality. Still, the sheer number of grand projects seems to be straining even Saudi Arabia's resources. With oil income falling below Saudi Arabia's spending needs, in 2024 the government announced that some big projects will be slowed. Additionally, it began large borrowing and transferred a $163 billion stake in its oil company, Aramco, to the PIF to help fund projects to modernize the economy.[24]

The government also has announced massive spending to develop its mineral wealth as a new pillar of the Saudi economy. In 2023 it created Manara, a joint venture between the PIF and the kingdom's mining company, Maaden. Manara captured the world's attention by quickly investing $26 billion in a Brazilian mining venture. Saudi officials say they'll invest another $15 billion in mining assets globally in the next few years.[25] At home, Saudi Arabia has large deposits of uranium, copper, iron, gold, zinc, phosphates, and rare-earth metals. At a Future Minerals Forum in Riyadh in 2024, the minister of Industry and Mineral Resources estimated untapped mineral wealth at $2.5 trillion, nearly double the $1.3 trillion estimate in 2016.[26]

Saudi Arabia has big plans and big money to develop its gigaprojects and its mineral wealth to create a flourishing economy beyond oil. But will it succeed? In truth, few nations have successfully diversified off oil.

One of the few success stories is Texas. The Texas oil boom began with a gusher in 1901 in a small town near Houston. Soon Texas was pumping more oil than the Russian Empire. Today it remains the country's largest oil-producing state, accounting for 42 percent of total U.S. oil production of 12.9 million barrels a day in 2023.[27] But Texas over the decades has found other sources of income too.

When oil prices plummeted in 1980, Texas, like Saudi Arabia now, began to diversify its economy. A high-tech boom in the 1990s produced strong growth despite weakness in the energy sector. The aerospace industry centered on NASA in Houston spawned other related industries like telecommunications, information technology, and the airline industry. Moreover, the fortuitous location of Texas halfway between the two coasts has helped the state become a travel hub. Texas Instruments, an early manufacturer of integrated circuits for the Pentagon, is a prominent example of early successful tech companies in Texas. So is Dell Computer Company, near Austin.

Successful tech companies just keep coming to Texas for its low taxes, cheaper housing costs, and friendly vibe. Oracle, Hewlett-Packard (now HP), Tesla, and SpaceX all have relocated in just the past few years. Around Dallas, prominent Wall Street firms like J.P. Morgan, Goldman Sachs, and Charles Schwab are expanding to what is called Y'All Street, making Dallas second only to New York City in the number of workers employed in financial services.

Texas's location on the Mexican border has provided a ready supply of immigrant labor even if in more recent years that influx has upset many Americans and helped catapult Donald Trump to the White House in 2024. Between 1980 and 2011, the Texas population grew nearly 80 percent, double the national growth rate. By 2022, its gross domestic product totaled $2.3 trillion, more than twice that of Saudi Arabia even though each has a population of roughly 30 million. In the first quarter of 2023, Texas posted the fastest revenue growth of any state in the union.

Texas is the United States' largest oil producer but also its top producer of alternative energy—primarily wind and solar. Renewable energy now accounts for one-third of the power generated in Texas, more than in any other U.S. state. MBS is pledging that Saudi Arabia will generate 50 percent of its power from renewables by 2030.

Oil and gas remain important contributors to Texas's gross domestic product. But the number is now 9 percent of GDP,[28] down from 15 percent in 1980.[29] This shift is what MBS seeks to emulate. He is not looking to replace oil entirely but rather to diversify and build revenue streams other than oil to keep Saudi GDP growing. Oil in 2023 was 46 percent of Saudi GDP.[30] As he stresses publicly and repeatedly, he expects the world to rely on oil until at least 2050 or longer. Given the huge demands for energy to operate AI data centers, that seems assured. And the kingdom, with its large oil reserves, expects to be the last oil producer standing. So Saudi Arabia believes oil revenue is a large part of its future but will be a declining proportion of its total revenues. It's very uncertain how much oil revenue the kingdom can count on in 2030 and beyond. Equally uncertain is how much revenue will be generated by MBS's risky bets on gigaprojects and massive investments in tourism, gaming, and sports.

Over the decades profligate spending by Saudi kings on big failed projects that promise a better life for Saudis but wind up enriching the rich while doing nothing to lift the poor have left the kingdom with a pharaonic image: the rich oil sheikh seeking to build new monuments for his glory.

Surveying all the grandeur of the kingdom's gigaprojects and plans for Neom, it's hard not to recall Percy Bysshe Shelley's poem "Ozymandias." The poet describes the crumbled statue of the once-powerful Pharaoh Ramses II as a metaphor for the transience of power no matter how great.

> And on the pedestal, these words appear:
> My name is Ozymandias. King of Kings;
> Look on my Works, ye Mighty, and despair!
>
> Nothing beside remains round the decay
> Of that colossal Wreck, boundless and bare,
> The lone and level sands stretch far away.

MBS seems supremely confident of a more lasting legacy in the sands of Neom.

CHAPTER EIGHT

The Sports of Kings

The "Battle of the Baddest" is about to begin. It's well after midnight. Boxing fans are restless, having sat through six undercard bouts followed by a risqué dance performance seemingly intended to underscore that religious restrictions in the kingdom are definitely a thing of the past.

Now the ring emerges from below the floor. As bright lights rise on heavyweight champions Tyson Fury and Francis Ngannou, twenty-six thousand mostly Saudi fans erupt in cheers. These featured boxers aren't the only celebrities in the house. A host of recognizable stars begin to crowd into VIP seats around the ring. Mike Tyson, paid by Saudi Arabia to promote the fight, enters with Evander Holyfield, Larry Holmes, and Manny Pacquiao, all former boxing greats. Cristiano Ronaldo, the Portuguese soccer star who recently located to the kingdom, is a current Saudi star. But the squeals and whistles are loudest when this mostly young Saudi audience spots Kanye West and Eminem.

This is definitely not your father's Saudi Arabia.

The contest is a thrilling ten rounds, with underdog Ngannou scoring a knockdown in the third round. Fury's six-foot, nine-inch body buckles and hits the floor. The audience gasps. Though Fury fails ever to score a knockdown the judges still award him a split-decision victory. From my ringside seat, the decision seems unfair. And many around me are also grumbling. But all eyes quickly return to the ring, where Oleksandr Usyk, a Ukrainian fighter, stands glaring at Fury, wasting no time promoting the next big championship fight in Riyadh.

This spectacle of famous fighters, popular celebrities, and suggestive dancers underscores how the kingdom is marketing itself as a destination for big-time sports. Just look at who already is here, is the implicit message. These high-profile sports events are part of MBS's plan to create a booming tourist industry that he believes can significantly supplement his nation's revenues as oil income gradually fades. For him, sports are a driver for Saudi tourism. Additionally, in a country that traditionally has had little entertainment—even sports—high-profile sporting events can also contribute to the country's social satisfaction and economic growth. And to altering Saudi Arabia's image abroad.

Finally, creating a vibrant society is one of Vision 2030's three broad goals along with a thriving economy and an ambitious nation. Sports is seen as boosting all three goals. Specifically, participation in sports can teach Saudis self-sufficiency and striving for self-improvement, insists a former president of Saudi sports, Prince Abdullah bin Musa'id. "Saudis prefer not to work if they can avoid it," he told me a decade ago, "so they don't train hard or try hard." Now, with the kingdom's focus—starting with MBS—on being top-tier competitors in a wide range of sports, that reluctance to exert for excellence is fading.

With this in mind, Saudi Arabia in 2023 spent an eye-popping $875 million to buy soccer stars to energize and improve its Saudi league teams. According to FIFA, the international governing body of soccer, Saudi Arabia outspent every European nation except Britain.[1] The kingdom's haul of illustrious players includes Portuguese stars Ronaldo and Ruben Neves, Brazil's Neymar, and

Ballon d'Or winner Karim Benzema. With these stars playing for Saudi Arabia, its league has signed deals with nearly forty different broadcasters.

Despite their extravagant price tags, these men are sound investments for the kingdom even if the Saudi competition is causing grumbling in other nations. Their star power on social media is marketing Saudi Arabia to hundreds of millions around the world, and their performance on the playing field is intended to lure some of those global sports fans to visit the kingdom as tourists.

Global sports revenues are roughly $500 billion and growing at 5 percent a year.[2] Saudi Arabia wants a "giga" piece of that and is aggressively going after it to make up for lost time. The kingdom trails other Gulf states in focusing on sports. Two decades ago, Dubai lured tennis icons Roger Federer and Andre Agassi to draw attention to its lackluster women's tennis tournament by hitting balls atop a seven-hundred-foot platform with no sides to prevent balls—or players—falling off. The world noticed.

The world also noticed when Saudi Arabia snagged Ronaldo with a $200 million annual salary, opening the door to a flood of interest by other soccer stars in moving to the desert kingdom. The world again noticed when Saudi Arabia's LIV Golf circuit, backed by its Public Investment Fund (PIF), agreed to merge with the PGA Tour, putting the PIF's riches behind one of America's preeminent sports institutions. The merger plan paused but didn't end an ugly battle between the PGA's prestige and the kingdom's money, which had lured major golfers like Phil Mickelson, Dustin Johnson, Brooks Koepka, and Jon Rahm, who is reported to have received $302 million up front, making him the highest-paid athlete in the world in 2023.[3] Saudi money won. PIF board chairman Yasir Rumayyan, a golf fanatic, is set to chair the joint venture board if the deal is ever finalized. A December 2023 deadline for a deal came and went. By late 2024 again the PGA and LIV Golf were talking of a final deal but details weren't released and any deal will have to be reviewed by the U.S. Justice Department to determine if it violates antitrust laws. President Trump met with the PGA and LIV and has expressed confidence their merger will soon be finalized.

All this lavish spending by the kingdom on big sports stars has prompted human rights critics to accuse the kingdom of "sportswashing." While Saudi Arabia clearly seeks to polish its reputation as a way to grow tourism, the Crown Prince also seeks to grow non-oil revenue. The presence of sports stars like Ronaldo, who boasts 100 million followers on X, promotes the kingdom as a new tourist destination. At the same time, the growing number of global sporting events held in Saudi Arabia, including Formula 1, boxing, soccer, and men's and women's tennis, gives sports fans around the world a reason to visit. In short, the kingdom is killing two birds with one stone—money.

"If sportswashing is going to increase my GDP by 1 percent, then we'll continue doing sportswashing," the Crown Prince told Fox News when asked about accusations of sportswashing in a televised interview.[4]

Still, the more successful the kingdom is at building its sports prowess, the louder the protests from human rights groups get. For instance, Saudi Arabia is the only bidder to host the FIFA World Cup in 2034 but human rights groups heavily lobbied FIFA members to reject the kingdom unless it released all political prisoners, created an independent judiciary, improved rights of migrant workers who will build all the new stadiums for the games, and enhanced women's rights by, among other things, criminalizing marital rape. "People are really dealing with the devil here," said Mark Pieth, a lawyer and one of three authors of the human rights report to FIFA.[5] The authors are threatening to sue FIFA unless it demands human rights changes in Saudi Arabia.

Tennis legend Rafael Nadal has defended the kingdom. He agreed in early 2024 to become Saudi Arabia's tennis ambassador, something that precipitated outcries from human rights activists. After playing in "The Six Kings Slam" in Riyadh in October, he defended his role. "In the end," Nadal told a Spanish interviewer, "by coming here we make events happen and tourists come, something that didn't happen four or five years ago. So, what do you want? For them to continue being bad, continue keeping the country locked up with more inequality?"[6]

Since becoming crown prince in June 2017, Mohammed bin Salman has made clear that Saudi Arabia intends to punch above its weight on the world stage. Reshaping global sports is simply the kingdom's latest ambition. It began in 2019 when Saudi Arabia organized a heavyweight title fight between Andy Ruiz Jr. and Anthony Joshua in the desert near Riyadh, with a staggering $60 million purse. That year Saudi also began hosting Formula 1 events and the world's richest horse race with a total purse of $35.5 million.[7] Crown Prince Mohammed personally crowned the winner in 2021 at the King Abdul Aziz Race Track, the site of his staged handshake three years earlier with a humiliated Prince Miteb, his cousin, shortly after releasing him from incarceration in the Ritz-Carlton.

The kingdom has moved beyond hosting sporting events to creating its own golf tour and buying major sports franchises. LIV was intended to "reinvigorate" golf, the PIF declared as it staged tournaments with team play and record-breaking prize money. The PGA accused Saudi Arabia of trying to buy golf. LIV sued the PGA for anticompetitive practices; the PGA countersued arguing LIV was using the game of golf "to sportswash the recent history of Saudi atrocities and to further the Saudi Public Investment Fund's Vision 2030 initiatives."[8] Notwithstanding the harsh rhetoric, secret negotiations already were ongoing between Yasir Rumayyan and the PGA's Jay Monahan, who shocked the golf world in June 2023 by agreeing to merge with LIV.

That shotgun merger prompted the U.S. Senate to hold hearings on potential antitrust issues. When asked during those hearings to explain the PGA's rationale for partnering with the Saudis, the chief operating officer admitted the PGA simply couldn't afford a protracted war with LIV. "We faced a real threat that LIV Golf, which is 100 percent owned by the Kingdom of Saudi Arabia, would become the leader of professional golf."[9] In short, David surrendered to Goliath.

But the LIV golf saga isn't over. When LIV and the PGA failed to conclude an agreement by their 2023 year-end deadline, the new year opened with a new bang. A group of sports industry billionaires agreed to buy a minority stake in the PGA, infusing it with needed cash and also complicating its negotiations with LIV. The billionaire bailout trio includes John Henry, owner of the Boston Red Sox and Liverpool FC; New York Mets owner and hedge fund titan Steve Cohen; and Atlanta Falcons owner Arthur Blank. Not only are they bringing money to the PGA, but according to the *Wall Street Journal*, many of the investors also have experience running successful sports franchises and could help the PGA Tour "reform its business operations to increase profitability."[10] Can the two competing leagues merge without raising antitrust issues? Or how will PGA players who turned down lucrative offers from LIV be compensated in a joint league for their loyalty to the PGA?

This hiccup hasn't dimmed Saudi sports ambitions. Because sport is a key building block for its tourism ambitions, a full calendar of sporting events is central.

In 2021, the PIF bought a majority stake in Newcastle, a British soccer team then ranked nineteenth in the Premier League, the highest level of English soccer. Two years later, bolstered by PIF spending, Newcastle finished fourth in the standings and earned a spot in next season's Champions League. Newcastle fans have overwhelmingly welcomed the Saudi takeover despite the club banning one local woman from its matches for three years for a tweet allegedly denigrating transgender individuals that was deemed "hate speech."[11] In 2022, the kingdom lured Ronaldo, arguably the world's greatest soccer star. In addition to playing on the pitch, Ronaldo was expected to pitch Saudi Arabia's plan to host the World Cup in 2034.

Not content with just one great soccer player, the Saudis reportedly offered Lionel Messi, the Argentine striker who holds a record seven Ballon d'Or trophies, $420 million to join the Saudi league before he signed with Inter Miami. Although he declined to join a Saudi soccer team, he did sign on as a goodwill ambassador for the kingdom's Ministry of Tourism. Messi won't have to run, sweat, or get knocked down to earn a cool $25 million a year. Beyond supporting Saudi World Cup 2034 ambitions, all he is required to do are a few commercials and make some social media posts to his 400 million followers, as well as post photos of an all-expense paid annual vacation with his family to Saudi Arabia. One additional requirement: he must not say anything that would "tarnish" the image of Saudi Arabia.[12] Some see this restriction as proof of sportswashing. It may be. But in reality, it is just another example of restriction on free speech that all Saudis endure under MBS.

The value of sports figures like Ronaldo to the kingdom's tourism marketing is priceless. When Ronaldo and his Spanish model partner, Georgina Rodriquez, visited historic Al Ula, a popular tourist site in Saudi, he posted a photo of himself on Instagram at Al Diwan, a spectacularly large chamber carved in rock adjacent to an even more spectacular narrow path between two high rocks, forming a dramatic opening. The photo earned 200 million likes.

"Sports is the way to reach hearts," says a Saudi prince. "Sports goes around religion, nationalism, everything. Sports figures reach people in ways others can't."

The kingdom clearly is determined to transform its own Pro League teams into international competitors on a level with the best in Europe. So the hunt continues. In 2023, Karim Benzema, the holder of soccer's coveted Ballon d'Or award and a Muslim, joined

Al Ittihad Club for a reported $112 million for each of the two coming seasons plus $20 million each year as a sports ambassador to help secure the 2034 World Cup. Another decorated French superstar, N'Golo Kanté, also a Muslim, will join his countryman on Al Ittihad. Another Saudi club, Al Hilal, offered Kylian Mbappe, a World Cup winner for France, a mind-boggling $1.1 billion salary and signing bonus but he refused to talk with their representatives. Regardless, the offer underscores Saudi Arabia's determination to use its wealth to challenge the likes of Real Madrid, Barcelona, and Paris St. Germain. The Saudi raids on Europe's best players clearly are reminiscent of European clubs buying the best talent from Africa, Asia, and South America over the years to build European soccer prowess. Regardless, European clubs are up in arms over what they see as an attack on the structure of European football.

Saudi Arabia also is seeking to break into tennis, the most truly global sport. Players from all over the world participate in every tournament throughout the competitive year. The kingdom won the right to host the so-called Next Gen tennis finals in December 2023, which features competition among the top players under twenty-one. That contract runs for five years. The young faces visible in the King Abdullah Sports Center in Jeddah in 2023 are intended to inspire Saudi Arabia's youthful population to get out and exercise. A "vibrant nation" is one of Vision 2030's three broad goals.

Saudis long have been sedentary since there was little opportunity for access to sports facilities for any but the wealthiest citizens who could afford membership in the very few sports clubs available. Prior to the recent reforms, most young males were largely left to kick a soccer ball in open fields often strewn with garbage—or sit home. And, of course, women were forbidden to exercise, at least in public, by religious ulama who insisted exercise would damage their reproductive ability.

The kingdom also is reported to be seeking to buy the United

Cup from Australia to have a regular place in the annual tennis lineup of major tournaments. This tournament features men's and women's matches and mixed doubles, giving the kingdom a chance to highlight both its new freedoms for women and its willingness to encourage the mixing of genders, once forbidden by the religious police. The competition is held in January as part of the run-up to the Australian Open in Melbourne.

In early 2024, after more than three years of private discussions between the Saudi Tennis Federation and women's tennis organizations, the Women's Tennis Association agreed to hold its year-end finals in Saudi for at least the next three years. Prominent former tennis greats Martina Navratilova and Chris Evert spoke out against the move, insisting women's rights in Saudi remain "token measures."[13] Daria Kasatkina, a Russian tennis star who has come out as bisexual, also expressed concern about playing in the kingdom. Asked about playing in Saudi, she said there were many issues concerning the country. "Honestly, tough to talk about." But, she added, "Money talks in our world right now."[14]

The first WTA finals in Riyadh in 2024 opened to sparse attendance, but by the time American Coco Gauff defeated Qinwen Zheng in a gripping three-hour final, all five thousand seats in the King Saud University Indoor Arena were full. While Chinese attendees supported Zheng, hijab-clad Saudi women chanted, "Let's go Coco." And Gauff, who was supportive but tentative as the tournament opened, seemed convinced eight days later that the WTA did the right thing by coming to Riyadh, despite doubts about its human rights lapses. "Just to show young girls that, you know, their dreams are possible," she said. "I'm literally no different than they are. We just maybe come from different places."

Female rights in Saudi surely aren't perfect. But the sweeping progress in the past half-dozen years would seem to make Saudi Arabia an excellent place to stage a tournament promoting women's equality. When the WTA was launched fifty years ago by Billie Jean King, its dream of equality for women was aspirational, not achieved. The WTA's successes over the years—for instance equal prize money with men—doubtlessly would inspire Saudi women far more than shunning the kingdom. Clear evidence of how far women's tennis has come: King earned under $2 million in prize money during her quarter-century career, less than half the $4.8 million prize purse Gauff received in Riyadh.

There's also a little hypocrisy in these organizations' position. After all, the WTA hosts tournaments in China, where Uyghur women undergo forced sterilization and abortion. And more reprehensible—and closer to tennis—Chinese female tennis player Peng Shuai temporarily disappeared from public after posting on social media site Weibo that a prominent vice premier had forced her to have sex. Her post was immediately removed and friends and the WTA couldn't reach her. While the official she accused remained silent, Peng Shuai, some months later at the Beijing Olympics in a tightly controlled interview with a Singapore newspaper, recanted her Weibo post. "I have never said or written that anyone has sexually assaulted me. . . . There's been a lot of misunderstanding." After a brief suspension of play in China, the WTA resumed its full schedule there in 2023 without opposition from its big stars.[15]

Beyond traditional sports, the kingdom also has huge ambitions for mixed martial arts as well as for esports. The Public Investment Fund (PIF) in August invested in mixed martial arts in the U.S. by buying a minority stake in the Professional Fighting League, started in 2018 and now valued at $500 billion. According to the *Financial Times*, the Saudi stake in mixed martial arts is valued at $100 million.[16]

To underscore its determination to be a dominant global sports power, the kingdom created SRJ Sports Investment. SRJ is pronounced "surge." SRJ Sports is entirely owned by the PIF and charged with continuing to invest in sports globally to raise the kingdom's profile and hopefully one day its profits.

If all this isn't enough, the kingdom is building an entirely new city forty miles from Riyadh, which it hopes will become the global hub for esports and videogaming as well as motor sports. When complete, Qiddiya, its planners say, will create 325,000 jobs and add $36 billion to Saudi GDP. Spread over an area twice the size of Washington, D.C., Qiddiya will have a racetrack, a Six Flags–type theme park, and FIFA World Cup football stadiums by 2034, the year Saudi will host the World Cup. Qiddiya planners say they expect some 48 million visitors annually with 2 million there purely to watch soccer matches.

The PIF, Saudi Arabia's sovereign wealth fund, launched Savvy Gaming Group in January 2022 to advance its gaming strategy. Crown Prince Mohammed, who chairs the board of Savvy, said, "Savvy Games Group is one part of our ambitious strategy aiming to make Saudi Arabia the ultimate global hub for the games and esports sector by 2030."[17]

Savvy has $38 billion to achieve the royal videogamer's ambitious goal. Acknowledging that the task won't be easy, the Savvy CEO expresses confidence of success. Everyone in Saudi, he says, has signed up to Vision 2030 so it's a "bullet train to the future."[18]

That is surely what MBS intends. As with the kingdom's outsize spending to lure sports stars, the spending on esports is intended to dominate the market and make Saudi Arabia a sports powerhouse in both physical and esports. Whether Savvy can successfully compete with Microsoft, Sony, and other major players in the gaming industry, it's clear the PIF will continue to invest aggressively in gaming just as it has in physical sports. The kingdom has a lot of gamers. Some 65 percent of Saudis are under thirty and roughly the same percent, some 23 million

Saudi residents, are gamers.[19] Worldwide the gaming industry generated revenues of $187 billion in 2023.[20] Remarkably, 100 million people viewed the League of Legends World Championship in South Korea in 2019, more than viewed the Super Bowl.[21]

Saudi Arabia hosted its first gaming event in the summer of 2023. Gamers 8, a series of tournaments, and a festival were hosted by Savvy Gaming Group. As with other Saudi forays into sports, the event featured an outsize prize purse of $45 million. At the completion of that competition, the Crown Prince himself announced that Saudi Arabia would host the Esports World Cup in 2024. That eight-week event in Riyadh offered a $60 million prize purse. The event drew one million visitors according to *Arab News*.

"The Esports World Cup is the natural next step in Saudi Arabia's journey to become the premier global hub for gaming and esports," the Crown Prince said, "offering an unmatched esports experience that pushes the boundaries of the industry."[22] The prince has long had an interest in gaming since he got his first Nintendo at age six. Now he's trying to transform a childhood passion into a profitable new industry.

CHAPTER NINE

Six Flags over Saudi Arabia

F un has come to Saudi Arabia, a remarkable change from the sober and somber Saudi society that MBS inherited.

The Crown Prince remembers a time not so long ago when public entertainment was nonexistent in the kingdom and he is determined to change that. To Wahhabi clerics, fun was a dirty word—a frivolous waste of time that should be devoted to focus on Allah. Indeed, the Quran advises, "Little is the enjoyment in this world. The Hereafter is far better for those mindful of Allah."[1]

These days there is a lot of amusement all over Saudi Arabia. Riyadh's streets, once abandoned after dark, now teem with Saudis enjoying new entertainment options that have popped up in the last half-dozen years. One of the most popular new sites is Boulevard World, a sprawling theme park patterned on Disney's Epcot Center in Orlando, Florida. A visitor to Boulevard World can tour the globe's major capital cities and sample international cuisine in each. Egypt was added this year, replete with pyramids and sphinx. It's all a bit garish but Saudis don't seem to mind.

When I take my fourteen-year-old granddaughter to visit around 8 p.m. on a January evening, the entire theme park is packed with groups of young men, groups of young women, and families pushing baby strollers. The evening is hot, so some of the young Saudi men are wearing shorts and T-shirts as if they were in Orlando, not Riyadh. Because of the heat even in January, Saudis typically go out after sundown and stay until midnight, when the park closes. Even elderly people in motorized wheelchairs are braving the hubbub to enjoy the ambience. Interestingly, perhaps because there is so much activity to capture a child's attention, I hardly ever see a crying toddler in Boulevard World though toddlers abound. Saudi families tend to include their young children when they go out to restaurants or amusement parks as family remains the key unit in Saudi society.

On a night like this, it's easy to forget that all this visible fun could have been created by an invisible exploitation: the labor of millions of underpaid, overworked migrants with few rights and little protection slaving through hot days to build many of the kingdom's new developments. Foreign workers, mostly from Southeast Asian nations or Egypt, willingly come in pursuit of wages, which, while low, are superior to what they can earn in their home countries. This desperation makes them easily exploitable as what human rights groups liken to indentured servitude. Employers often seize workers' passports and withhold their wages since the kingdom bans labor unions. Regardless, there are no accusations that Boulevard World—built in only eighty days in late 2022 by a team of seventy contactors working three shifts a day on a 24/7 job site—exploited foreign laborers.

Tonight, Saudis are enjoying, if perhaps not truly appreciating, what these workers produced. At Boulevard World, three little girls watch in anticipation as their mother, clad in a black abaya and hijab, tosses basketballs at a hoop, vainly seeking to win a five-foot purple velour banana. She fails. But no tears from the toddlers. This, of course, is a game of chance, or gambling, once strictly forbidden by Wahhabism.

Seeing so many Saudis smiling, relaxed, strolling happily among each other despite the crowded conditions is in sharp contrast to a decade ago. Then, shopping malls were about the only places open in evenings and because they were patrolled by the religious police, many Saudi women were reluctant to go. Young single Saudi men were forbidden by religious restrictions to enter a mall for fear they might prey on women. So those who did enter malls looked somber, not relaxed.

All this began to change in 2016. That year the kingdom founded the General Entertainment Authority (GEA), to bring once-forbidden entertainment to the kingdom. Religious officials immediately labeled it the General Evil Authority. Its first director, Ahmed al-Khateeb, invited me to join him in Jeddah to see its inaugural event—ILuminate, a New York–based group whose show features dancers in the dark with their bodies lit only by flashing lights on their bodysuits. To watch male and female dancers in such proximity onstage with women's breasts daringly outlined in red lights was shockingly at odds with my forty years of kingdom visits. It was also shocking to see thousands of Saudi men and women and foreigners sitting together after decades of gender segregation. Yet the audience cheered and whistled, seeming to enjoy this startling new entertainment in their kingdom.

"When you go to entertainment you are smiling, you accept others," al-Khateeb told me. "When you sit home bored, you may go out with bad people." Indeed, entertainment had two primary goals: to distract young Saudis from contemplating terrorism and to create new sources of revenue for the kingdom, which hoped to build a tourism industry.

From that small start, entertainment options have exploded. Today Boulevard World features Thailand, an Asian nation renowned for its pretty women and risqué lifestyle. This Thailand, like the real one, offers visitors massages—but only for their "hands, feet, back, or neck." The purchaser enters an open hall where women provide the service in an area visible to all other customers. The door is guarded by a woman who allows entry only after surrendering a ticket. Still, the whole experience lacks any policed feel. It's just normal. Public massages now normal in a country that once forbade even hair salons.

Indeed, what is most striking from several hours walking around Boulevard World is how normal Saudi men and women seem to feel mingling close together on crowded sidewalks. Observing them now, one would never know such mixing was strictly forbidden until 2016. Most of those at Boulevard World are Saudis, not foreigners. The majority of Saudi women even today are wearing black abayas, though it is no longer required. Some also cover their heads and faces, some cover only their heads, and some, though a minority, have bare heads and faces.

A visitor can't help but be struck by the relaxed smiles of Saudis as they walk through "Morocco," stopping to listen to a band playing loud Moroccan music, or pose for photos in front of the Eiffel Tower or London's giant Ferris wheel, known here as the Riyadh Eye, not the London Eye.

The relaxed atmosphere attests to how quickly and dramatically the Crown Prince has changed Saudi culture. The once-austere demeanor of society has given way to happiness at little pleasures. For instance, families at Boulevard World are allowing their children to have their faces painted to resemble cats. Less than a decade ago, creating any human likeness was forbidden because only God creates life and man must not imitate God. Yet the Saudi women painting these children's faces don't appear to fear hellfire. They laugh and chat with the happy children as they work.

Our guide at Boulevard World is a young Saudi female lawyer, twenty-eight years old. Her youth and teen years were spent in a kingdom where none of these entertainment venues existed. Her entertainment, she recalls, was walking to the park or playing cards with her friends. Or she and her friends could watch mostly Egyptian movies at home on television. Like other wealthy Saudis, she traveled abroad with her large family and saw all the entertainment other nations had to offer, but only in very recent years has she been able to avail herself of pleasure in her home country. The United States, she says, is her favorite country to visit. Ironically, the U.S. at Boulevard World isn't represented by New York or Florida but by a California freeway featuring an Edsel Ford car in front of gasoline pumps, a freeway sign, and a Harley-Davidson motorcycle.

One of the most entertaining rides at this theme park is a fleet of small convertible cars with propellers that allow passengers to travel about what purports to be the largest man-made lake in the world. These propeller-driven convertibles putter around the lake giving visitors at least a glimpse of the entire theme park without having to walk. The little cars can hold two passengers and a driver. The driver rolls down a ramp using wheels and then enters the water, where a propeller takes over and quietly moves the car about the lake. We are so low in the water one can easily drag a hand over the car's side.

Every national venue offers products for sale from that country as well as national food. There is snack dining such as crepes in France or souvlaki in Greece, or numerous sit-down restaurants offering, for instance, pasta in Italy, sushi in Japan, or fish and chips in England.

If one tires of Boulevard World, one can take a sky tram to nearby Boulevard City, a 900,000-square-meter entertainment facility built in one year and opened in 2019. The site is divided into nine subzones featuring outdoor cinemas, fine restaurants, and cafes and hookah lounges where Saudi women in their twenties and thirties relax smoking *shisha*, a heated, specially prepared tobacco with smoke drawn through water into a long, flexible tube to reach the smoker's mouth. During its first year, this venue hosted what it called the Color Run, or "the Happiest 5K Race on the Planet." Runners—men, women, and children—were dashed at the start of each kilometer of the race with different color powders.

It's truly hard to think of anything less traditionally Saudi than a mixed-gender run. While the Prophet is said to have run races with his preteen wife Aisha, recreational running isn't something most Saudis ever imagined doing.

One of the main features of this venue is a Times Square look-alike. As in New York's Times Square, huge signs flashing different colors continuously light the area along with brightly lit advertisements for a host of brands, from Dunkin' to Starbucks to Lululemon and something called Fat Sal's hamburgers. Tables and chairs line the sidewalk. A young Saudi woman, seemingly oblivious to all that is going on around her, sits at one table engrossed by the computer in front of her. For young children there is a horror house featuring a giant *Tyrannosaurus rex* and something called the Avalanche, a long slide for young children to swoop down.

Again, the most gripping sight is none of the attractions but the opportunity to watch Saudis and some of their Gulf neighbors who visit this venue looking so relaxed and happy as they walk past beautifully lit fountains, holding the hands of their children or stopping at small green food trucks called "Munch and Move" to buy chips or candy or water. Here again Saudi men and women happily toss basketballs toward round hoops hoping to win the five-foot velour bananas far too big for their small children to carry.

Nearby Wonder Park, with seventy rides, two arcades, and thirty-one restaurants, offers another opportunity to spend an evening having fun among Saudis. The park is especially suited for children, with a butterfly house where over one thousand species live in a rain forest atmosphere. One can see the butterflies at all stages of development before they fly about their barnlike home where walls are hung with beautiful fresh flowers. Here I saw for the first time a Saudi toddler cry when a butterfly frightened him by landing on his arm. He screamed hysterically, then fell into continuous sobbing on his dad's shoulder once the offending butterfly was removed. His young brother looked on in embarrassment.

The centerpiece of this park, which is divided into three sections—blooms, trees, and butterflies—is a towering red and blue lit pole called "Drop Tower" where the truly brave can experience free falling. The daredevil visitor is strapped into a small seat that ascends slowly to a height of 160 feet, where the white-lit chairs swing in a circle visible from everywhere in the park before falling to the ground at 70 miles an hour.

This ride is much like Disney World's Tower of Terror (which closed in 2023), except there the rider was encased inside the tower so that the fall resembled a 130-foot descent in an elevator. Drop Tower at its height gives the rider a panoramic view of Boulevard World and Boulevard City—and the ground far below at Wonder Park—before plunging to the ground. My companion at the park had the misfortune to be stuck once at the top of this ride, dangling 160 feet above the ground for two hours.

Most of these theme parks are either free or have entry fees that low-income Saudis can afford. Boulevard City is free and Wonder Park costs about $2.50 per adult; children are free. This allows one to wander through the entire ninety-three acres of the park. Amusement rides or games cost extra. One favorite game here is trying to toss a hoop around the top of a jar. If one succeeds the reward is a free iPhone. My group failed utterly, as did everyone else we watched. But lore has it that one Saudi was banned from this game after he won an astonishing 128 times.

As if all this isn't enough, the kingdom is building an entirely new city some forty miles from Riyadh, dedicated to "playfulness" and "joy." Qiddiya was announced in 2018 by King Salman, with plans to be near completion by now. The project is far behind its original schedule. Crown Prince Mohammed challenged its planners to come up with a theme that would capture how Qiddiya's three elements—entertainment, sports, and culture—would enrich Saudis' lives. The team came up with the theme that connects all Qiddiya will offer: "Freedom, Joyfulness."

The Crown Prince's response: "That's it."

"Our culture is built around play," says Abdullah al-Dawood, managing director of Qiddiya. "We want to provide in everything a dollop of playfulness, escapism that the rest of the world isn't having. Society is now at a point where it can think about being playful, not just working."[2]

So, instead of an amusement park, the new concept for Qiddiya is a city built from scratch. This new city isn't just about diversifying the economy, he insists, but harnessing the Saudi smile. "We want to show the world Saudis are friendly, hospitable."

Already, once-taciturn Saudis display a friendliness toward foreign tourists that not so long ago was reserved only for rare foreigners they knew very well. When I ask directions or questions of Saudis on the street these days, they smile and respond fulsomely, not tersely. If they don't speak English, they touch a hand to their hearts as if asking forgiveness for their inability to help.

On a recent trip I ask a young man how to find Masmak, the old fort in Riyadh that Abdul Aziz conquered in 1902 as he began his battles to reestablish Al Saud rule. He smiles and asks where I am from. When I say New Jersey, he tells me he attended university there. He doesn't give directions but escorts me to the fort. The omnipresent photos all over Riyadh of a smiling Crown Prince Mohammed seem to be inspiring his populace to smile too.

Qiddiya will be nestled into the Tuwaiq Mountains, a limestone range stretching five hundred miles through central Arabia. Saudis call the mountains the "edge of the world." They like to compare the dramatic structure of these mountains to Arizona's Grand Canyon, though the Tuwaiq Mountains reach a height of only 2,000 feet, about one-fourth of the highest elevation of the Grand Canyon.[3] Still, the site is indisputably dramatic from a distance, and that drama will be integrated into Qiddiya. The planned water park will pass over the Formula 1 racetrack, heightening the thrill for both groups. Diners relaxing over a meal will see race cars through a glass whizzing in front of their tables.

As always with Saudi projects, Qiddiya boasts a world's record: Its roller coaster will be the longest, tallest, and fastest in the world, say its planners. The so-called Falcon's Flight will be two and a half miles long, nearly one mile longer than the Steel Dragon in Japan, currently the longest roller coaster. Falcon Flight's top speed of 155 mph will break the record held by Abu Dhabi's Formula Rossa at Ferrari World, which has a top speed of 150 mph. And the roller coaster at 650 feet high will be the world's tallest, beating out Kingda Ka at Six Flags Great Adventure in Jackson, New Jersey.[4] As always here, it's big, bigger, best.

Beyond all these existing and envisioned entertainment venues, Riyadh features a host of pop-up events. On a recent visit I attend Fashion Week, an event displaying Saudi Arabia's emerging fashion industry. The festival was located on a street in the JAX District, the core of a $20 billion project to revitalize the surrounding urban area. In one building, Saudi designers are displaying their creations. One, Yousef Akbar, thirty-eight, says he earned a degree in Australia and hoped to return and design clothes for women. But in 2006, when he graduated, strict gender segregation in Saudi Arabia meant a fashion career was out. So he remained in Australia to design and is thrilled to be able at last to design in his native country, where only a decade ago women's fashion was essentially an oxymoron. All women were fully covered in black abayas. While many wore stylish outfits under their abayas, those dresses were visible only at female events where abayas could be removed. The visible fashion statement of old was an expensive handbag.

This night the fashion festival features Kate Moss, a British supermodel who rose to fame in the early 1990s for her size-zero figure and collaborations with Calvin Klein. She mingles with the Saudi women who are enjoying a warm evening sitting on white leather poufs munching finger food and sipping mocktails, the nonalcoholic fruit drinks increasingly popular in Saudi. The diversity of dress is notable. While there are women in black abayas, many others are wearing fashionable high heels, shimmering silver pants, or tight-fitting black dresses revealing legs or leather pants paired with a sleeveless top. Individuality seems to be the object of the night as they relax and listen to a British-Lebanese rapper, Laughta, perform onstage.

It's just a normal night in the new Saudi Arabia.

Not surprisingly, all these social changes are beginning to alter Saudi culture. Once men worked and women stayed home to care for children. But these days, with more working couples, Saudi parents come home tired from a day's work and, like their American counterparts, allow children to play on iPads or watch television. This fixation with screens and gaming apps is producing young Saudi children who speak English before Arabic. I meet the grandson of a King Saud University sociology professor who enthusiastically describes his favorite game, *Duck Life*. A duck farm is destroyed and one egg survives, he says. He must grow the egg and buy things to adapt the new baby duck like feet, feathers, and so on. Like so many American children, this nine-year-old can't sit still as he speaks in English to describe studying Arabic as a second language with boys from Finland and Pakistan.[5] His eleven-year-old brother too acknowledges his English is better than his Arabic. (English is the traditional second language in Saudi schools, though the Crown Prince also introduced Chinese in Saudi schools in 2019.)

"The whole dynamic of family life has changed," explains an accomplished professional woman. Men who marry professional women know that entails a level of independence. But once they live together, men often are frustrated at their wives being gone so much for work or to socialize with female friends. "Most men are looking for more traditional wives," she says, but then adds, "It's still not okay for a woman to be more successful than her husband."

Still, culture is changing all around, she says. Her teenage son introduces her to his friends. This would have been a source of deep shame in earlier Saudi culture, to so expose your mother to strange males. Her brother never allowed his male friends even to know his mother's name, she recalls. And he constantly castigated her if a hair was visible from under her scarf. Now that same brother, she says, is reporting to his younger sister in their business.

Further evidence of cultural change, says this professional woman, is the growing tendency of women to split restaurant checks with male colleagues. Because the Quran says a woman's money is her own, more conservative Saudi women disapprove of this egalitarian practice.

And, despite all the advances for women and the many amusements available to Saudis, many parents remain protective of their daughters. A mother describes a class at the Kingdom School, a prominent private school in Riyadh, planning its first-ever school trip outside the city. The school's seniors will visit Al Ula, an area famous for its ancient Nabatean tombs. Of eighty young women in the class, only twenty-five secured their parents' permission for the trip, and the mothers of nearly a third of those girls accompanied their daughters. "It's a sign of how conservative we still are," says this mother.

Indeed, the new Western-style amusements the Crown Prince is introducing carry a risk. While many Saudis clearly were tired of the hypocrisy of Al Saud princes imposing strict religiosity on their people while indulging themselves abroad, Saudi society remains fundamentally conservative, traditional, and tribal measured against any Western standards. Changing that—if it truly changes—will take time. Meanwhile, all the playfulness of Qiddiyya and the new sports competitions are a modern equivalent of first-century Rome's "bread and circuses." The Roman emperors sought to distract their citizens from any discontent by providing free food and violent public entertainment like gladiators. Today's amusements in the kingdom help distract young Saudis from the arduous task of reforming the kingdom's economy, something that requires totally transforming its inferior education system and its work ethic. Both tasks will require at least a generation.

Meanwhile, the risk is that economic changes the Crown Prince is promising could fail to produce enough jobs for young Saudis now patiently accepting the promise of a brighter future. Will bread and circuses then suffice?

CHAPTER TEN

Pied Piper

For millennia, Saudis struggled to survive in a vast desert under searing sun and shearing winds that deplete a man's energy as he searches for a wadi of shade trees and water, which are few and far between, living on only a few dates and camel's milk. These harsh conditions made Bedouins suspicious of anyone outside their own tribe. Even as Saudis urbanized over the past half century, they continued to live clannish lives behind high walls. Divided by tribe, region, religion, culture, and even gender, Saudis have been trapped in a metaphorical maze constructed by the Al Saud to keep them isolated enough so they won't coalesce around common frustrations.

Now Mohammed bin Salman is seeking to destroy those divisive walls of religion, tradition, and gender. Like a modern-day Pied Piper, he is offering a new tune of nationalism and seeking to lure the 65 percent of Saudis under thirty years of age to follow him.

"We are half of the present, but all of the future," he said in his graduation speech from King Saud University in 2007. Now that future dominated by his young generation has arrived. No longer is deference to elders the dominant social imperative.

In MBS's new Saudi Arabia, the celebrated citizen isn't the one who blindly obeys religious clerics or memorizes the Quran.

The new role model is the entrepreneurial young man or woman committed to developing Saudi Arabia economically, not living off government handouts. "We are each personally responsible for our own futures," he said in his Vision 2030. In short, MBS, much like the youthful American president John F. Kennedy in 1960, is essentially telling young Saudis, "Ask not what your country can do for you but what you can do for your country."

Just as Kennedy assumed power after the sedentary presidency of Dwight Eisenhower, MBS is taking leadership after decades of elderly do-nothing kings. JFK inspired young Americans by pledging to put a man on the moon by the end of the decade. With his Vision 2030, MBS is pledging to transform his stodgy, oil-dependent nation into a modern, diversified economy playing a major role on the world stage—and, yes, also getting to the moon. He constantly underlines the importance of young Saudis as the real hope for creating this new Saudi Arabia.

MBS's open talk of nationalism is a breathtaking break from Saudi Arabia's past. The kingdom's religious establishment insisted that Saudis are members of a transnational community of believers, the umma, not of any nation state. Religion, not nationalism, was the glue that bound a very diverse Saudi population to each other and to their Al Saud rulers. Indeed, when the late King Abdullah in 2005 announced that Saudi Arabia would celebrate September 23, the founding day in 1932 of the third Saudi state by his father, King Abdul Aziz, religious leaders vigorously protested. Venerating any day other than the two religious holidays marking the end of Ramadan, the holy month of fasting, and the end of hajj, the Muslim pilgrimage to Mecca, is heresy.

Yet under MBS, the government has literally rewritten the history of the kingdom's founding to diminish religion and promote the prominence of the Al Saud.

For nearly three hundred years, the founding story has been that the first Saudi state was born in 1744 of a covenant between the

Al Saud and Sheikh Mohammed ibn Abd al-Wahhab. The sheikh and Mohammed ibn Saud joined forces and Islamic jihad helped the Al Saud conquer Arabia. Since then, the Al Saud and Wahhabi religious leaders have been partners off and on—until now.

Abruptly in 2022, King Salman proclaimed February 22, 1727, as the founding day of the first Saudi state. According to this new myth, Mohammed ibn Saud alone created the first Saudi state eighteen years before he ever met ibn Abd al-Wahhab. This resetting of the clock to expunge ibn Abd al-Wahhab's formative role is the outcome of "extensive historical research," explained the *Arab News* in reporting the king's decree.[1]

Poof. By royal decree, out went the narrative of the founding covenant between the Al Saud and its religious partner. It's as stunning as if George Washington suddenly were written out of a founding role in America after more than two centuries of extolling his role as the leading Revolutionary War general.

Indeed, instead of being central to the foundation of the state, ibn Abd al-Wahhab's meeting with Mohammed ibn Saud is now explained as an invitation to visit Diriyah, the capital of the Al Saud's already existing state. "In short," wrote the *Arab News*, "it was not the alliance of Sheikh and Imam that made possible the foundation of the First Saudi State but rather it was the existence of that state, already politically and economically strong, that made possible the spread of the message of reform."[2]

So let it be written. So let it be done.

Is it really possible to diminish the role of religion in a country where the life of Prophet Mohammed is deeply embedded in the geography of the Arabian Peninsula, especially in the holy cities of Mecca and Medina? In truth, the Crown Prince isn't seeking to remove Islam from his country. Indeed, he craves the extra influence that comes from controlling Mecca and Medina and being seen to represent the world's 1.8 billion Muslims. "We aren't Islamic," he told me in our first meeting, implying that the word *Islamic* has been co-opted by radicals. "We are Muslims." His goal is to eject Wahhabism and bring Saudi Muslims back to the more tolerant religion of the Prophet, who accepted women as equals in Allah's eyes. In short, he wants to separate Al Saud legitimacy from religion and place it firmly in his family's history in building Saudi Arabia.

The new history King Salman outlined not only expunged ibn Abd al-Wahhab from a key role but also deepened the part the Al Saud played in Saudi history. Imam Mohammed ibn Saud didn't just create the first Saudi state, according to the new history; the Al Sauds first settled in the vicinity of current day Riyadh way back in the fifteenth century, founding the city of Diriyah in 1446.

To glorify the Al Saud family, the site now is the center of a $62 billion development project to transform Diriyah into a heritage site and tourism attraction.[3] Already fine restaurants serving international cuisine dot Diriyah's Al Bujairi heritage park. To bring alive the Al Saud family, the government pays young Saudi men to dress like the late King Abdul Aziz and walk about the sprawling old town greeting visitors just as cartoon characters greet visitors to Disney World.

The dramatic backdrop to Diriyah's streets is the old mud palace of the Al Saud destroyed by the Ottomans in 1818 and restored a century later. It now includes a museum that features a massive family tree tracing the Al Saud's thousands of princes from 1727 right through to MBS's three young sons. Seeking to further stoke Saudi pride, MBS is promoting a Saudi Culinary Arts Commission to preserve traditional recipes, discover local chefs, provide a source of livelihood to Saudis, and "present the best of Saudi culture and hospitality locally and globally through our culinary heritage."[4] So Diriyah also features eateries that serve traditional Saudi food, including the national dish, *jareesh*, a heavy porridge of cracked wheat, vegetables, meat, and aromatic spices.

Saudi press and commentators piled on to spread the new history with a straight face. "Founding Day came to confirm the

Crown Prince Mohammed bin Salman, thirty-nine, de facto leader of Saudi Arabia since 2015. *Bandar Aljaloud/Saudi Royal Palace via AP*

المملكة العربية السعودية

KINGDOM OF SAUDI ARABIA

King Salman bin Abdul Aziz, eighty-nine, suffers from fragile health and leaves most governance to his son Crown Prince Mohammed. *Bandar Aljaloud/Saudi Royal Palace via AP*

Young MBS with his father,
HRH Prince Salman, at a
public gathering.
*King Abdulaziz Foundation
for Research and Archives*

Riyadh Governor Salman
with his teenage son
Mohammed in an undated
photo.
*King Abdulaziz Foundation
for Research and Archives*

Saudi Crown Prince meets with Palestinian Authority leader Mahmoud Abbas in Riyadh in 2024 to discuss the Palestinians' future in the wake of the Gaza war.
Palestinian Presidency/Handout/Anadolu via Getty Images

Saudi Crown Prince Mohammed meets Iranian President Raisi in Riyadh in 2023 after the start of the war in Gaza and months after establishing diplomatic relations in an effort by MBS to protect his kingdom's massive development projects from potential attacks by Tehran.
Iranian Presidency/Hanout/Anadolu via Getty Images

President Trump with Saudi Crown Prince Mohammed bin Salman in 2017. The president hopes to persuade the prince to open diplomatic relations with Israel during his second term. *AP Photo/Evan Vucci*

Mohammed bin Nayef was deposed as crown prince in 2017 and replaced by Mohammed bin Salman, his cousin. In 2020, MBN was charged with treason and remains in detention. *AP Photo/Jacquelyn Martin*

Saudi Arabia is on a building spree, making it the world's largest construction market. Here, King Salman Park, set to be completed by 2025, will be the world's largest urban park. *Peter Bogaczewicz*

The Haramain high-speed electric railway, inaugurated in 2018, connects the holy cities Mecca and Medina to Jeddah. *Saudi Press Agency*

The seventy-six-story Public Investment Fund (PIF) Tower is the tallest building in Riyadh's King Abdullah Financial District.
Saudi Press Agency

Aramco's Jubail Refinery Company, established in 1981, processes numerous products from oil even as the kingdom seeks to reduce its dependence on petro-dollars.
AP Photo/Hassan Ammar

Top: Work advances in Qiddiya City, a future entertainment hub near Riyadh.
Saudi Press Agency

Middle: The Line, a car-free, $1 trillion smart city intended to model sustainable living in harmony with nature.
Saudi Press Agency

Right: Hegra, also known as Mada'in Saleh, was shunned by Wahhabis as cursed by Allah but is now a major tourist site.
Photograph courtesy of the author

Saudi women often sat outdoors before the kingdom began offering mixed-gender restaurants and other entertainment options. *Peter Bogaczewicz*

Qinwen Zheng of China in typical tennis attire competes before abaya-clad Saudi women at the first women's tennis finals in Riyadh in 2024. *Katelyn Mulcahy/Getty Images Sport via Getty Images*

Two women smoking a hookah, or waterpipe, in a Riyadh restaurant. *Photograph courtesy of the author*

historical depth of the Saudi royal family whose chain of rule dates back nearly 600 years since the foundation of the city of Diriyah by King Salman's grandfather thirteen generations removed," gushed the *Saudi Gazette.*[5]

To deepen the revised founding myth, a new national logo was unveiled with the slogan "The Day We Started." At its center, the logo features a man carrying a banner surrounded by four symbols, carefully described by their government creators to glorify the benefits of Al Saud rule. The first is dates, said to signify life, growth, and generosity; the second is the symbol of a council, signifying unity and cultural harmony; the third is an Arabian horse, the symbol of bravery shown by the state's princes; the final symbol is for a market, representing economic activity and diversity. Interestingly, there is no symbol for religion. Nor does the banner the man is waving include the words on the Saudi flag: "There is no god but God and Mohammed is the messenger of God." This leaves open whether the national flag too may one day be revised.

Founders' Day is a three-day holiday for kingdom residents. The actual day is lavishly celebrated by once-forbidden music and dancing. To add dazzle, an elaborate sky show featuring fireworks, pyrotechnics, and a fleet of drones marked the first Founders' Day celebration in 2022. Key visual components symbolizing three hundred years of Saudi history were woven into the show in a night sky.[6] The twenty-minute display was broadcast live on four networks in the Saudi region so not only Saudis but the kingdom's neighbors could witness the celebratory change in Saudi history.

All this seeks to embed Al Saud legitimacy in nationalism, not religion. Crown Prince Mohammed bin Salman is the primary leader of these nationalism efforts and seeks also to be their biggest beneficiary. Youth is his priority. And he expects them to make Saudi Arabia theirs by pledging unquestioned loyalty to him, his vision, and his leadership. The prince is young and modern and sees himself as a role model for young Saudis. They appear to agree. He portrays an active lifestyle young Saudis aspire to. For instance, he shows up in public at Formula E races the kingdom hosts and is filmed riding a dune bike on the sandstone hills of Al Ula, home to the ancient Nabatean region he is developing as a tourist attraction.

In 2019, he appeared at the Formula E electric-car races wearing a navy-colored Barbour jacket over his traditional Saudi thobe, Tom Ford aviator sunglasses, and a pair of black Adidas Yeezy Boost 350 trainers. His photo was all over social media and hundreds of Saudis shared their purchase receipts of the British Barbour jacket.[7] A few years later, he showed up at a new outdoor restaurant called Somewhere in Al Ula, wearing a Brunello Cucinelli zip-up vest in beige and white. The vest retails for $6,900 on luxury marketplace FarFetch. Young Saudis began immediately looking for the vest on lower-priced websites and sharing advice with each other on how to get the look.[8] The smiling prince also posed for photos with Saudi diners at Somewhere and many quickly posted those photos to social media. Because MBS is young and visible, he creates a sense among young Saudis that they belong, along with him, in a new Saudi Arabia shedding its religious rigidity and economic stagnation. He gives young Saudis so much that was denied, including movies, concerts, gender-mixing, and females driving and working.

"We never had a ruler like this," a young Saudi woman tells me in 2017. "He knows all what he is talking about and he cares enough to explain it to us. This is new. We should support him," she says. Though from a conservative family, this single woman works at the Saudi stock market.[9]

Another professional woman the same year expresses joy at the prospect of soon driving. "My mother wanted to do that all her life and now we will get to drive," she says. "I am living my life as I want to. I feel like I'm in Dubai." Yet she frets that MBS is using the many social changes to distract Saudis from growing political repression. "He should meet with the people or take questions by phone from people," she says. "We can't do or say anything. If you cross the line on Twitter, they take you to prison."[10]

In his bid to build Saudi nationalism, MBS has crossed the line into once-forbidden pre-Islamic times. Under Wahhabism, anything pre-Islamic was *jahiliyyah*, or ignorance, and therefore forbidden. For more than two thousand years, Hegra, a walled city in the Al Ula region of Arabia, lay largely unknown to most Saudis. Hegra is famous for huge tombs carved in sandstone by Nabateans, two centuries before Christ. Hegra's anonymity is starkly at odds with its world-famous twin city, Petra in Jordan.

That anonymity ended in June 2017 when Crown Prince Mohammed rode into the sand dunes around Al Ula with a party of friends on four-wheel dirt buggies, startling the small local population. Dressed in a black thobe, he apologized for the noisy entry and posed for selfies, which, of course, were spread on social media, beginning the unveiling of Al Ula to Saudis. Al Ula is a tourist site not made by modern man. It needs no PIF press releases to leave visitors in awe. Its sandstone mountains stretch for vast miles around Hegra, its crown jewel.

Placing Al Ula as the centerpiece of the kingdom's new tourism strategy is deeply ironic. As noted, the kingdom's Wahhabi religious establishment taught that anything before the Prophet Mohammed's time was *jahiliyyah*, or ignorance. Yet here is MBS not only reviving but glorifying pre-Islamic history as part of his bid to replace Islam with nationalism as the source of Al Saud legitimacy. A new Royal Heritage Commission is painstakingly researching and restoring ancient remnants of history all across Saudi Arabia, including Hegra, also known as Mada'in Saleh.

Even more ironic is MBS's spotlighting this particular site. Many conservative Saudis believe Mada'in Saleh is cursed by Allah. The Quran recounts how the Thamud people, who lived in northern

Arabia, ignored repeated pleas by Prophet Saleh, a precursor to Prophet Mohammed, to acknowledge Allah. They ignored the Prophet and also killed a miraculous she-camel that Allah had sent them as a sign of his existence. According to the Quran, God then destroyed the Thamud by a shriek, an earthquake, a thunderbolt, and a blast.[11]

After my first visit to Al Ula in 2019, a deeply devout Saudi woman with whom I lived a decade earlier to experience life in a conservative home shakes her head in sadness. "I could never go there," she says, making clear she would not violate Allah's commands as I had done. News of the curse was omitted from my tour and is dismissed by Mohammed al Essa, secretary general of the Muslin World League and a key Islamic scholar for MBS. "The idea that Mada'in Saleh is cursed is superstition," he tells me. "I am religious and I've visited Mada'in Saleh. I wouldn't go if God said not to."[12]

Of course, ignoring religious history that some conservatives attach to the area simply underscores the Crown Prince's message that his new nation is open and inclusive; his nationalism is intended to transcend sectarian and ethnic divisions and regional and gender divides. It is a new Saudi Arabia where all Saudis can take pride in their history and all foreigners can feel welcome in the present, bringing their minds and their money. In short, MBS is reviving what the famous fourteenth-century philosopher-historian Ibn Khaldun called *asabiyyah*, or social solidarity. Ibn Khaldun warns that this social solidarity usually dissipates over four generations, or about 150 years, leading to the fall of the ruling dynasty.[13] MBS, who read much Islamic and Arab history under his father's tutelage as a boy, understands not only the importance of creating a new legitimacy for Al Saud replacing religion, but also the importance of national pride and social solidarity around achieving new goals—Vision 2030.

In addition to the alluring historical setting, Al Ula features a modern concert hall built in just three months to host the first group of internationally renowned performers that organizers hope will begin to establish Al Ula as a global arts center. Several hundred lucky listeners sit in plush white leather chairs facing a stage where Lang Lang, a Chinese pianist, performs. Through the glass wall behind him, the rose-lit sandstone mountains are as beautifully captivating as his music.

This concert hall is itself a piece of art. Maraya, meaning mirror or reflection in Arabic, is a mirrored structure 100 meters by 100 meters by 26 meters. Essentially its length and depth are the size of an American football field. Nestled in the sandstone mountains, its mirrored walls reflect that front range, creating a dizzying but mesmerizing mirage.

Making foreigners comfortable in Saudi Arabia is a key driver for this new nationalism. To truly transform the kingdom beyond new myths and consultants' proposals for gigaprojects, the Crown Prince needs foreign expertise, foreign tourists, and most of all foreign investors. Multitudes of foreigners will not come to a country that lives as if it were a museum for Islamic practices of centuries past; where women can't drive and are segregated from men; where shops close for prayer five times daily; where there is no public entertainment, not even cinema. So, all the modern pleasures in the new Saudi Arabia from concerts, theaters, five-star restaurants, and luxury resorts are intended not just to transform the Saudi economy off oil but also to lure the foreign dollars and international expertise needed to help execute that transformation. Even with all this, regional upheavals like the Gaza war, Iran's missile attack on Israel, and Houthi missiles attacking Red Sea ships have discouraged foreign investors from flocking to the kingdom as MBS had hoped.

By emphasizing national culture, the Crown Prince seeks to bury—or at least subdue—local narratives among various Saudi communities who romanticize their differing Bedouin histories.

Determined to diminish these tribal divisions and loyalties, Abdul Aziz through brief marriages to hundreds of different tribal women created the Al Saud as a "supertribe," or one vast family to which all tribes could express loyalty.[14]

By his own count in 1930, Abdul Aziz had consummated marriages with 135 virgins and about 100 other women. Many of these were widows of tribal chiefs he conquered and married for one night. Henceforth, he told a friend, he would limit himself to two new wives a year. If so, by his death, his marriages totaled about 275.[15] Divorce was quick and easy. A man simply says, "I divorce thee." The woman has no choice. Abdul Aziz duly divorced women to ensure he never exceeded the Islamic limit of four wives at one time. Despite his marriage spree, tribal segmentation remains to this day.

Some 80 percent of Saudis say they identify with a tribe. The kingdom has dozens of major tribes with hundreds of branches and some three thousand recognized tribal chiefs whom the government pays to interface between their tribe and the government bureaucracy.[16] Each chief seeks to get the most government services and other largesse for his tribe. In the early 2000s camel beauty contests among various tribes competing as tribal units so aroused old tribal loyalties and passions that the late King Abdullah's government forbade them. Instead the late king organized a camel competition among individuals, not tribes, and an Al Saud prince was the judge. MBS attends these camel beauty contests, falcon competitions, and other Bedouin events to demonstrate he is one of the people. It is clear that King Abdul Aziz's effort to eradicate tribal loyalties with religion was only partially successful. Indeed, Prince Salman told me a decade ago when he was governor of Riyadh, "Saudi Arabia was many kingdoms. Every tribe was a kingdom. We have pride in our Islamic beliefs that collected all the races as democracy did in America. If you take away Islam, our country will be dismantled."[17]

As indicated in this statement by the kingdom's current king, there are risks inherent in shifting the legitimacy of the Al Saud from religion to nationalism. While the Crown Prince clearly isn't removing Islam from the kingdom, he is deemphasizing its centrality as he stresses the territorial history all Saudis share and the nationalist future they can build together under Vision 2030.

The truth is that the religious establishment was something of a buffer for the Al Saud rulers. From the early days of cooperation between ibn Abd al-Wahhab and Mohammed ibn Saud, the religious leader set strictures on what the Saudi people could do. While the Al Saud ruler was responsible for political decisions, the sheikh was the primary voice on religious responsibilities of the citizens. Through the centuries Saudis grew accustomed to the idea that the religious officials had significant power that curbed what their government could do. Therefore, lack of reforms could be blamed on the religious establishment, shielding the Al Saud from public upset. And when Crown Prince Faisal sought to replace his elder brother, King Saud, in 1964, the religious establishment provided its authority to endorse the move, giving the royal family cover for replacing an incompetent king with a younger brother. Thus the change in leadership was portrayed as religiously sanctioned change, not evidence of a power struggle in the royal family.

Over the years, the Al Saud became adept at using the religious shield behind which they pursued their own social, economic, and political priorities. The regime was careful to balance conservatives on one hand and calls for reforms on the other. Because almost all Saudis were dependent on government for their livelihood—jobs, education, health care—overt opposition was rare. The social contract gave citizens their life necessities, while levying no taxes on the populace, in exchange for obedience—and no requests for representation.

When Islamists challenged the Al Saud's religious legitimacy in the 1990s for inviting infidel U.S. troops into Saudi Arabia, the regime jailed their leaders. But the success in recent decades of Islamism, from the Muslim Brotherhood through the Islamic State, has shaken the Saudi royal family and helped drive this shift to nationalism. Saudis were schooled at home on the same Islamist teachings from which these movements evolved. Thus their messages attacking the Saudi government for apostasy resonated with some Saudis. Increasingly, the government realized it can't control Islamists while it relies on Islam for its legitimacy.[18] Moreover, in the post-9/11 world the brutality of ISIS and other Islamist organizations is often ascribed by the international community to the influence of Wahhabi doctrine being spread abroad by the Saudi government. So nationalism not only gives young Saudis a way to channel their aspirations outside of Islamism, but also differentiates Saudi values from those of the Islamic State.

To diminish radical Islam's appeal in Saudi Arabia with its two holy sites, the kingdom has led an international effort to create a pan-Islamic set of principles that support anti-extremism and religious and culture diversity, and oppose hate and violence. The so-called Mecca Charter, approved by Islamic leaders of 139 countries in 2019, was spearheaded by Mohammed al-Essa, MBS's chief adviser on Islam, and the new head of the Muslim World League. "If someone is not tolerant or doesn't accept another faith or culture and believe in its right to exist, he is going against the will of the creator," al-Essa tells me in 2023. Living out his words, he signed a memorandum of understanding with the American Jewish Committee to further Muslim-Jewish understanding and also visited Auschwitz.

Despite all this, there is a dark side to the new nationalism. Since 2017 the nationalist narrative has become jingoist, with a loud faction attacking fellow Saudis who don't adopt their excessively nationalist views. Think Proud Boys support of Donald Trump's nationalist rhetoric. Some have even begun to call for prosecution of those considered to have offended Saudi leadership, culture, or values.[19] While most of the nationalists on social media support the government's regional policies, especially its assertive "Saudi First" stance, they disagree on domestic issues. Some conservatives are beginning to argue that the government needs to filter entertainment to protect Saudi culture and identity.[20] The kingdom has been daring in its willingness to allow controversial entertainment. For instance, the government allowed movie theaters to screen *Barbie* while countries across the Middle East banned the movie for undermining traditional gender norms.

Traditional media in the kingdom tend these days to mirror social media. Indeed, as in the U.S., some traditional media simply rely on reporting the content of tweets rather than developing their own reporting. All this is driven in part by an increasingly narrow band of permissible discussion in the kingdom as the Crown Prince continues to intensify political repression against perceived critics. Once TV shows in Saudi hosted genuine debate among political or religious figures or talks by outspoken scholars like Salman al-Awdah, imprisoned since 2017 for a tweet deemed unsupportive of the Saudi government's blockade of neighboring Qatar. He remains in prison charged with "terrorism-related crimes." al-Awdah, a prominent Islamist sheikh, was first jailed in 1994 by King Fahd. When released, he moderated his views and was permitted to host his own popular television show during the late King Abdullah's reign before being rearrested under MBS's rule.

Whether the Crown Prince's sanctioned nationalist narrative will eventually clash with the grassroots nationalism increasingly emerging across many public platforms remains an open question. Just as the late King Abdullah criminalized criticism of government, the new Saudi regime has arrested waves of people as "threats to national security" for offenses such as speaking with some foreigners, including foreign journalists. Loujain al-Hathloul, a proponent of allowing women to drive, was arrested in 2018 on the eve of the kingdom's lifting the driving ban and accused of using her relations with foreign governments and journalists to "pressure the kingdom to change its laws" and of "attempting to destabilize the government." Initially analysts speculated that the Crown Prince wanted credit for letting women drive and didn't want the appearance it had occurred under pressure from activists like al-Hathloul. (Al-Hathloul was released from prison in 2021 but remains in Saudi Arabia under a travel ban.)

But subsequent arrests since 2018 have made clear the government no longer seeks to balance competing requests among its citizens as in the days of earlier Saudi kings but now assumes responsibility for providing reforms based on its own judgment and its own timetable. Grassroots activists are not to lobby or protest for change. "The new nationalism is about the state—not the society," wrote Eman Alhussein, a nonresident analyst at the Arab Gulf States Institute in Washington, D.C.[21]

While young Saudis are expected to follow the Crown Prince, he works to retain their devotion and build their motivation. To deepen ties with this group, the Crown Prince's MISK Foundation hosts hundreds of programs to bring together young Saudis. His goal is to create national camaraderie among them and provide motivational training. MBS launched the foundation in 2011 by taking remnants of his father's charities and folding them into his own foundation focused on youth education. MISK organized meetings for young Saudis in the U.S. when MBS visited in 2018 and at the United Nations in subsequent years. It also hosts a "Youth Majlis" each year in Davos, Switzerland, where young Saudis meet with youth from around the world. The first such dialogue in 2022 welcomed some 1,700 visitors from forty-two countries during the three-day Davos forum.[22]

During a MISK Global Forum in November 2023, some forty thousand Saudis registered and tens of thousands can be seen strolling the historic pathways around Diriyah, the old Al Saud capital, or attending a multitude of different lectures occurring simultaneously. The three-day event is grandiosely titled "The Big Now." MISK's CEO opens the event by urging young Saudis to "act now to transform dreams into reality."

At dusk on this perfect fall evening, the Crown Prince's older half brother, energy minister Prince Abdul Aziz bin Salman, takes the stage. Unlike the tightly wound MBS, Prince Abdul Aziz is a tall, erect, erudite man who exudes a calm, philosophical demeanor. One can imagine his reading Marcus Aurelius's *Meditations*, or even privately writing his own. A graduate of King Fahd Petroleum University, he worked at the Ministry of Energy for more than three decades mastering the portfolio before finally being named minister of energy in 2018 by his father, King Salman.

"I was a sidelined person," the prince tells the young crowd. "If you can use that time to say, 'I will have the opportunity,' that's good. I was fortunate to have my opportunity at a later date." In short, keep striving. As the lights on the mud palace of his ancestral home nearby create a halo in the growing twilight, he assures young Saudis their Bedouin heritage is compatible with being citizens of the world. "Can Bedouins become global citizens?" he asks. "Yes. We can prove we are no different than others."[23] In sum, dream big but don't abandon your Saudi heritage. MBS, educated only in Saudi Arabia, personifies this pride in Saudi heritage, not imitating the West.

Consistent with that, the government in 2024 issued a ruling that Saudis working for the government must wear formal Saudi attire at all times in the office. Men must wear their head coverings, not show up and remove them in the office.

Promoting nationalism carries a risk for MBS. If he disappoints these young people by failing to produce the economic opportunities he is pledging, he can't use religion as a buffer of blame. These days MBS clearly is calling the tune and therefore accountable for the success or failure of his reform agenda. The next five years or so will provide hard evidence on whether the $1 trillion spent on gigaprojects will produce jobs, grow non-oil revenue, and create a more sustainable economy or produce a host of white elephants.

The Crown Prince seems supremely confident that he and the young generation he leads can achieve his grand vision for Saudi Arabia. In his mind, previous generations hobbled the kingdom by their low expectations. That's surely a mistake he's not guilty of.

"My father's generation came to Riyadh when it was just sand," he told Jared Kushner, the prince's youthful interlocutor during the first Trump presidency. "They look around at this city with airports, buildings, and schools and they say, 'We can't believe we accomplished this in our lifetime.'" But, he added, "My generation, we look at this and say we are not achieving even ten percent of our potential. We have unbelievable natural and human resources beyond oil."[24]

Classic MBS. To him the glass is only 10 percent full but he will fill the rest.

CHAPTER ELEVEN

Venturing Forth into the World

From the outset of his father's rule, MBS has demonstrated a determination to put Saudi Arabia first. With oil prices at a nadir in 2015, he persuaded Russia to join members of the Organization of the Petroleum Exporting Countries (OPEC) in cutting production to lift prices, creating the so-called OPEC Plus. It worked: oil prices grew 50 percent over the next year. So when Covid lockdowns in 2020 sharply cut global oil demand and sent prices plummeting, MBS again sought production cuts to bolster oil prices. President Putin refused. An angry MBS announced price discounts to buyers of Saudi oil to grab market share from Russia. His impulsive action triggered a free fall in world oil prices causing particular pain for U.S. shale oil producers.

Within a month, President Trump called the young prince with a blunt message: unless Saudi Arabia cut its oil output to stabilize prices, he would be unable to stop Congress from passing legislation forcing the withdrawal of U.S. troops from Saudi Arabia.[1] Essentially, Trump told the shocked Crown Prince, "We are defending your oil industry while you're destroying ours."[2]

"Drill, baby, drill" had been a favorite slogan of candidate Trump. And by 2018, large gains in shale oil production had made the U.S. the world's largest oil producer. Now the sharp decline in oil prices was seriously threatening U.S. shale oil producers, whose cost to extract oil from shale was at least four times the cost of producing a barrel of Saudi oil. Ten days later, the Saudis and Russia led the oil cartel in agreeing to slash production by nearly 10 million barrels a day, the largest production cut ever negotiated.[3] That production cut, plus another in 2022, remains largely in place as this book goes to press. And U.S. shale oil production hit a record average 13.2 million barrels a day in 2024.

Fast forward to President Trump's second term. Instead of demanding higher prices to help U.S. shale oil producers, he is now demanding lower prices to help American consumers. Sure enough, Saudi Arabia quickly obliged. In February 2025, Riyadh led OPEC Plus to boost oil production and to pledge further increases, which immediately sent prices below $70 a barrel. Russia's President Putin joined the production increase, repaying Trump for his strong support of Russia over Ukraine as Washington seeks to end that three-year-old war.

The Crown Prince learned he wasn't the only leader who could play hardball to advance his nation's interests.

But under Joe Biden's presidency, the Crown Prince continued to surprise the White House with his bold focus on Saudi first. When the U.S. sought to punish Putin for Russia's invasion of Ukraine in 2022 by organizing a boycott of Russian energy, Saudi Arabia refused to go along. Riyadh began buying discounted Russian oil, flouting Washington's wishes to cripple Russia's economy and erode its fighting ability in Ukraine. While China and India are the largest buyers of Russian oil, Saudi Arabia has regularly purchased small quantities of fuel oil from Russia for its power plants. All this clearly has helped Russia evade Western sanctions and perpetuate its war against Ukraine. Bolstering Russia in Ukraine is a vivid example of how Saudi Arabia's new independence can hurt U.S. interests. As the war dragged on, support in Congress has ebbed. And President Trump has quickly sided with Russia in his efforts to get an end to the war. The president called Volodymyr Zelensky a "dictator," falsely blamed Ukraine for starting the war, implied Russia could hold on to conquered Ukrainian territory, and said that Ukraine would not be welcome in NATO. A clear win for Russia in Ukraine will doubtless erode U.S. credibility with allies like South Korea, Japan, and Taiwan, all of whom depend on the U.S. to protect their security from China's expansion in East Asia and the South China Sea. While tearing down Zelensky, President Trump boosted the Saudi Crown Prince by choosing Riyadh to host Russia-U.S. talks to end the war in Ukraine.

Clearly, Saudi Arabia's activist crown prince isn't just transforming his kingdom but also roiling global politics, often with negative consequences for U.S. security interests. Beyond defying the U.S. on Russia, he also is declining to confront Yemen's Houthis, who began shooting missiles at ships in the Red Sea in 2023, very much including U.S. military ships there to counter the Houthis and keep the Red Sea lanes open. The U.S. outraged Saudi Arabia in 2016 by refusing to help it in its war against the Houthis, even cutting arms shipments to the kingdom. As a result, the Crown Prince isn't going to risk his own 2022 ceasefire with the Houthis to help the U.S. now.

For most of its modern history, Saudi Arabia was a hermit kingdom content to sell its oil and otherwise to hide itself behind veils of religious piety. No longer. Crown Prince Mohammed has made it clear that, unlike his elderly uncles who ruled for the past half century, he isn't going to dwell in the desert with his falcons, or sit for months on his royal yacht off Spain, or hang out at his royal stables admiring his Arabian Thoroughbreds. He is going to reshape the world—and Saudi Arabia's role in it.

Instead of playing junior partner to the United States, the young Crown Prince is contending to operate alongside the elderly men leading China, Russia, and the U.S. and play them all off against each other to get what's best for Saudi Arabia. He is also determined to forge cooperation with other middle powers like South Korea, Turkey, and Indonesia. He sees himself as not only the voice of Arabs but also of the world's 1.9 billion Muslims, whether in Asia, Africa, or the Mideast. His immodest goal is to use his nation's wealth and his ambition to occupy a place alongside the U.S., China, Russia, and India as arbiters of global governance. These geopolitical divisions create new opportunities for ambitious nations like Saudi Arabia to maneuver among the so-called big powers.

"My mandate from my leadership is very clear," said Saudi foreign minister Faisal bin Farhan. "Saudi Arabia's foreign policy is a tool for its domestic prosperity. That is our top priority." But he acknowledges, "You cannot build prosperity in a turbulent region. . . . If we want to protect our pathway to sustainable prosperity, we must be engaged in the world."

All of this is being put to the test by Israel's war in Gaza and the Crown Prince's desire to resolve the long, intractable Israeli-Palestinian issue to stabilize the Mideast and thereby protect his nation's huge investments in modernity. His overriding preoccupation is money and peace. He needs money to fund his economic modernization and peace to protect what he's building from the mounting threats all around the kingdom.

As with everything the Crown Prince sets his mind to, he is pursuing his goal for world influence with a relentlessness that would exhaust a leader not blessed with his youth. In the space of one month after the war in Gaza began in 2023, MBS hosted a dizzying spate of summits:

- The Association of Southeast Asian Nations (ASEAN) came first. Asia's wealthy tigers are role models for Saudi's economic transformation. A smiling MBS greeted each leader, posed for an animated photo, and acted as if only that leader mattered to him.

- Next a tête-à-tête with South Korea's president. A South Korean company is one of the contenders to build the kingdom's first two nuclear power units and another will manufacture cars in Saudi Arabia, assisting its economic diversification.
- Then MBS hosted the first-ever African Summit with fifty African leaders to discuss trade and humanitarian assistance by Saudi Arabia, which pledged $50 billion to African nations.
- One day later he hosted an extraordinary Arab-Islamic Summit, attended by dozens of leaders, including the late President Ebrahim Raisi of Iran, with which Saudi restored diplomatic relations a few months earlier. The Muslim leaders unanimously condemned Israel's war in Gaza against Hamas, the terrorist organization that attacked Israel on October 7, 2023, killing 1,200 Israelis and taking 250 more as hostages.
- A few days later dozens of Caribbean leaders gathered in Riyadh for the first-ever Caribbean Summit, intended to build new partnerships and open trade cooperation between the kingdom and that distant region.[4]

No nation is too small to entice the Crown Prince. Nor is any issue too large. After the spate of summer summits, MBS in August convened an international summit on the war in Ukraine, attended by forty nations excluding Russia. It was evidence that all roads increasingly converge in Saudi Arabia. A year earlier the Crown Prince had gotten involved in Ukraine by helping negotiate a Russia-Ukraine prisoner release of nearly three hundred people, including ten foreigners.[5] As summit host, MBS placed himself between the U.S. national security adviser and the top Chinese representative, seeming to encourage warmer relations between his longtime security partner and his largest trading partner. The summit produced no peace in Ukraine and no improvement in U.S.-China relations.[6] With Russia absent, President Vladimir Putin soon made his own pilgrimage to see the Crown Prince in December.

For most of Arabia's many millennia, it wasn't a place of summits but of solitude. The Prophet Elijah sought refuge there after Israel's Queen Jezebel threatened to murder him for killing pagans who were worshipping her false god, Baal. A thousand years later Apostle Paul trekked to Arabia to spend three years contemplating the meaning of his dramatic conversion to Christianity on the road to Damascus. The onetime persecutor of Christians departed Arabia as the Bible's most prominent proclaimer of Christ.[7]

Throughout history, the million square miles of Arabian deserts were mostly traversed by traders on camels plying the Silk Route with goods from China bound for the Levant. Indeed, until the death of Prophet Mohammed in 632, what happened in Arabia largely stayed in Arabia.

After the Prophet's death, his successors launched a movement that thrust Arabs out of the peninsula and into world history. In quick succession they conquered Iraq, Palestine, Syria, Egypt, and part of modern Tunisia before expanding through Algeria and Morocco to the Atlantic Ocean.[8] Within one hundred years the Arabs had reached the Indian subcontinent, occupied much of Spain, and entered France, where their advance finally was halted at Tours in 732.

Arguably, Mohammed bin Salman is the first Saudi leader to seek a prominent role in global politics since that Islamic conquest 1,400 years ago. One big reason for his assertiveness is that the world itself is changing. The unipolar world dominated by the U.S. since the fall of the Soviet Union now is being replaced by growing competition—and tension—between the U.S. and China. That competition is leading other nervous nations to jockey for position—and for advantage—by playing the big powers off against each other. America's holiday from great-power geopolitical competition is "unmistakably over," wrote political scientist Hal Brands in 2023, "as China challenges for hegemony, Russia seeks dramatic revisions to the European balance, and an array of revisionist actors test Washington and the international order it leads."[9] It's certainly true the Mideast these days has no clear hegemon.

It's also true that one of the actors jockeying for power there is MBS, a cocky and calculating young prince. But he is hardly the only leader of a so-called middle power with ambition to assert more control over the global order to influence outcomes in favor of his nation. Turkey, Iran, Qatar, the United Arab Emirates, Brazil all come to mind. But the combination of Saudi Arabia's strategic location, its oil wealth, and its ambitious and aggressive young leader make the kingdom the leading example of a nation bent on balancing all powers to its advantage.

Beyond modernizing his kingdom, MBS's primary goal is to make Saudi Arabia the power center of the Middle East. He envisions the kingdom as the key link between India and Europe through a corridor that connects Saudi Arabia and Israel. Saudi and the Jewish state would not only become a technological powerhouse but also the pathway for moving goods, data, and energy from the Indian Ocean to the Mediterranean Sea. Some of MBS's ministers already refer to him as Saladin, the famous twelfth-century Kurdish leader who freed Jerusalem from nearly a century of Christian dominance and united Arab lands from Arabia through Palestine, Syria, and Egypt. The Crown Prince doesn't intend to conquer Jerusalem but rather cooperate with Israel to meld its technological prowess with Saudi money to transform the kingdom into a new Silicon Valley of entrepreneurship. After all, ambitious goals are synonymous with this crown prince.

In the early years of his leadership, MBS was so confident he even dared to snub the U.S. president. As a candidate, Joe Biden labeled Saudi Arabia a "pariah" and promised to isolate the kingdom. Saudis are accustomed to such hot rhetoric during U.S. elections. But when the U.S. president doubled down by publicly announcing he wouldn't even speak to MBS, the kingdom's de facto leader, that crossed a line for MBS. When Biden sought to call the Crown Prince to seek more oil production to ease gasoline prices and help Democrats in the 2022 midterm elections, the Crown Prince refused to take his call. Things got still worse.

In the summer, Biden flew to Jeddah to personally make his request for more oil and to reset frayed U.S.-Saudi relations. MBS was eager to move past Biden's opprobrium for the murder of Jamal Khashoggi. The photo of a perfunctory fist bump between the U.S. president and an unsmiling Crown Prince was worldwide news. After their meeting, Biden boasted to reporters that he had blamed MBS to his face for Khashoggi's death. For his part, the Crown Prince simply declined to boost Saudi oil production. Their summit humbled the president who had sought to humble the prince.

Meanwhile, until just recently the kingdom tried to prop up oil prices by holding down production. In 2023 it voluntarily cut its production by one million barrels a day and in 2024 extended that cut as oil prices remained stubbornly around $80 a barrel, below the $90–100 the kingdom needs to meet its development budget.

All of this underscores that Saudi Arabia has options other than its so-called special relationship with the U.S. If the American president wanted to denounce the kingdom as a pariah, Riyadh would simply deepen its cooperation with Russia and China.

Both nation's leaders had stood by MBS after the death of Jamal Khashoggi in 2018 when most world leaders shunned him. At the G-20 summit shortly after Khashoggi's death, a laughing Putin gave the Saudi Crown Prince a big high-five greeting. A few months later the Chinese president warmly welcomed the Crown Prince to

Beijing. A photo shows a smiling MBS posing with President Xi Jinping. Look who's standing beside one of the world's most powerful leaders, seemed the implicit message in MBS's broad smile. The two countries signed a $10 billion deal to develop a refining and petrochemical complex in northeastern China.[10]

Saudi dealing with China isn't new. What's new is the kingdom's flaunting close ties with Beijing to humiliate Washington. In 1986, when Saudi Arabia had no formal relations with China, the kingdom secretly purchased fifty Chinese medium-range nuclear-capable missiles sold with conventional warheads. The Saudi missile purchase came after the American Congress blocked its request to buy U.S. F-15 jet fighters to enhance its security. At that time, Saudi Arabia feared both Israel and Iran.[11] When the U.S. discovered the missile installations near Riyadh in 1988, an immediate diplomatic crisis ensued. President Ronald Reagan demanded through diplomatic channels, not publicly, that the missiles be removed. The late King Fahd adamantly refused. Once the story broke in the *Washington Post*, it became a public rift, but still both sides operated within the context of Saudi dependence on the U.S. for its security. There was no gratuitous public embrace of China by Riyadh. The missiles have never been used and were visible publicly only once, at a parade in 2014 honoring a Pakistani visitor.[12]

Nonetheless, this opening to China soon led Saudi Arabia, a staunchly anticommunist nation throughout its history, to establish diplomatic relations with Beijing in 1990. Saudi Arabia was the last Arab nation to do so. One year later, the first barrel of Saudi oil arrived in China.[13] Nearly a quarter century later, China is the kingdom's largest trading partner due to its deep dependence on Saudi oil imports. In recent years Saudi has invested tens of billions of dollars in Chinese petrochemical plants in China to ensure a long-term market for its oil. Saudi Aramco believes the market for turning oil into chemicals will last beyond the uses of oil for gasoline.

While MBS is well aware that China cannot replace the U.S. as the ultimate guarantor of Saudi security, the China-Saudi relationship has grown over the past three decades, especially under MBS and President Xi. China has passed the U.S. as Saudi Arabia's largest investor with investments from 2021 to October 2024 totaling $21.6 billion, nearly double the U.S. $12.5 billion foreign direct investment in the kingdom.[14] The late King Abdullah was the first Saudi king to visit China in 2005, signaling a turn to the east. At that time, a group of prominent Saudi ministers, unhappy with the U.S. invasion of Iraq and George W. Bush's constant promotion of democracy, told me over dinner in Riyadh, "If you Americans aren't careful, in twenty years you'll find us all speaking Chinese." Today, nearly two decades later, MBS has mandated teaching Chinese (along with English) in Saudi schools and his own children are studying the language.

At first glance, the president of China and the Saudi crown prince would appear to have little in common. But a closer look reveals many similarities. Both believe American decline offers them an opportunity to play a dominant role in world affairs, sometimes at U.S. expense. They also share a distaste for American democracy, especially what they regard as Washington's sanctimonious democracy promotion to the world.

Both see themselves as symbols of proud and ancient civilizations that are superior to the West. They are offended by Washington's assertion that individual liberty and human rights are universal values.

While both face frequent condemnation from human rights groups, that's clearly not a criticism raised when they meet. After President Xi warmly welcomed MBS to Beijing a few months following Khashoggi's death, MBS returned Xi's hospitality by expressing support for China's brutal suppression of Muslim Uyghurs. China has imprisoned at least one million Uyghurs in detention camps. Whatever their private conversation, both leaders publicly insisted that Saudi-Chinese relations are "trouble-free." One of the Saudi ministers traveling with MBS told me later, "MBS managed President Trump but he meshed with President Xi."

As trust in U.S. reliability declines, Saudi Arabia has continued to work not just with China and Russia but a growing constellation of partners. After an initial period of pugnacious policies, including a war with Yemen and strained relations with Tehran, Qatar, and Syria, the Crown Prince more recently has pursued a peace offensive. Early in 2022 the Saudi-led coalition announced it would cease hostilities in Yemen; that ceasefire was still holding in 2024 when Yemen's Houthis began firing missiles at ships in the Red Sea, but not at Saudi Arabia.

In 2023, MBS concluded a détente with Iran, partially brokered by China, which enjoys good relations with both Iran and Saudi Arabia. As the Gaza war spawned numerous attacks by Iranian proxies, Tehran in 2024 hadn't yet attacked Saudi Arabia, and China is said to be discouraging Iran from precipitating a wider Mideast war. Saudi also has restored relations with Qatar, improved ties with Turkey, and had welcomed Bashar al-Assad back into the Arab fold before he was subsequently driven from Damascus by Islamic insurgents in late 2024.

Regardless all the maneuvering among big powers, what Saudi Arabia most wants is a reliable security partnership with the United States, the only country with the military capability to protect the kingdom. But how can Riyadh be confident the U.S. actually would come to its rescue in a crisis?

At the nadir of U.S.-Saudi relations in the summer of 2022, the Biden administration began to seek a new phase in relations with the kingdom. When Putin invaded Ukraine that spring, the U.S. sought to deprive him of economic resources by banning imports of Russian oil, gas, and coal to the U.S. and encouraging allies to do likewise.

Instead, Saudi not only purchased Russian oil but led oil producers in cutting production to raise prices, thus helping Russia finance its war on Ukraine. Saudi Arabia's ability—and willingness—to undercut U.S. strategic interests with Russia raised questions in Washington of how the kingdom might seek to thwart America's competitive advantage with China, already Riyadh's largest trading partner. The Biden administration came to recognize that in a world of emerging nodes of power rather than one superpower, Saudi Arabia's energy and its location make it a pivotal power in this new world.

As a result, the Biden administration began negotiating with Saudi Arabia to provide a security treaty that would grant the kingdom reliable access to purchase U.S. weapons and pledge Washington to defend the kingdom in exchange for Saudi establishing diplomatic relations with Israel. Such a U.S.-Saudi security treaty would require confirmation by two-thirds of the U.S. Senate, something Washington deemed unlikely without the popular sweetener of Saudi-Israeli relations. The proposed security commitment isn't a promise to go to war on behalf of the kingdom, but one akin to the U.S. promise to Japan to "meet the common danger in accordance with its constitutional provisions and processes." The war in Gaza disrupted all this.

If there is a U.S.-Saudi security deal anytime soon, it likely will be a less fulsome one, similar to promises the U.S. has made in recent years to protect other Gulf states like Bahrain and the United Arab Emirates. In short, it's a presidential pledge that may or may not be kept by the next U.S. president. It's this on-again, off-again partnership that so frustrates Saudi Arabia and keeps it seeking a real security treaty confirmed by the U.S. Senate. "What we've had since FDR and Abdul Aziz in 1945 is just words," says a former Saudi official. "We need more."

So, while MBS has significantly reshaped his kingdom, despite all his diplomatic maneuvering he hasn't yet succeeded in reshaping the Middle East. The Israeli war in Gaza following a brutal Hamas invasion of Israel has greatly complicated his hope for Saudi-Israeli normalization that would allow him to pursue his dream of economic partnership with Israel to boost foreign investment and international tourism in the kingdom. For now the war in Gaza has put MBS atop a potential explosion that he is powerless to control.

He has watched as Israel devastated Gaza, killing tens of thousands of Palestinians, including many women and children. He watched the Israeli army maim thousands of Hezbollah operatives by booby-trapping and then exploding their pagers. He watched Israel murder Hamas leader Ismail Haniyeh with a bomb hit on a presidential guesthouse in Tehran and blow up Hezbollah leader Hassan Nasrallah in Beirut. Less than a month later it was Hamas's new leader Yahya Sinwar in Gaza. Three assassinations in three months. While Saudi Arabia has no love for these terrorist organizations, all this has greatly complicated MBS's vision for his kingdom's economic and security future tied to cooperation with Israel.

"MBS wants to rearrange the living room furniture," says Norman Roule, a retired U.S. intelligence official who served in both Saudi and Iran, "but he can't do so during a hurricane."

The Gaza war has lasted much longer than the Crown Prince hoped. Yet to curtail the Israeli assault, leaving more than 10,000 Hamas terrorists alive, would create a latent risk not only to Israel but to nations around it, including Egypt, Jordan, and Saudi Arabia, all of which are vulnerable to Hamas terrorists or homegrown imitators. To understand the damage to regional stability these surviving Hamas terrorists could perpetrate, look at Iraq. The U.S. unleashed chaos in Iraq by toppling Saddam Hussein and then disbanding his army, leaving thousands of disgruntled soldiers with weapons. Many became insurgents against U.S. efforts to stabilize Iraq, with repercussions to this day. Neither Israel nor Saudi Arabia wants to see that fiasco repeated in Gaza.

Still, the prolonged war on Hamas doubtlessly also is breeding new Hamas recruits. A post on X shows Sinwar sitting in a bombed-out building, his face covered in ashes. As he watches an Israeli reconnaissance drone filming him, he defiantly tosses a wooden stick at the drone before he dies as the building collapses. This defiance to the bitter end has inspired many Palestinians to post their admiration for the dead leader.

Beyond the problem of how to end the turmoil in Gaza is the trauma that will follow in both Israel and among Palestinians. Political infighting among both Israelis and Palestinians will seriously delay any efforts to create new Palestinian leadership. Indeed, even after the death of Sinwar, Israeli prime minister Benjamin Netanyahu continues to reject any Palestinian sovereignty in Gaza. West Bank Palestinian leader Mahmoud Abbas, eighty-nine, continues to reject yielding his leadership to a younger, more capable, and less corrupt Palestinian leader.

So MBS is in a wait-and-see position. He has emphatically ruled out diplomatic relations with Israel absent agreement for a two-state solution. "The kingdom will not cease its tireless efforts to establish an independent Palestinian state with East Jerusalem as its capital," he said in September 2024, "and we affirm that the kingdom will not establish diplomatic relations with Israel without one." And since Donald Trump's election victory, MBS has toughened his public criticism of Israel. "The kingdom reiterates its condemnation and absolute refusal of the collective genocide, committed by Israel against the brotherly Palestinian people," he told leaders of Islamic nations gathered in Riyadh. And he called on Israel to respect the sovereignty of "the sisterly Islamic Republic of Iran."[15] Whether this is a genuine reflection of his mindset or an attempt to bolster his leadership role among Islamic nations is impossible to know. Or is it simply an effort to enhance his personal security?

Saudi officials say the Crown Prince would be putting his life at risk were he to recognize Israel when his own young population and that of other Arab states is deeply incensed by images on social media of Israeli devastation and death in Gaza. "Seventy percent of my population is younger than me," the Crown Prince is quoted as telling the *Atlantic*. Most of them are being introduced to the Palestinian issue for the first time through the war in Gaza, he explains. "Do I care personally about the Palestinian issue? I don't but my people do," the magazine quotes him as telling Secretary of State Antony Blinken. Saudi officials insisted the Crown Prince was inaccurately quoted without providing further information. Regardless, it's clear that both the Saudi Crown Prince and the Israeli prime minister see the Palestinians as a distraction from their real threat: Iran's nuclear ambitions.

The Crown Prince continues to work with Arab, U.S., European, and international institutions to end the fighting and create a peacekeeping force in Gaza that would clear the path for reconstruction and negotiations for a Palestinian state. He has made clear that Saudi Arabia will help pay for reconstruction of Gaza only if there is a two-state solution. He also continues to meet with Abbas and urge the Palestinian leadership to get its act together. But without the ability to organize a new Palestinian leadership and until there is Israeli leadership more open to a Palestinian state, MBS is largely stymied. Perhaps for a long time as a two-state solution appears to be far in the future—if not a mirage.

"He can take steps not to make things worse," says Roule, "but there is little he can do to make things better."

Despite all these obstacles, the Saudi Crown Prince finds himself in a position to play a pivotal role in seeking to cut this Gordian knot. He alone has a dialogue with all the key interlocutors in the rising risk of a wider Mideast war. He has a dialogue with Iran and with Israel and is the Arab leader closest to President Trump. As a result, the kingdom is poised to be a linchpin in achieving any Mideast peace deal.

If there is an Arab leader willing to take risks for genuine peace, MBS is the most likely. His foreign minister, Faisal bin Farhan, has repeatedly emphasized that the kingdom will not participate in what he called a "resetting of the status quo" but is interested only in a permanent peace that brings economic benefits to Palestinians and Israelis. "As long as we're able to find a pathway to a solution, a resolution, a pathway that means we're not going to be here again in a year or two, then we can talk about anything," he told CNN's Fareed Zakaria at Davos.[16] Indeed, MBS's top priority is avoiding a wider war in the region that could destroy the vast sums he is spending to modernize his country. Moreover, his decisiveness and his penchant for taking risks, coupled with his desire to create a greater economic cooperation with Israel, are reasons he could play a lead role in seeking to secure a genuine peace between Israel and Palestinians.

Netanyahu clearly speaks for a large majority of Israelis traumatized by Hamas's invasion of Israel. The Palestinian issue has defied peaceful solution for more than a century. "The only difference between October 7 and the 1929 Hebron Massacre is that you can kill more Jews with automatic weapons than you can with axes," one former Israeli official tells me. (The Hebron Massacre involved the murder of sixty-seven Jews in violence precipitated by rumors the Jews were planning to occupy the Temple Mount in Jerusalem, then part of the League of Nations Mandatory Palestine.)

Even if Arabs and Israelis can find a solution to their deep differences, Iran surely will try to disrupt anything that removes the Palestinians as a card it has played at will for decades to roil the region through its proxies. All of this means the whole world is likely to continue to feel the political and economic repercussions of Mideast turmoil, including higher prices due to shipping disruptions and, of course, the risk of a hot war with all the shocks that could unleash. Optimists like to point out that after the 1973 Yom Kippur War, when, like October 7, Israel was surprised and its military initially performed poorly, the result was Anwar Sadat's surprise visit to Jerusalem in 1977 to offer peace with Egypt. Perhaps, just perhaps, this war will still yield such a momentous result.

Some Israelis even dream that the Saudi Crown Prince, like Sadat, could appear at the Israeli Knesset to announce diplomatic relations with Israel if the Israeli government could publicly announce willingness to resume acceptance of a two-state solution. Those who know the Crown Prince well say don't count on that.

For now, all eyes are on Donald Trump. Israel's troops are exhausted. They've already achieved unprecedented victories in Gaza, against Hezbollah in Lebanon, and exposed Iran's vulnerability. Can Trump persuade Prime Minister Netanyahu to resume his earlier position on the Palestinians: "In my vision of peace, there are two free peoples living side by side in this small land, with good neighborly relations and mutual respect, each with its flag, anthem, and government, with neither threatening its neighbor's security and existence," he said at a speech at Bar Ilan University in 2009. Or will Netanyahu continue to resist a Gaza ceasefire to postpone an accounting for his personal legal problems and an investigation into his government's responsibility for a security lapse that led to Hamas's October 7 invasion?

Both Saudi Arabia and Israel are happy with Trump's victory. The Saudi Crown Prince was one of the first world leaders to speak with Trump after his lopsided victory, expressing "the kingdom's aspiration to strengthen the historical and strategic ties between the two nations." And the Israeli prime minister spoke early and often to the new president-elect.

But things dimmed for Riyadh after President Trump shocked the world by proposing to displace 2.2 million Palestinians from Gaza into neighboring Jordan and Egypt and transform their war-torn homeland into a vacation resort owned by the U.S. The Palestinians would not be permitted to return, the president said before walking that back. The whole Arab world rejected the Trump plan.

Still, he doubled down on his proposal at a White House press conference with Israeli prime minister Benjamin Netanyahu, his first foreign visitor, beside him. Saudi Arabia immediately issued a statement of its adamant opposition. The kingdom "will continue its relentless efforts to establish an independent Palestinian state with East Jerusalem as its capital and will not establish relations with Israel without that."

Despite Trump's braggadocio, he's unlikely to change anytime soon the deep hatred and suspicion between Israelis and Palestinians. A century-old scab freshly bleeding from wars in Gaza and growing Israeli settlements on the West Bank, complicated by a lack of Palestinian leadership and an Israeli leadership expressing adamant opposition to a Palestinian state, has no easy fix. And on top of all that is the potential for growing turmoil in post-Assad Syria that could spread into Iraq.

As for Iran, Trump encouraged Israel to "hit the nuclear first and worry about the rest later," at a North Carolina campaign rally in October. But he hasn't talked of the U.S. under his presidency following that advice and he has said he won't seek regime change in Tehran.

In this regional tumult, not only can Saudi Arabia be a useful partner for the U.S. but it greatly needs American military protection. Despite the Saudi-Iranian détente, Tehran is warning Arab nations that it may attack American military assets in Saudi and other Gulf states to thwart Israeli assaults on Iran—or in retaliation for such Israeli attacks. While Iran's proxies look weakened by their bloody, humiliating encounters with Israel, and Iran is weakened by its humiliation in Syria, Iran isn't giving up. Its foreign minister personally visited Riyadh in late 2024 to warn Crown Prince Mohammed not to allow Israel to use Saudi airspace to attack Tehran.

MBS, long accustomed to acting decisively, now finds himself forced to learn patience. Watching Iran's shocking missile barrages against Israel and the lack of U.S. response, the Crown Prince has learned a sobering lesson: there isn't enough air defense in the U.S. arsenal to protect Saudi Arabia and other Gulf states so they must remain neutral toward Iran. The U.S. sent its very limited Terminal High Altitude Area Defense (THAAD) missiles to protect Israel, not any Gulf state. (The U.S. has only nine THAAD missile batteries, each costing more than $1 billion.) And it previously withdrew its Patriot missiles from Saudi and other Gulf states to send them to Ukraine for defense against Russian missiles. Moreover, while the U.S. possesses the ability to detect a missile launch within seconds and retaliate by knocking out the missile launcher, the Biden Pentagon didn't utilize that offensive capability against Iran. To make matters worse, as noted already, Tehran has underscored that any Israeli attacks on Iran may prompt retaliation against U.S. military installations in Saudi Arabia and other Gulf locations without regard to host nation consequences. Should that happen, "We will protect ourselves," said a senior Saudi official.

The Crown Prince is walking a tightrope. He wants his kingdom to be a superpower alongside the U.S. and China with Riyadh's power derived from its energy dominance and its representation of 1.9 billion Muslims worldwide. To be seen as a true superpower the kingdom shouldn't host foreign troops. Yet without U.S. protection the kingdom risks an attack by Iran that could destroy its energy and thus its financial power and possibly all the developments the Crown Prince has worked to create over the past decade. That risk rises if Israel, as expected with President Trump's support, launches strikes against Iran's nuclear program.

Beyond managing the Iranian threat, the Crown Prince continues to work with Arab, U.S., and international officials in frantic diplomacy to craft a viable framework for an end to the Gaza war that doesn't leave Israel, backed by the U.S., expanding its power far beyond Gaza deeper into the broader Mideast. Israeli officials insist they still want normalization with Saudi Arabia but will not pay the "too-high" price of allowing the creation of a Palestinian state. Some Saudi officials indicate that President Trump may find a way to secure Saudi diplomatic recognition of Israel even without a Palestinian state, despite the Crown Prince's adamant claims to the contrary. "We can't allow our interests to be forever hostage to Palestinians who can't get their act together," explains one source close to MBS.

With risk all around, the Crown Prince easily could pull his head in and, like a turtle, close his shell. But he continues to work to protect the kingdom's relations with China, Russia, and Iran while seeking to strengthen ties to the U.S. Those close to him say that despite all the obstacles, his vision for the region remains unchanged. What he most wants is to be in the U.S. fold, but not as a supplicant, rather as a leader with political clout. Saudi Arabia lacks that clout in the U.S. So the only way he can get it is by joining with Israel which has strong political support in the States. So he continues working to advance his idea of the kingdom as a technological center ready one day—whenever Mideast politics permit—to link up with Israel's high-tech capabilities for commercial success and its political clout to enhance the kingdom's security. He has attracted numerous artificial intelligence investments, including a $5.3 billion deal with Amazon Web Services to create a data center infrastructure in Neom. "His long-term vision is unchanged," says one of his ministers. "His vision for both development and security includes Israel. It's just going to take longer to get it done."

CHAPTER TWELVE

Persian Peril

O f the many challenges facing MBS, none is greater than the threat from Iran. The Islamic theocracy in Tehran remains dedicated, as it has since its birth in 1979, to assuming global leadership of Islam by removing the Al Saud monarchy from the holy cities of Mecca and Medina and capturing Saudi oilfields.

For Saudi Arabia to flourish while Iran's economy struggles galls Tehran. Only hatred of the U.S., labeled the "Great Satan" by Ayatollah Khomeini when Iran seized fifty-two American hostages in 1979, and the "Little Satan," Israel, top Saudi Arabia on Iran's enemies list. Iran's gross domestic product (GDP) is less than half that of Saudi Arabia, while its population is more than four times as large.

Tensions between Iran and Arabia didn't begin with the Islamic Revolution. They date back at least 1,400 years to when Muslims from Arabia invaded Persia, ending its control west of today's Iran.[1] After centuries of more conquests by yet other powers, Persia finally was reunified as an independent state in 1501 and ruled by a monarch for the next four centuries until Ayatollah Khomeini overthrew the Shah in 1979. Since that time, Iran-Saudi relations have ranged from troubled to tense with rare periods of respite. Recently the two nations reestablished diplomatic relations with the help of China after a seven-year break.

This latest Saudi-Iranian détente, however, has done nothing to dissipate the deep distrust and enduring enmity between the two Persian Gulf neighbors. Each seeks to dominate the region. The restoration of relations with China's help isn't a marriage of love, but a desperate shotgun wedding: Iran needed a pause to deal with mounting economic and political problems at home and Saudi Arabia hoped its surprise détente with Iran would wake the Biden administration to the true threats posed by the Iranian theocracy and its proxies across the entire Middle East.

"We have to face reality," the Crown Prince told me at the time. "There is not a high chance of the U.S. intervening in Iran." In short, U.S. timidity at confronting Iran's mischief in the Mideast—and its growing nuclear program—required the kingdom to ease tensions with Tehran. That necessity has only grown as Iran's missile attacks directly on Israel have raised the risks of a wider Mideast war. Israel's devastating retaliatory strikes on Iran's military sites and air defenses have seriously exposed Iran. And the sudden collapse of Bashar al-Assad's brutal regime gravely weakened Iran's ability to make mischief in Syria and use its territory to resupply its Hezbollah allies in Lebanon. All this is good news for Saudi Arabia but the risk that Syria will turn into a snake pit of confrontation among Islamic terrorist groups has to gravely concern Riyadh. So diplomatic relations with Iran still make sense for the kingdom even if the two remain wary of each other.

When the two established diplomatic relations in 2023, each nation's interest in the other was so tepid that it took six months for Tehran and Riyadh to get around to exchanging ambassadors. Even then, about the only public diplomatic intercourse between them involved Saudi Arabia sending a representative to an international conference in Tehran on combating sandstorms.[2]

Things changed abruptly when Hamas, an Iranian proxy,

invaded Israel on October 7, 2023. The Saudi Crown Prince, eager to avoid wider hostilities that could threaten his expensive development plans, quickly invited the Iranian president to a tête-à-tête in Riyadh. He offered aid to Iran's sanction-strapped economy if Tehran would promise not to widen the Israeli-Hamas war either by launching attacks itself or encouraging its proxies, Hezbollah in Lebanon or the Houthis in Yemen, to get actively involved.[3]

These days Iran is isolated economically and politically from the West. At home it is weakened by the sudden death of its president in a helicopter crash in 2024 and the uncertainty surrounding the health and longevity of its supreme leader, Ayatollah Ali Khamenei, eighty-five, the longest-serving leader in the Middle East. Additionally, Iran has been rocked by domestic protests sparked by the murder of a young woman in the custody of morality police for allegedly not wearing the hijab, or scarf, to hide her hair. It has an economy beset by high inflation and low revenue due to Western embargoes. On top of all that, it's been ejected from Syria.

Nonetheless, it continues to pursue its nuclear program and to surround a militarily weaker Saudi Arabia with assertive proxies in Yemen, Iraq, and, to a lesser extent, in Lebanon. And Tehran harbors the hope of rebuilding relations with whatever faction emerges on top in Syria. In April 2024 Iran launched its first-ever direct military attack on Israel. Iran's new president, Masoud Pezeshkian, inherits an impoverished and divided nation battered by sanctions and its government's spending to support proxies abroad. But thanks to new relationships with Russia and China, Tehran, before its fall in Syria, enjoyed more sway in the Mideast than at any time since the 1979 revolution that brought the theocracy to power. China is buying Iranian oil, providing an economic lifeline to Tehran, and Russia is buying Iranian drones for its war in Ukraine.

"We live in an environment where we have Iran as the main driver of chaos," a senior Saudi official told me in 2024.

Unquestionably, Iran and Saudi Arabia have different visions for their region. The Saudis seek economic power that would underpin their dominant influence in the region while Iran seeks to dominate first through proxies and in the end to eliminate the Al Saud monarchy and establish their Shia theocracy as the Mideast hegemon. This forty-five-year-old dream continues to recede in reality but remain alive for Iran's powerful mullahs.

For its part, Saudi Arabia under Crown Prince Mohammed was initially more pugnacious toward its nemesis. Previous Saudi rulers were less overt about confronting Iran's hostilities. "These vile and ungodly Wahhabis are like daggers which have always pierced the heart of the Muslims from the back," Ayatollah Khomeini said in 1979 as he called on Muslims to overthrow the U.S.-supported regime of the Al Saud.[4] More recently, his successor, Ayatollah Khamenei, blasted Saudi Arabia for banning Iranian pilgrims from the holy cities and called the Al Saud rulers "small puny Satans who tremble for fear of jeopardizing the interests of the Great Satan (the U.S.)."[5] Rather than turn the other cheek, the Crown Prince launched a shooting war against Iranian proxies in Yemen in 2015 and compared Iran's supreme leader to Adolf Hitler.

The Crown Prince labeled Khamenei the "new Hitler of the Middle East" and asserted that the ayatollah "made Hitler look good."[6] The Saudi leader said Iran's overreach into Syria, Lebanon, Iraq, and Yemen is evidence of its expansionist designs on the Middle East just like Hitler's on Europe. "We learned from Europe that appeasement doesn't work," he said. "We don't want the new Hitler in Iran to repeat what happened in Europe in the Middle East."[7] The Iranian Foreign Ministry spokesman immediately called the Crown Prince a "delusional naïve person who never talks but with lies and bitterness" and urged him "to ponder upon the fate of famous dictators in the region,"[8] a reference to the demise of late Iraqi president Saddam Hussein.

Within a year of the fall of the Shah, Saddam invaded Iran, believing victory over a nation gripped by Islamic fervor would be quick and easy. Instead his war with Iran resulted in an eight-year stalemate and economic devastation for both countries. The Iran-Iraq War took an estimated one million men, with Iran suffering the larger losses, and maimed many millions more.[9] The memories of that brutal war are alive today in Iran. So is the fact that Saudi Arabia supported Saddam with big war loans.

With war tensions high, Saudi relations with Iran got much worse in 1987 when Iranian pilgrims in Mecca clashed with Saudi Arabian National Guard troops, killing at least four hundred people. Shia pilgrims began shouting "Death to America" and "Death to Israel," as they had routinely done for years during the annual pilgrimage. But this time Saudi security forces blocked their route, leading to a deadly confrontation. Angry Iranians attacked the Saudi embassy in Tehran, causing more deaths. Calling the Saudis "heartless and murderous," Ayatollah Khamenei challenged the kingdom's control of the two holy mosques.[10] Saudi Arabia ended diplomatic relations with Iran and put limits on Iranians allowed to make future pilgrimages to Mecca.

There also have been brief happier interludes in Saudi-Iranian relations. In the 1990s, after Saddam Hussein invaded Kuwait and threatened Saudi Arabia, it was Iraq, not Iran, that became the kingdom's major concern. So, the bitter enemy of my enemy might be my friend. Something of a thaw developed between Saudi and Iran. Diplomatic relations were restored in 1990.

In 1997, then–Crown Prince Abdullah visited Tehran to attend an Islamic summit, becoming the first senior Saudi to visit Iran since the overthrow of the Shah. This launched a prolonged effort by the late Crown Prince Abdullah to warm his country's relations with Iran. In 1998, former Iranian president Akbar Hashemi Rafsanjani visited Saudi Arabia for an extended stay that took him not only to the holy Muslim cities of Mecca and Medina but half a dozen others. His host was Crown Prince Abdullah, with whom he sought to build a personal relationship.[11] The following year, Iranian president Mohammed Khatami visited the kingdom, the first Iranian president to do so since the 1979 revolution.[12] In 2001 the two nations signed a security pact to cooperate on terrorism, money laundering, and drug trafficking. The pact was never implemented.[13]

Soon the brief thaw was back to a freeze. President Mahmoud Ahmadinejad came to power in 2005 and unleashed a hardline foreign policy that saw Iranian proxies in Lebanon, Syria, and Iraq challenge Saudi interests. During the Arab Spring of 2011, Saudi was so concerned about Iranian expansionism that it sent troops to neighboring Bahrain, a Sunni monarchy, when Shia protesters there seemed to be gaining support. That year, two Iranians were accused by the U.S. Justice Department of plotting to kill the Saudi ambassador to the United States at Café Milano, a Georgetown, Washington, D.C., restaurant famous for its prominent clientele. Still, King Abdullah in 2012 greeted Ahmadinejad to Riyadh for a gathering of Islamic heads of state and seated the Iranian leader next to him.

Regardless, things only got worse. Iran's growing nuclear program frightened Riyadh, and the Obama administration's 2015 decision to end sanctions on Iran in exchange for a vague promise to curb its nuclear program was even more unnerving. Finally, already raw relations were severed in 2016 by Saudi Arabia after an Iranian attack on its embassy in Tehran.

For most Europeans and Americans who are more secular, it's impossible to really understand the sectarian bitterness between the Shia of Iran and the Sunnis of Saudi Arabia. This sectarian divide dates to a dispute in the seventh century over who rightfully should succeed Prophet Mohammed as the leader of Muslims. Trouble among the believers over succession resulted in the murders of three of the Prophet's first four successors, including his beloved son-in-law, Ali. To this day, Iranians see all caliphs after Ali as usurpers, not leaders of the faithful. And they see Al Saud control of Mecca as simply the latest usurpation.

Saudi control of Mecca gives Al Saud rulers considerable sway with Muslims around the world. To underscore the Al Saud role in Mecca and Medina, Saudi kings since the late King Fahd have called themselves "custodian of the two holy mosques," not king. After all, kings are plentiful, but there is only one custodian of the two holy mosques. Iran's resentment of Saudi Arabia is both religious and political. The majority of Iranians of all types hate Arabs, an Iranian professor recently told an Iranian weekly. "Persians will never forget their defeat at the hands of Arabs," he said. He called that defeat 1,400 years ago a fire that "keeps seething under the ashes" and "waiting for a time to explode."[14]

Iran's regime sees the U.S. as the big obstacle blocking Tehran's conquest of Saudi Arabia. Without U.S. support, the kingdom is no military match for Iran. As a result, Iran resents Western sanctions on its nuclear program and its support of what the U.S. regards as terrorism by the Houthis, Hezbollah, Hamas, and Palestine Islamic Jihad. These sanctions by denying Iran needed technology have crippled its oil industry and cut production to roughly 3.5 million barrels a day compared to nearly 10 million a day for Saudi Arabia. The U.S. embargo on Iranian oil has cut its exports to around 1.5 million barrels a day, mostly to China, which ignores the U.S. embargo and buys Iranian oil at a deep discount. By contrast, Saudi Arabia exported 7.4 million barrels a day in 2023, earning $310 billion, or 35 percent of all revenue earned by OPEC producers.[15] With oil prices averaging around $80 a barrel, Saudi Arabia's new crown prince has been spending lavishly to develop and modernize the kingdom's economy while Iran suffers mounting poverty and nearly 40 percent inflation in 2023.[16]

Iranian resentment of Saudi Arabia prompted Tehran to fire a warning shot at Saudi oilfields in 2019 with a massive drone attack on Abqaiq and Khurais in the kingdom's Eastern Province. The attack knocked out half of Saudi oil exports and prompted an immediate 10 percent hike in world oil prices. But the kingdom's rapid repair of the damaged facilities and restoration of its oil exports prevented what could have been a devastating blow to world oil supplies and prices. An emotional Prince Abdul Aziz bin Salman, the kingdom's oil minister and a brother of the Crown Prince, told me a month after the attack that he was devastated after viewing the destruction. But by morning, he said, he wept "tears of pride" after Aramco engineers assured him they could quickly repair it. The repairs took about six weeks and Saudi maintained its oil exports to the world by dipping into its reserves. The minister, who had been on the job only six days at the time of the attack, joked to me that Iran celebrated his appointment with "fireworks."

"This was not an attack on Saudi Arabia, as President Trump said," the minister insisted. "This was an attack on every household in the world. An attack of this magnitude is an attack on the world."[17]

Although eager to avoid a conflagration with Iran, Saudi leaders nonetheless see the U.S. failure to retaliate for the attack on its primary oil facility as evidence Washington is no longer a reliable protector of the kingdom. Actually, doubts about U.S. reliability began earlier when President Obama declared a red line in Syria against the use of chemical weapons and then failed to punish President Bashar al-Assad's 2013 attack on rebels in Damascus with sarin gas.

But the U.S. ignoring a direct attack by Iran on the kingdom was far more shocking for Saudi leaders. After all, the U.S. had a special relationship dating back to President Franklin Roosevelt's 1945 meeting with King Abdul Aziz al-Saud on an American cruiser in the Suez Canal. More recently, the U.S. had sent 500,000 American troops to Saudi Arabia in 1990 to protect against a possible invasion by Saddam Hussein's Iraqi forces, already occupying Kuwait. In short, Iran's attack only briefly damaged Saudi oil resources but it devastated the kingdom's trust in the United States.

That distrust only grew when Joe Biden assumed the presidency pledging to isolate Saudi Arabia as a "pariah" state for its role in the murder of Jamal Khashoggi. Worse yet, from Riyadh's view, he insulted the Saudi government, saying there is "very little social redeeming value in the present government in Saudi Arabia."[18] Hardly a comment intended to encourage changed behavior in Saudi Arabia.

Biden's dogged efforts throughout his presidency to revive the Iran nuclear deal further angered and disillusioned Riyadh. The U.S. president lambasted Saudi human rights violations while ignoring those of Iran, which, by the reports of human rights experts, exceed those of Saudi Arabia. Both nations are guilty of gross violations of their citizens' rights to any semblance of personal freedom. Arbitrary arrests, torture, unfair prosecutions, and, of course, executions are common in both nations. While China is the world's most prolific executioner of its citizens, Iran ranks second and Saudi Arabia is third, according to Amnesty International. For instance, Iran executed 901 people in 2024, some simply for exercising their right to protest. But Iranian executions were nearly triple the 338 executions in Saudi Arabia in 2024.

Ever since the Abqaiq attack, Crown Prince Mohammed has been seeking new ways to protect the kingdom's oil and its huge investments in economic development from another, possibly more devastating Iranian attack. He has warmed Riyadh's relations with China, worked closely with Russia to control global oil prices, healed the kingdom's rifts with Qatar and Syria, sought to end his war with Yemen, deepened cooperation with Israel, and in 2023, as noted earlier, even restored diplomatic ties with Iran. All of this was intended to get the Biden administration once again to see Saudi as the pillar of U.S. interests in the Middle East, not the pariah that President Biden often labeled the kingdom until recently.

Indeed, David Petraeus, a decorated U.S. Army general for leading combat in the Mideast and former head of the Central Intelligence Agency, insisted in 2024 that "the Saudi-US relationship is back, it's revitalized."

After trash-talking Saudi Arabia for two years, the U.S. president in 2023 began a serious effort to conclude diplomatic relations between Saudi and Israel, which, from the Saudi perspective, must include security guarantees for the kingdom from the U.S. To secure congressional approval of an upgraded Saudi-U.S. security relationship, the kingdom would need to recognize Israel to secure enough votes in Congress to ratify a new U.S.-Saudi security pact. Saudi officials insist that normalizing relations with Israel will increase the risk that Iran and other avowed enemies of Israel, including Hezbollah and Hamas, might retaliate against Saudi Arabia for cooperating with the Jewish state. "The Saudi dilemma is this: Do we open ourselves up to terrorist attacks to secure Saudi-Israeli peace?" said one senior Saudi official.[19]

Beyond security advantages in a Saudi-Israeli relationship, the Crown Prince understands that to transform Saudi Arabia into a thriving commercial bridge between Asia and Europe as he seeks to do, he would benefit from normal relations with Israel. The kingdom hasn't yet started to build the Saudi portion of a railway that is intended to link India via ports to the United Arab Emirates and then by rail from the UAE to Saudi, Jordan, and Israel, cutting three weeks off the time needed to transport goods from Asia to Europe by ship. His ambitious goal of a modern, high-tech economy central to boosting the economies of all the Mideast nations can best occur with close cooperation with Israel's high-tech capabilities and those of other Western high-tech companies more likely to set up in a Saudi Arabia that has diplomatic relations with Israel.

Already Saudi-Israeli intelligence cooperation is close. When Iran attacked Israel with a missile barrage in April 2024, Saudi

Arabia was among the Arab countries with no formal relations with the Jewish state that shared intelligence, opened their airspace, and helped track Iranian missiles. In fact, Saudi-Israeli cooperation began in the 1960s when the kingdom opened its airspace for Israel to drop weapons to Yemen Royalists resisting a military coup that both Israel and Saudi viewed as a threat. Then and now, Israeli-Saudi intelligence cooperation stems from a shared view of threats and pragmatism. Over the years, Saudi ambassador Prince Bandar bin Sultan visited Israel, and Mossad leaders have visited the kingdom, according to intelligence and political sources in Israel and the U.S. These high-level visits aren't as important as the day-to-day operational cooperation among intelligence operatives in both countries. One Israeli with intimate knowledge says the two services' cooperation over the past decade is "extensive," primarily on Iran but also on the Muslim Brotherhood and global threats from Islamic State terrorists in Syria, Sinai, Iran, and around the world. Full diplomatic relations wouldn't much improve intelligence cooperation, he says.

But to truly develop deep economic ties and commercial relations, normal relations are needed to allow companies and investors to operate in the open and feel their investments in Saudi are secure. To make peace with Israel, Riyadh will have to grasp the nettlesome issue of the Palestinians. Almost any deal with Israel, which directly controls nearly 60 percent of the occupied West Bank and has devastated Gaza with its war on Hamas, will not satisfy many Palestinians, especially Hamas and other terrorists who want Israel destroyed. All this became painfully clear when Hamas attacked Israel in October 2023. Officials in both Saudi and Israel believe Hamas's primary goal with its October 7 invasion was precisely to disrupt Saudi-Israeli rapprochement. Hamas succeeded—at least for a time. So, terrorism is a continuing and potentially growing threat to both Saudi and Israel—and the wider world—as threats in 2024 to attack a Taylor Swift concert in Vienna illustrated.

"There is a recognition that no other country in the world can do what the U.S. is doing in the greater Mideast," says General Petraeus. "The chill that followed the Khashoggi affair in some quarters in the U.S. has thawed in recognition that this is among the most important relationships in the region; the common interests [of the U.S. and Saudi Arabia] are too substantial not to have a very strong relationship."

Beyond its ability to exploit terrorism, Iran also uses its Shiism to roil Shia citizens in Sunni-dominated countries like Saudi Arabia and Bahrain. Saudi Arabia is particularly vulnerable, as the majority of its Shias live in the Eastern Province, which is home to the kingdom's oilfields and much of its oil infrastructure. Shias are only about 12 percent of the kingdom's 20 million citizens, but they total roughly 30 percent of the population of the Eastern Province.[20] The execution of a Shia cleric in the Eastern Province in 2016 prompted Iranian Shias to attack the Saudi embassy in Tehran. Riyadh severed diplomatic relations, restoring them only in 2023 with the launch of its new détente with Iran.

Shias in the Eastern Province routinely complain about discrimination. Even as the late King Abdullah launched an interfaith dialogue at the United Nations in 2008, Shias in Qatif, a majority-Shia town, complained that what happened in New York stayed in New York. Despite the king's interfaith dialogue, Shias in Al Khobar, another town in the Eastern Province, were forbidden to build mosques and so were forced to either pray in their homes or drive thirty-six miles to Qatif. When some Shias began praying in a Sunni mosque, they were told not to come. With no permit for a mosque, no permit to pray, and being forbidden to pray in a Sunni mosque, Shias began praying in the streets of Eastern Province towns.[21]

While things have improved marginally under Crown Prince Mohammed's rule, Shias continue to be treated as second-class citizens in the kingdom. Human rights officials note that Sunni

Muslims too suffer from lack of due process from government, so it's not always possible to establish religious discrimination in treatment of Shias. But when the Saudi government executed forty-one Shia men in 2022, it allowed no opportunity for a final meeting with their families and refused to turn over the bodies to the families for funerals. Of the executed men, only three were convicted of murder; the others were charged with attempted murder of police, inciting strife, and spreading chaos. All were executed nonetheless.[22]

Riyadh's fear that Iran will exploit Saudi Shias as a fifth column inside the kingdom prompts tight government control of Shias and their constant oversight, humiliation, and arrest. These very Saudi tactics, of course, risk making the government's fears come true. Iran also is accused of seeking to sow mischief among Saudi tribes, like the Huwaitat who inhabit the Saudi-Jordan border area and are disgruntled with the Crown Prince's cutbacks of spending by the National Guard, which once dispensed money to key tribes in its ranks. Furthermore, Iran also is using these tribes to export unprecedented quantities of captagon, a pill form of amphetamine, from Syria through Jordan to Saudi Arabia, the largest drug market in the region and home to half of all Mideast drug seizures.[23]

To combat captagon, the Saudis have erected checkpoints in large cities to catch captagon smugglers. In late 2024, they confiscated 1.3 million pills hidden in marble mixing material near the Jordan-Saudi border. Saudi officials also dismantled a Riyadh drug ring that included more than a dozen government employees. Still, the pills keep coming as young Saudis keep buying them.

By far the greatest tension in Saudi-Iranian relations stems more recently from Tehran's nuclear program. While most of the world believes that Iran's nuclear ambitions began with the Islamic Republic, they actually started under the Shah. In the 1950s President Eisenhower launched the Atoms for Peace initiative to help developing nations use nuclear energy for peaceful purposes. The

Shah believed nuclear energy would not only solve his energy needs by replacing oil, but also attract high-tech industries that would modernize his nation.[24]

Just like the Saudi Crown Prince these days, seeking a nuclear enrichment program, the Shah had ambitions to enrich uranium not only for his reactors but to sell abroad. Also like MBS, the Shah insisted his ambitions were entirely peaceful, but if his regional neighbors developed nuclear weapons, Iran would too, he said in 1974—"without a doubt and sooner than you think."[25] Nearly half a century later, MBS has made a similar public statement: "Saudi Arabia does not want to acquire any nuclear bomb, but without a doubt if Iran developed a nuclear bomb, we will follow suit as soon as possible," he told CBS in March 2018.[26]

The U.S. helped Iran with nuclear technology, nuclear fuel, training, equipment laboratories, and power plants, all for the purpose of generating electricity. In 1967, Iran received its first small, 5-megawatt research reactor powered by highly enriched uranium. A German company was building a large nuclear plant at Bushehr on the Persian Gulf when the Islamic Revolution broke out in 1978.[27] That ended Western help to Iran's nuclear program. Still, it is ironic that the U.S. helped lay the foundations for the Islamic Republic's nuclear capability.

After the Islamic Revolution, Iran briefly dropped its efforts, arguing that pursuing nuclear capability would make it dependent on Western technology, violating one of the revolution's principles—independence from infidel influence. But the bloody Iraq-Iran War during the 1980s and Iraq's use of chemical weapons on Iranian troops and cities changed the regime's thinking. It isn't known precisely how and from whom Iran acquired its nuclear technology, but it is believed by U.S. and Israeli intelligence services that both Pakistan and North Korea assisted the Islamic Republic.[28]

Two decades of diplomacy failed to stop Tehran from enriching uranium far above the 20 percent allowed by President Obama's nuclear deal. The U.S. director of national intelligence warned in July 2023 that Tehran's stockpile of 60 percent–enriched uranium had reached 251 pounds and that uranium enriched to 60 percent purity is only a technical step away from 90 percent enrichment needed to make a bomb.[29] In 2024 U.S. intelligence agencies escalated their threat warning: Iran has "undertaken activities that better position it to produce a nuclear device if it chooses to do so."[30] Iran now is believed to be able to produce a bomb within two months of a decision to do so, according to the Arms Control Association.[31]

Veteran nuclear inspector David Albright warned in a 2024 report that the world should be watching Iran's weaponization efforts as it already has enriched uranium to a sufficient level it can achieve "breakout" (90 percent enrichment) in days once it develops a delivery system.[32] "Once they get to ninety percent it's too late," warns a senior Saudi official. "The time to take military action is before that point." Prior to Israel's attacks on Iranian military sites in 2024, Iran had the largest number of ballistic missiles of any Mideast nation,[33] allowing it to threaten the security of all its neighbors. So far Iran has seemed content to torment the region by being on the verge of nuclear weapons without actually building a bomb that surely would invite military action by Israel, with or without U.S. cooperation.

But even an Iran on the verge of a nuclear bomb is understandably a major security concern for Saudi Arabia, now spending trillions of its oil dollars developing an economy built on tourism, high tech, and clean energy and positioning itself as a commercial bridge between Asia and Europe. Despite the exchange of ambassadors between Iran and Saudi in August 2023, Saudi distrust of Iran remains deep. Almost every senior Saudi official I speak with expects war with Iran in three to five years as the Vision 2030 developments reach advanced stages of completion. So, bolstering Saudi defense capabilities at home and beefing up security ties with partners like the U.S. remain paramount goals of MBS.

So is access to its own nuclear enrichment capability. It is widely assumed that in extremis the kingdom can procure nuclear weapons from Pakistan, an Islamic nation that successfully tested its first nuclear weapon in 1998. While no Saudi official has publicly confirmed a role in assisting Pakistan's nuclear program, it is conventional wisdom among U.S. diplomats and security officials that Saudi Arabia provided financial funding in the 1980s and '90s to the Pakistani nuclear effort and thus could call on Islamabad for nuclear payback.

For his part, the Crown Prince has made clear that Saudi Arabia will get its own civilian nuclear capability one way or another. If the U.S. refuses to share nuclear technology, the kingdom is talking with China, South Korea, and France to purchase nuclear reactors. Of course, purchasing nuclear reactors to produce power is a long way from securing weapons capability. China is believed to strongly oppose assisting any nation to achieve nuclear weapons capability and the U.S. likely would use its clout to block South Korea or France from transferring nuclear technology to Saudi Arabia, intelligence sources say.

Saudi Arabia possesses 5 to 7 percent of the world's uranium. Therefore, both the Crown Prince and his brother, Abdul Aziz bin Salman, the kingdom's energy minister, have stressed their determination to enrich uranium for use in Saudi nuclear power reactors but also to sell to other nations. Acknowledging U.S. opposition to Saudi Arabia enriching uranium, Prince Abdul Aziz told me in 2019, "What's wrong with enriching your own material?"[34] Two years later, he said publicly that Saudi will develop "the entire nuclear fuel cycle which involves production of yellowcake, low enriched uranium, and the manufacturing of nuclear fuel both for our national use and of course for export."[35]

The capacity to enrich uranium for peaceful purposes, of course, creates the possibility of enriching uranium to greater purity for use in a nuclear weapon unless stringent safeguards are in place to ensure transparency. In August 2024 the kingdom took a significant step toward securing U.S. help to develop a nuclear energy program by signing a protocol that would permit the International Atomic Energy Agency (IAEA) to operate inside the kingdom.[36] Still, Riyadh remains coy about its willingness to accept unannounced inspections of its nuclear facilities by IAEA inspectors. Saudi leaders insist that uranium mining and enrichment are simply part of their Vision 2030 strategy to diversify the Saudi economy off oil. Using more nuclear energy from Saudi uranium and also selling enriched uranium to other nations, they insist, is a significant step toward the kingdom's economic diversification. So the kingdom marches on, announcing plans to build sixteen reactors in the next three decades for its energy needs and hoping to conclude a security pact with the U.S. that would permit nuclear enrichment facilities in the kingdom.

Given the deep enmity between Iran and Saudi Arabia, the world's nightmare is that these two antagonists both become nuclear powers and put the whole Mideast on a hair trigger as each nation fears first use by the other. It is a nightmare with deep roots in reality.

CHAPTER THIRTEEN

The Human Element

I f Iran and its proxies pose the greatest regional threat to Saudi, the kingdom's restrictive human rights policies are likely its greatest challenge in sustaining strong relations with Western partners and protectors in the U.S. and Europe.

Under Crown Prince Mohammed, social and economic freedoms have grown markedly while political freedoms have shrunk. Women's freedoms have exploded in recent years to include equal employment opportunities, equal pay, and the freedom to divorce, control finances, and leave the country without a male guardian's permission. Yet every time the kingdom invests in a new sport, procures the right to host women's tennis finals, or wins hosting the 2034 World Cup, human rights activists point to Saudi Arabia's rights record and try to block its integration with the world at a people-to-people level. While most of these efforts fail, Saudi human rights pose a continuing threat to its relations with the West and are pushing it increasingly toward the Global South, where many countries' human rights records are far worse.

For critics of Saudi Arabia, human rights have long been the whip of choice. Since the 9/11 attack on the United States by predominantly Saudi hijackers two decades ago, many Americans view Saudi Arabia as a nation sponsoring murderous Muslims bent on destroying Western civilization. Jamal Khashoggi's death in 2018 revived this Western revulsion.

At the same time, a growing wave of authoritarianism in China, Russia, North Korea, Turkey, and Venezuela is widening the opportunity for the Saudi Crown Prince to find common cause with these dictators to pursue benefits for his nation—often at the expense of the U.S., once his kingdom's primary ally. As the Saudi Crown Prince grows ever more assertive in his domestic and international actions, human rights likely will become a more contentious issue between the U.S. and Saudi Arabia. Because this is yet another challenge confronting the Crown Prince—and a U.S.-Saudi relationship essential to both nation's security—it is important to examine and understand both Saudi and U.S. views of human rights.

Congressional leaders, presidents, and celebrities such as tennis greats Chris Evert and Martina Navratilova criticize the kingdom for criminalizing the LGBTQ community and for a long record on human rights at odds with Western standards. The differing standards of human rights once were quietly kept in diplomatic channels and largely out of public view. But now a U.S. president dared to publicly label the kingdom a "pariah" and pronounce he wouldn't even speak to its crown prince. For his part, the Crown Prince publicly rounds up prominent Saudis, imprisons them, releases some, and holds others without charges for years. Beyond that, he regularly arrests and jails a stream of Saudis on accusations of criticizing the monarchy. Indeed, in 2020 he arrested Prince Ahmed bin Abdul Aziz, his father's eighty-three-year-old brother who has been critical of MBS and declined to approve MBS's elevation to crown prince. Prince Ahmed is believed to still be under house arrest.

"MBS doesn't have a moral bone in his body," a former high-ranking U.S. naval official who served in the Mideast tells me. "So how can we really connect with him?"

Just how pervasive the American public's negative view of Saudi human rights is can be illustrated by a group of high school girls in conservative Alabama. After my granddaughter visited the kingdom with me in 2024, the most persistent question asked by her fourteen-year-old classmates: "Don't they kill a lot of women there?"

Despite these negative views of the kingdom by some Americans, Washington's strong commitment to the security of Israel and its nearly half century of growing confrontation with Iran mean the U.S. must remain involved in the Mideast to protect its own interests. Saudi Arabia sits in the center of waterways accessing the Suez Canal, the Strait of Hormuz, and the Bab el-Mandab Strait, three chokepoints through which the world's oil and commerce flow from Asia to Europe, meaning the kingdom's security is paramount to all the world. Given Saudi Arabia's hold over global oil prices that impact every nation's economy, the U.S. can't ignore the kingdom. (Yes, the U.S. is a major oil producer, but the world price of oil is still determined largely by Saudi production and export.) Moreover, the U.S. strongly supports Saudi Arabia's desire to recognize Israel even if that possibility has been badly set back by the war in Gaza.

"Las Vegas rules don't apply in the Mideast," says General David Petraeus. "What happens there doesn't stay there. Because of that, the idea of the U.S. leaving the Mideast has been shown to be similar to Michael Corleone trying to leave the mafia."[1]

As a result, the U.S. can't escape the Mideast nor the impact of Saudi Arabia. Joe Biden discovered this in 2022 when gasoline prices rose precipitously as midterm elections approached, forcing him to visit the "pariah" state and speak, at last, to MBS to beg him to pump more oil. The Crown Prince said no. The kingdom needs high prices to fund its ambitious developments.

MBS isn't bothered by irritating Washington nor embarrassed by his country's lack of freedoms. In 2023, the kingdom ranked

154 of 164 nations on Freedom House's Human Freedom Index, which measures a broad range of personal civil and economic freedoms. Saudi Arabia came in slightly ahead of Iran at 159, trailed by laggards like Yemen, Venezuela, and Syria.[2] The U.S. ranked 17. This index measures the absence of coercive measures so it's a broader gauge of human rights than that which measures personal abuse of individuals.

For instance, Saudi Arabia's rules governing social media and the internet are among the world's most restrictive. Posting satirical content that "mocks, provokes or disrupts public order, religious values, and public morals" is punishable by up to five years in prison and a 3 million Saudi riyal ($800,000) fine.[3] Violations of this cybersecurity law have been used to jail thousands of people. Shortly after MBS became crown prince, the government also posted a message on its own Twitter account urging Saudis to report immediately on each other any posting of "terrorist or extremist ideas." After arresting between 6,000 and 7,000 individuals for social media violations over half a dozen years, the government quietly began to release them in 2025. When I asked an official why this decision wasn't announced, he said, "actions speak louder than words."

The general lack of personal freedoms partially explains Saudis' silence on human rights abuses in their country. But more to the point, Saudis have never known rule of law or individual rights. Their king appoints all members of the country's Potemkin parliament and all its judges. He also outlaws any political parties and most associations. Indeed, since the founding of the first Saudi state, one Al Saud ruler or another has made the rules under which all Saudis live. For much of that time, impoverished Saudi tribes were far more interested in a full stomach than in free speech. And the ruler's duty was to help secure and share sustenance. Obedience was the accepted price that tribes paid for that security.

These days prosperity is more widespread in Saudi Arabia, with oil prices high and the government promising to spend nearly $3 trillion to create new gigaprojects and a growing private sector that offers jobs for Saudis. Still, the government's control of most of the economy means it can dispense favors to supportive citizens— or withhold them. Thus government abuse of power, including ignoring its own laws, is still accepted as the price for participating in the security and prosperity that government provides its citizens.

For Americans, whose forefathers fought a war to throw off arbitrary rule by an English king, individual rights and the rule of law are inalienable rights. How can Saudis and citizens of many other nations not want and demand the same? The answer: different history and different cultures produce different national priorities.

As egregious and gruesome as the Khashoggi murder was, Saudi Arabia doesn't actually top any analytical list of most abusive governments. Indeed, even most human rights groups, who are uniformly critical of the kingdom, rank its abuses well behind those of nations like Iran, China, Russia, and North Korea. (Iran is the second-worst human rights violator after Yemen. China is number 3, North Korea 8, Russia 12, and Saudi Arabia 22.)[4] Yet U.S. officials—and to some extent the American people—hold Saudi Arabia, a longtime ally, more accountable for its human rights shortcomings than they do adversaries like China, Russia, and Iran. And Americans remain largely ignorant of the sweeping changes in Saudi Arabia over the past half-dozen years. As a result, decades of U.S. criticism of Riyadh along with America's diminishing role in the Mideast have badly frayed U.S.-Saudi relations in recent years without yielding any improvements in Saudi government behavior toward its citizens.

Still, as the Crown Prince seeks to modernize Saudi Arabia, it's not surprising that modern Western nations hold the country to a higher standard. At the founding of the relationship, FDR struck a

202 ◇ THE MAN WHO WOULD BE KING

partnership with MBS's grandfather without any recorded concern that slavery was legal. It wasn't until JFK that an American president lobbied the kingdom to abolish slavery in 1962.

MBS's removing the religious police from Saudi streets in 2016 freed all Saudis from the fear of running afoul of those heavy-handed and arbitrary oppressors. Saudis at last could feel safe leaving their homes, walking the streets, and enjoying new entertainment now available in Saudi Arabia.

But social liberties definitely haven't led to political liberties. At first, when MBS locked up wealthy businessmen and prominent princes in the Ritz hotel for alleged financial corruption, the public cheered after decades of complaining about that. But soon scores of Saudis, including women, were being detained and sent to prison without explanation or any idea how long they'd be incarcerated. Indeed, the U.S. State Department's annual human rights report discusses a litany of abuses including arbitrary killings, enforced disappearances, political imprisonment, torture, life-threatening prison conditions, and so on.[5] The imprisonments continue. Most recently two brothers of a Saudi dissident living in exile in London were convicted for "publishing posts that harmed the security of the homeland on social media websites."[6] Mohammed al-Ghamdi, whose X account had only nine followers, was sentenced to death in July 2023 and his brother, Assad, was given a twenty-year prison sentence in July 2024. "Saudi courts mete out decades long sentences to ordinary citizens for nothing more than peacefully expressing themselves online," says Joey Shea, a Saudi Arabia researcher at Human Rights Watch.[7] In 2024 the Saudi Appeals Court overturned the death penalty for Mohammed al-Ghamdi but hasn't yet made clear if he will be retried.[8]

Some of the detainees were well-known, like Salman al-Awdah, one of the most charismatic Saudis I've met. A Muslim scholar, he once was such a fierce fundamentalist that he was arrested in the 1990s for his criticism of the regime. Freed five years later, he moderated his views and worked to help the regime dissuade young Saudis from terrorism. By 2007 he had become a multimedia phenomenon with a newspaper column, videos, books, and lectures in addition to a very popular weekly television show.

"Saudi society is slow to change and has no plan," he told me in 2010. "So, what is coming is a spontaneous change." al-Awdah's focus was on teaching young Saudis to deal honestly with each other. "If we can change the young, they might change the country."[9] His prediction of spontaneous change supported by the young proved correct. MBS unleashed his revolutionary reforms widely supported by young Saudis who saw in him their own frustration at a rigid and repressive society that had lacked any plan for securing their future. So far, ubiquitous entertainment seems to outrank restrictions on free speech for most of these young Saudis.

But al-Awdah found himself again imprisoned in 2017, charged with incitement against the ruler and spreading discord. Apparently his offense was to send a tweet to his 14 million followers that offended the Crown Prince. "May God harmonize between their hearts for the good of their people" was an apparent call for reconciliation between Saudi Arabia and Qatar, a diplomatic spat MBS had instigated.[10] The Crown Prince made up with Qatar in 2021 but al-Awdah remains in prison facing the death penalty.

Most of the arrested individuals were less well-known. Loujain al-Hathloul, a Saudi female activist, was jailed in 2018 for supporting a campaign to legalize driving for women. Other women also were arrested for this offense. al-Hathloul was charged with sharing information with foreign diplomats and journalists. This charge greatly enhanced the fear of Saudis to speak to journalists like me. Most Saudis believe their phone conversations are monitored; they no longer talk unless no phones are present. al-Hathloul accused the government of torture, including electric shocks, during her incarceration. She was strongly backed by international human rights groups and quickly became the face of MBS's human rights abuses in 2018—until the death that October of Jamal Khashoggi. She was released in 2021 but is forbidden to travel.

Obviously, the Crown Prince didn't oppose women driving, something he legalized in 2018. So Saudi conventional wisdom is that he jailed her and the other women promoting driving to underscore that the government alone decides what reforms to initiate and when. And that citizen protests are unnecessary and will not drive his decisions. Whatever the rationale, her arrest has intimidated Saudis from critical public tweets and discouraged the making of even private remarks to visitors by many Saudis.

Beyond the high-profile prisoners are the forgotten ones. Mohammed Fahad al-Qahtani was imprisoned in 2013 by the late King Abdullah's government for "breaking allegiance to the ruler" and "questioning the integrity of officials."[11] His ten-year prison sentence was set to end on October 24, 2023. When his wife called the prison to ask his whereabouts, she was told he had been moved to a new prison but she was offered no details and no proof of life.[12] al-Qahtani was released in January 2025 according to a knowledgeable Saudi official and is at home maintaining silence on his experiences.

Dr. al-Qahtani is a chubby, cherub-faced man determined, as he told me in 2009, to "challenge and change the system legally" so that his young children would live in a freer society. When I met him in 2006, he was an economics professor at Riyadh's Diplomatic Studies Institute. After earning a PhD in economics at Indiana University, he had returned to Riyadh, where he lived a middle-class life in a small apartment shared with his wife and three children. His day job was teaching at the institute, which trained diplomats for the Ministry of Foreign Affairs. But he talked openly of improving human rights in Saudi Arabia. Indeed, he is one of the few independent human rights advocates I ever met in Saudi, as the others with whom I spoke worked for government-sanctioned human rights organs. In 2009 he founded the Saudi Civil and Political Rights Association, dedicated to advocating laws to protect human rights and also to documenting human rights abuses.

One abuse he and many other Saudis talked about was the continuing incarceration of scores of Saudi men held without charges since their arrests in a spate of terrorist incidents in the kingdom between 2003 and 2005. As the Arab Spring democracy demonstrations roiled publics across the Mideast in 2011, more than one hundred women protested in Riyadh and in the capital of Qasim Province, north of Riyadh, demanding that their jailed relatives be freed or charged and tried in a public court. These weren't the only protests in 2011, a year that saw demonstrations and protests in numerous Saudi cities. But these were essentially the last public protests in the kingdom. Criticizing government or religious officials was forbidden by royal decree on penalty of imprisonment.[13]

A year later al-Qahtani crossed a red line by asking then King Abdullah to remove his crown prince, who during nearly four decades in charge of internal security had imprisoned any number of Saudi citizens without charges. This defied the explicit ban on criticizing the royal family. al-Qahtani was arrested and charged with eleven counts, including setting up an unlicensed organization, describing Saudi Arabia as a police state, and turning international organizations against the kingdom.[14] His human rights organization was disbanded and he was sent to prison.

His pregnant wife took her three children to New York State, where she lived and studied while her husband served his sentence. Some years ago, when we met in New Jersey, she recalled her young daughter, Layla, born shortly after her father's imprisonment, asking her one morning, "Mom, do I have a dad?" Of course, she assured her daughter, you talk to him on the phone.

"No, but do I have a dad?" Layla persisted. Her three older

206 ◇ THE MAN WHO WOULD BE KING

siblings can talk about things they did with their father, an enthusiastic hiker and camper. But Layla can't. Still, Maha al-Qahtani
draws strength from the fact that some of the world's most successful leaders, who, like her husband, sought change, had great
impact on history without a father beside them: men like Moses,
Jesus, and Prophet Mohammed. Layla, eleven, still has no father
beside her.

Another Saudi human rights and democracy activist, Mikhlif
al-Shammari, was sentenced about the same time as al-Qathani for
defending Shias in the kingdom. al-Shammari, a writer, took me to
visit a Shia husband who had been forcibly divorced from his Sunni
wife by a judge at the request of her brothers, not her husband. The
wife, of course, had no say. al-Shammari's activism subsequently
led the government to sentence him in 2014 to two years in prison
and two hundred lashes.[15]

Another Saudi friend of mine who worked for the government
has similarly disappeared. Abdullah al-Shammary, who helped
me as a translator when I spent six years visiting Saudi Arabia
to write my first book, became a friend. I would visit his home to
see his family and friends on my subsequent visits to Riyadh. In
all the years I spent time with him, I never heard him speak critically of the Crown Prince. Abdullah and I contacted each other
on WhatsApp, as he didn't like to use a mobile phone. Because
WhatsApp is supposed to be encrypted, most Saudis prefer this
method of communicating. In 2021 my WhatsApp messages to
Abdullah stopped being answered. Either he has disappeared or
is too nervous to respond. Some others with whom I met freely
for the first book similarly have stopped responding or profess to
be out of Riyadh and thus not available to meet. The silence is
deafening.

It is easy to understand why most Saudis keep their opinions
to themselves. Their silence isn't just fear or intimidation. It also
stems from irrelevance. Saudi citizens understand they have no

role in selecting their king or crown prince and little influence on government policy. So they render unto Caesar that which is Caesar's. Full authority over them.

Indeed, politics is as irrelevant to most Saudis as the Christian Bible. Instead they focus on the economic well-being of their extended family and tribe, seeking to use whatever contacts they have to secure the most for themselves. They do blame government if it imposes price hikes and taxes, as it did in 2018 to offset huge budget deficits compounded by low oil prices. Balancing the budget, Saudis believe, is the job of government, not people who have no influence on government spending. But those complaints are voiced in private conversations, not in public demonstrations. And, after the first few years of austerity under King Salman, MBS has kept spending high and thus prosperity possible for almost any Saudi willing to work.

"We believe in the notion of human rights," MBS told a CBS interviewer in 2018, "but ultimately Saudi standards are not the same as American standards."[16] He is far from the only world leader to make that point.

Therein lies the frequent friction between the U.S. and Saudi Arabia. Despite the U.S. becoming the world's largest oil producer in 2023, it continues to need to cooperate with Saudi Arabia because U.S. allies in Europe and Asia require Saudi oil and Israel needs stability in the Middle East that only the U.S. can bring to the region. So regardless of Saudi Arabia's human rights record, the United States' own interests require cooperation with Riyadh to check Iran and its proxies from creating turmoil—and potentially war—in the Mideast. Iran's human rights record is far worse than that of Saudi Arabia. The Islamic Republic has reversed women's rights in marriage, child custody, and divorce—even lowering the marriage age to nine—while Saudi has moved in the opposite direction. Moreover, when Iranian women defied compulsory head covering to protest the death of a woman in police custody in 2023, police opened fire on the women.[17] But, as noted earlier, the Crown Prince's determination to make Saudi Arabia a modern nation open to the world means that much of the civilized world now expects his government to show its citizens greater respect of their individual rights.

In today's atmosphere of heightened geopolitical tension, it is more tempting than ever for Saudi Arabia's American critics to use the kingdom's human rights record to try to block arms sales. While Saudi Arabia is the United States' largest recipient of foreign military sales, with more than $100 billion, it receives no American economic aid. The kingdom pays for all its arms purchases. (Ukraine and Israel are the largest recipients of U.S. military and economic assistance.)

Despite paying for its arms purchases, both Democratic as well as Republican senators in 2023 introduced a resolution that could have forced the Biden administration to prepare a report on Saudi Arabia's human rights record and cease all security assistance if Congress found the human rights record deficient. In reality, the Biden administration notified Congress of some $10 billion in proposed weapons sales to Saudi. So the restraining resolution didn't become an issue. Still, it needled Riyadh and eroded cooperation by making Washington look unreliable. So it's a vicious circle: threats to use human rights erode trust between the two countries, and reduced trust in the U.S. becomes a reason for Saudi Arabia to explore other partnerships, such as China and Russia, that reduce U.S. trust in Saudi.

While Saudi Arabia has greatly increased social liberties for its people since MBS came to power and chained the religious police, undeniably it remains a state where the ruler is absolute. What he feels is necessary to protect his political and personal survival always takes precedence over everything else—U.S. entreaties, human rights standards, or international outrage. Ali Shihabi, founder of the Arabia Foundation and graduate of Harvard and Princeton, is well-connected in the Saudi government although he's a private businessman. He argues that the U.S. needs to cut MBS some slack; the Crown Prince "inherited a sclerotic monarchy and reactionary religious establishment" and had to break some china to change those two institutions. Yes, he acknowledges, the Khashoggi murder and arrests and alleged mistreatment of women activists all "deserve censure." But he insists that an honest assessment of MBS's performance must balance these failures with the many things he got right in a very short period.[18]

Shihabi makes a good case that much positive change has occurred even as free speech and political freedom have shrunk. For me the test is less the past than the future. Now that he's "broken china" to jump-start economic reforms and taken repressive steps to ensure his political ascension, what does he do? Will he show the confidence to ease up on repression or will he continue to be an authoritarian survivor always seeing some new risk to his rule that needs crushing?

The renowned philosopher Niccolò Machiavelli argued in the sixteenth century that a republic is superior to a principality because a prince "unchecked by laws will be more ungrateful, unstable, and imprudent than a populace."[19] While leaders such as MBS take big, bold decisions, they often make big, bold, costly mistakes— the murder of Khashoggi, going to war against Yemen, severing relations with Qatar, to cite a few. Machiavelli thought the test of a prince isn't merely to rule wisely during his life, but to leave institutions that serve the state after he is gone.

"He whom the heavens give such an opportunity [to rule a state] should consider that there are two paths: one that will make him secure during his lifetime and glorious after his death, and the other that will make him lie in constant anguish and after his death leave behind a legacy of everlasting infamy," Machiavelli wrote.[20]

That is the challenge Crown Prince Mohammed is confronting. Absent some huge blunder, MBS could easily rule Saudi Arabia for the next fifty years. Can he be wise enough to ensure that his lavish spending on gigaprojects at home and his determination to assert Saudi power abroad will leave Saudi Arabia a more just country with a more sustainable economy in a more stable region than the kingdom he and his father inherited in 2015?

CHAPTER FOURTEEN

Gambling on the Future

P lotting the future of Saudi Arabia's economy is like playing
roulette on a long-spinning wheel. The Crown Prince has
placed multibillion-dollar chips on multiple options for transitioning
his economy off oil, hoping that many are at least partial winners
and some hit big. But, to extend the gambling analogy, the ball in
this particular roulette wheel is circling so slowly the winning bets
won't be truly paid for decades.

The list of unknowns the Crown Prince and his government
are juggling is formidable. When will demand for Saudi oil run
out? What energy sources will replace oil? How fast will global climate goals drive production of renewable energy alternatives? How
quickly will new technologies make those alternatives affordable to
worldwide consumers? What damaging effects will global warming have on an already hot Arabia? Will the trillions being spent
on gigaprojects yield a return sufficient to sustain the kingdom's
economy as oil dollars dwindle? At what rate can foreign talent and
foreign investors be attracted to help achieve the kingdom's new
economy? And can Saudi education truly be reformed in order to
prepare future generations of Saudis to fill the sophisticated jobs in
the new economy the Crown Prince seeks to create?

Firm answers to all these questions are elusive. Still, the Crown Prince is gambling his future and that of his people on an unprecedented high-wire act: he will end Saudi reliance on oil revenue before climate activists and technology succeed at ending the world's reliance on oil. Never mind that the kingdom has utterly failed to curb its addiction to oil revenue despite half a century of five-year plans pledging to do so. He now has a brand-new plan for transitioning its economy beyond oil.

In short, that plan focuses on continuing to sell oil, investing at home and abroad in promising technologies to create new energy sources from "all of the above": solar, nuclear, green hydrogen, and transforming crude oil to chemicals. In short, a chip on every possible source for transitioning off oil in a decarbonized world. The Crown Prince tells friends it's better to try to do a hundred things and achieve fifty than focus on only five and achieve four. That sentiment guides his strategy for transitioning beyond oil.

"I will not sit and watch without making plans to rectify any challenge," he told me in our first meeting, when he was still only deputy crown prince. "I am in a hurry. I don't want to see it as a challenge. I want to focus on what is the region in ten years. What is our position economically in ten years?"[1]

To position itself for whatever the future brings, Saudi Arabia is investing heavily in renewables for its own energy needs as well as for export. At present Saudis consume more oil per capita than any nation on earth. The kingdom uses 3.7 million barrels a day of oil, behind only the U.S., China, and India, despite a population that is a tiny fraction of any of those nations. The Crown Prince is promising to generate 50 percent of Saudi domestic electricity consumption from renewables, mostly solar and wind, by 2030, cutting Saudi oil consumption by 500,000 barrels a day. At present renewables account for under 1 percent of power generation. As renewables replace oil in generating Saudi power, more oil will be freed for export to finance the Saudi economy. But if new technology produces affordable renewable alternatives, the global appetite for Saudi oil could recede quickly.

If the world weans itself off oil before Saudi Arabia's economic reforms can provide jobs for the 65 percent of young Saudis under thirty years of age, the Crown Prince could face a major domestic challenge. These young Saudis have enthusiastically backed his Vision 2030 reforms precisely because he promises a new nation whose modern economy and open culture will offer better jobs and a panoply of new entertainments. In short, a life of security, opportunity, and fun.

But delivering on that promise will be hard. By 2030, the number of Saudis age fifteen and older is expected to increase by six million, with four million working-age Saudis seeking jobs. This means the Crown Prince between 2016 and 2030 will need to create almost three times as many jobs for Saudis as government produced during the boom years of 2000 to 2014.[2] It's a very tall order. Since he has alienated the religious conservatives and many of his royal relatives, young Saudis are his major base of support.

Yet it all still starts with oil. Saudi Arabia is the world's second-largest oil producer, slightly ahead of Russia but behind the U.S., which produced an unprecedented 13.2 million barrels a day in 2024.[3] Oil has traditionally accounted for about 75 percent of Saudi Arabia's fiscal revenues and 40 percent of its GDP. If it continues to export oil to other nations at current levels and doesn't discover any new oil, its reserves would be exhausted in about twenty-six years, well after the International Energy Agency predicts world oil demand will peak in 2030. The peak, the IEA predicts, will be followed by a plateau in demand that will last for "many years" and produce emissions too high to limit global warming to 1.5 degrees Celsius called for by the Paris Climate Accords of 2015.[4] Saudi Arabia has flatly refused to simply curtail its oil and gas production as climate advocates seek because it believes the world will need oil for decades beyond 2030.

"We will monetize every molecule of energy this land has, period," oil minister Adul Aziz bin Salman told a global audience of financiers in Riyadh in 2024. "We are committed to maintaining 12.3 million barrels a day of crude capacity and we are proud of that." He insisted oil production isn't at odds with climate goals. "We are not ashamed of our record when it comes to emissions," the minister said. "We are proud of it but the pundits try to create a smoke screen not to allow us to be on the so-called higher moral ground."[5]

Despite this defiant assertion, Saudi officials are navigating the unknowns by insisting the kingdom will remain a major producer of energy though not necessarily of oil. "We as a country, we are no longer called a leading oil-producing country . . . we would like to be called an energy-producing country of all kinds of energy," Prince Abdul Aziz bin Salman, the kingdom's energy minister, a half brother of MBS, says. Another minister adds, "We believe oil will be needed in 2040 and well beyond." Interestingly, what had been called the Ministry of Petroleum and Minerals since its founding in 1960 was changed to just the Ministry of Energy in 2019 to underscore the kingdom's shifting focus from oil to energy.

Saudi Arabia is believed to possess 6 percent of the world's known uranium reserves. As a result, the government is planning to build nuclear reactors to provide some of its energy needs and to enrich uranium to sell to other nations as a future new revenue source. Saudi Arabia also is building the world's largest solar farm. The new plant, under construction in Mecca Province, is set to be operational in late 2025. The government wants to make Saudi Arabia the world's low-cost producer of renewable energy for export.

"We see ourselves as an energy exporter to the world," Adel al-Jubeir, minister of state for foreign affairs and Saudi Arabia's new climate envoy, told a Davos audience. "We want to be able to sell you the nuclear energy that you can then plug in and get energy out of it. We want to sell you oil and we want to sell you gas, we want to sell you green energy, renewable energy, we want to sell you the whole litany of energy products."[6]

Toward that end, the kingdom is building the world's largest carbon-free green hydrogen plant in Neom, its futuristic new development near Aqaba on the Red Sea. The plant is a joint venture by ACWA Power, Air Products, and Neom and is set to begin production of so-called green ammonia in 2026 (green in the sense that it is produced entirely by renewable energy). The Neom Green Hydrogen Company (NGHC) will use only solar and wind energy to produce up to 600 tons per day of green ammonia as a source to power the global transportation and industrial sectors.[7] Other countries, such as Japan, Australia, the Netherlands, and Britain, also have plans to use green ammonia to store and export their renewable energy surpluses.[8] Britain and Japan also have experimental green ammonia plants powered by wind.

Beyond producing alternatives to oil, Saudi Arabia has delayed but not yet dropped plans to invest to increase its oil production. Energy Minister Abdul Aziz bin Salman believes passionately in the need to balance climate goals with advancing the economic livelihood of poor nations. To do that, poor nations must have access to affordable energy. In 2021 he told me that he sees three key pillars that must be carefully balanced: energy security, sustainable economic growth for the billions around the world living in poverty, and, "yes, attending to the serious issue of climate change." His conclusion: "We must do all three pillars at once and not put one above the other. We can't compromise on any of the pillars."[9]

The kingdom's plan to invest $300 billion to raise oil production capacity to 13 million barrels from 12 million at present was blasted by climate activists. "This is a hedge to protect the world economy," Finance Minister Mohammed al-Jadaan told me in 2021. "We can't have clean energy today," the minister said. "For the past fifty years coal, gas and oil supply eighty percent of the world's energy."

The so-called hedge, of course, also protects Saudi Arabia's ability to earn continued revenues from oil if the energy transition to clean fuels is slower, as Saudi experts expect it to be. To further protect oil revenues, Saudi Arabia is pursuing technologies to clean oil, so-called carbon capture, utilization, and storage (CCUS). These technologies can be retrofitted on existing power and industrial plants, allowing their emissions to be stripped of carbon. "Some want to see fossil fuel as evil," says al-Jadaan. "But we underestimate human ingenuity. It's very plausible that fossil fuel can be made as clean and cheap as renewables."[10]

Recent events indicate that the world's transition off oil won't be either swift or smooth. An estimated 700 million people around the world still are so poor they have no fuel other than wood fires, which produce much more carbon dioxide than oil or natural gas, according to the International Energy Agency.[11] Indeed, at COP 28 in Dubai, oil producing nations blocked any call for phasing out fossil fuels. Producers did sign on to a tripling of new investments in renewable energy and "transitioning away" from fossil fuels at an indefinite time. While hardly a ringing call for rapid transition off fossil fuels, the COP 28 final decision was the first time that fossil fuels were singled out by COP delegates for their role in producing greenhouse gases.[12] But a year later at COP 29, producers led by Saudi Arabia blocked any plans for ending fossil fuel use.

More important than decisions of international climate groups is the question of what damaging effects global warming will have on the kingdom and its economic future. A new in-depth study by King Abdullah University of Science and Technology (KAUST) concludes that Saudi Arabia is witnessing climate change at an accelerated pace compared with other regions. Temperatures in the kingdom are on track to rise 3 degrees Celsius by the end of the century and under KAUST's extreme scenario could rise 5.6 degrees Celsius. The report notes none of this is in stone; if the kingdom pursues aggressive mitigation policies, the worst climate change risks are still avoidable. But, the report concludes, the kingdom's mitigation policies aren't yet sufficient to meet its pledge to reduce greenhouse gases by 278 million tons of carbon dioxide equivalent by 2030 and reach net zero emissions by 2060.[13]

The government, while continuing to produce oil and gas, has actively sought to position the kingdom as a supporter of coordinated global climate actions. "Climate action is not lip service by Saudi Arabia," says Faisal al-Ibrahim, minister of economy and planning. "It is a serious matter to us as we live in one of the most heat- and drought-distressed areas in the world."[14]

The biggest climate threat to Saudi Arabia is its combination of high temperature and water shortage. Rising temperatures combined with intensive energy actions to allow society to survive the inhospitable conditions have created what KAUST researchers call "a positive feedback cycle where the insatiable energy appetite of modern cities drives further pollution and greenhouse gas emissions: amplifying the very conditions we seek to safeguard against."[15]

Saudi Arabia now endures roughly 125 days per year with temperatures above 95 degrees Fahrenheit (35 degrees C), which necessitates air-conditioning and water consumption. That number of extreme heat days will rise to 180 by 2050 according to a recent climate study by the RAND Corporation. Saudi relies almost entirely now on gas and oil for its electricity. Moreover, 50 percent of Saudi Arabia's water comes from desalination, a highly energy-intensive process. As a result, some 20 percent of the kingdom's total carbon emissions result from desalination.[16]

As the Saudi population rises, so too does the demand for water and electricity. Population is forecast to increase from 32 million to about 42 million by 2050. As temperatures rise, ironically the way solar technology works to convert sun to energy becomes less efficient, says RAND researcher Jeffrey Martini.[17] All this helps underscore why Saudi Arabia's crown prince is driving his country to take steps to become more energy-efficient and to increase production of clean energy. For instance, Saudi Arabia, which has so little groundwater, is organizing to become the world's largest user of recycled wastewater, behind only the U.S. and China. Wherever one visits these days along the Red Sea or at Neom, the kingdom's new gigaprojects are focused on sustainability. Decorative plants at chic new resorts are watered with recycled wastewater. Electricity to power the new hotels, airports, and businesses is produced by fields of solar panels.

Saudi Arabia also has launched its Saudi Green Initiative, which is intended to unite environmental protection, energy transition, and sustainability programs with the aim of reducing emissions and increasing the kingdom's use of clean energy. This initiative, among other things, calls for planting 10 billion trees across Saudi Arabia as a carbon sink. Two years into the initiative, 18 million trees have been planted, according to the *Arab News*. Some sixty sites have been set aside for planting trees that absorb carbon from the atmosphere and also help reduce high temperatures. Organizers intend to engage Saudi schoolchildren by each planting a tree to save the planet, helping sensitize youth to climate change issues. Additionally, Saudi Arabia has a so-called Middle East Green Initiative to coordinate climate mitigation actions with neighboring states, including underwriting some mitigation steps by its poorer neighbors.

"We are a responsible actor in the global community and we don't want to follow the standards; we want to set the standards for how countries should conduct themselves . . . and what initiatives they put in place domestically, regionally, and internationally to help meet the challenge of climate change," says Adel al-Jubeir, the kingdom's climate envoy.

If the world is slow to abandon oil, that may prove a mixed blessing for the kingdom. Sustained oil revenues will allow Saudi Arabia more time to develop other industries like transportation, mining, and tourism. Foreign tourists may shun the kingdom if rising temperatures indeed leave Saudi Arabia with temperatures above 95 degrees over half the year. While beachgoers may tolerate such temperatures, the absence of alcohol thus far in Saudi public places could push sunbathers to select a non-Saudi site. Given that alcohol sales are allowed for diplomats in Riyadh since January 2024, there is much speculation at the Red Sea projects that once more hotels open, alcohol also will be allowed at Red Sea resorts. Alcohol was served at the October 2024 opening of Sindalah Island resort in Neom, one of the first Red Sea projects completed. The island features eighty-six yacht berths, restaurants, and hotels. More alcohol seems likely as a Saudi friend shared a photo of a Red Sea hotel basement with empty storage shelves alongside a sign that reads "Liquor Storage." To date, "The wish is father to the thought," to paraphrase Shakespeare.

Another large risk for the kingdom as it undergoes the energy transition from oil to dependence on its new economy is the lack of skilled workers. "Human capacity" is the response every minister offers when asked the greatest challenge confronting Vision 2030's success. While hundreds of thousands of Saudis have been educated abroad in major universities, only in 2024 did a Saudi university break into the top one hundred. That year, the Shanghai Rankings rated King Saud University in Riyadh at 90 while the better-known *U.S. News & World Report*'s Best Global Universities ranked KSU 142, up from 212 a year earlier. That's clearly progress but the kingdom's goal is for KSU to rank 10 by 2030. Many young Saudis today are educated and motivated to transform their country. But far too many Saudis in their forties and fifties have neither the talent nor interest to work productively. Today's forty-year-old was born in 1983, just after the Iranian Revolution led the Saudi government to impose rigid religious rules on society to ensure that its religious establishment didn't turn on the royal family as the Iranian clerics had on the Shah of Iran. So that generation grew up studying Islam in school and at after-school programs and all too often majored in Islamic studies at university. With no marketable skills, most went to work for the government. So that generation has little interest in the hard work of private sector jobs or in transforming the Saudi economy. Indeed, the hard work of reforming the Saudi education system from kindergarten through university is a gargantuan task not yet truly tackled.

Saudi Arabia is heavily dependent on foreign workers in both private and public sectors and especially for domestic laborers like housekeepers. Foreign workers total nearly 13 million or nearly three times the 3.9 million Saudi employees. Monthly wages for Saudis average roughly 2.5 times that of expats. While employment of Saudis has grown in the private sector by some 35 percent over the past five years, reducing the unemployment rate from roughly 12 percent in 2016 to 7.1 percent in 2024, foreign employment has grown even faster.[18]

The burst of economic success in recent years in the kingdom has been largely driven by the Crown Prince's empowerment of Saudi women. Because Saudi females account for 58 percent of university graduates, most women studied to be teachers, about the only career open to them before MBS allowed them to drive and work anywhere in 2018. Once allowed to work, they flocked to the private sector, unafraid of hard work and eager to seize opportunity. Their skills and their spending have helped fuel recent economic growth. Saudi GDP increased 8.6 percent, the strongest growth among the G20 economies in 2022. But cuts that year in Saudi oil output reduced the kingdom's oil revenue, turning GDP growth negative in 2023 and marginal in 2024 and transforming a budget surplus into deficits until at least 2027 according to the ministry of finance.

The next booster for growth likely will have to come from hiring more foreigners to overcome the skills gap necessary to achieve Vision 2030 goals. The Ministry of Human Resources and Development acknowledges the country must attract "foreign talent to help train Saudis and transfer knowledge" and therefore must make the Saudi labor market "an attractive destination for high skill/income foreign talent." In 2023 the total number of foreign workers, highly skilled to unskilled, was 7.8 million, up from 6.9 million in 2019.[19] This need to attract high-skilled yet easily mobile foreign talent is one of the reasons for the many cultural changes—cinema, concerts, sporting events, fine restaurants, and allowing women to drive—that the country has undertaken in recent years.

Whether the Crown Prince's crackdown on free speech will complicate his efforts to attract the best and brightest is not yet clear. Foreigners seem to have more leeway in criticizing the government than Saudi citizens do. At the 2023 Formula 1, British driver Lewis Hamilton, who had earlier called Saudi Arabia's anti-LGBTQ+ laws terrifying, said publicly that he felt his sport was "duty-bound to raise awareness and try to leave a positive impact." He competed in the race without any official reaction or criticism of his comments.

As the kingdom pursues its goal to diversify the economy not just into tourism and manufacturing but also into complex sectors like AI, technology, and renewable energy, officials acknowledge there won't be sufficient Saudi talent. "We have to improve our ability to attract human talent—Saudi and foreign—by improving health care, education, personal rights laws, and quality of life," says one minister.

Despite a dearth of talent, Saudi Arabia is determined to become the world's preferred location for global AI data centers by meeting their enormous energy needs at the lowest price. In 2024, Amazon Web Services agreed to invest $5.3 billion to create cloud-based technology solutions in the region. Microsoft and Oracle also have pledged to invest $2.1 billion and $1.5 billion respectively to create new cloud areas in Saudi Arabia. A willingness to train Saudis for new high-tech jobs is part of all these commitments. In short, the kingdom is using its strength—cheap energy—to try to overcome its weakness—insufficiently trained Saudi talent. Because the energy demands for AI are so gargantuan, Saudi officials are seeking to exploit their competitive advantage in low-cost energy to draw even more of these data center investments.

Additionally, the Saudi Public Investment Fund has signed a partnership with Google Cloud to establish an advanced artificial intelligence hub in Dammam, located in the kingdom's oil rich Eastern Province. "As part of Saudi Arabia's rich technology ecosystem, we aim to create highly skilled jobs for Saudis and opportunities for global businesses to fuel growth through cloud adoption," said Ruth Porat, president and chief investment officer of Google and Alphabet. The kingdom hopes to attract foreign expertise with its low cost energy. "You are going to have the lowest cost energy to build data centers anywhere in the world because this is the place for it," Saudi Aramco CEO Amin Nasser told a Riyadh gathering of global business executives worried about both the supply and the cost of energy to run the world's new data centers.[20] Whether cheap energy is enough to overcome the kingdom's political and social restrictions to attract foreign talent to help train local Saudis remains an open question.

Those close to the Crown Prince say that while he seeks a modern economy, he is absolutely determined to avoid a Western culture. These individuals say MBS believes (not unlike Putin) that Western culture is decadent, especially the United States, which has diminished its focus on family and values. The Saudi Arabia he is building will offer its people Western entertainment—dancing in the streets, movies, travel, fine dining—but will not openly approve gay marriage or LGBTQ+ rights. Traditional family will remain the core of Saudi society.

Saudi Arabia ranks 43rd out of 46 popular expatriate destinations for foreign work, according to HSBC's Expat Explorer Survey.[21] The most significant objections to life in Riyadh are pollution, climate, and lack of tolerance, again according to that survey. The availability of affordable quality housing and good education for children are additional reasons foreigners give for shunning Riyadh despite high salaries offered by the Saudi government. So, despite living costs in Riyadh being at least one-third cheaper than Dubai, one of its main Gulf competitors, many expats still prefer Dubai as a place to live and work.[22] "Foreign talent needs more schools, spouses to be able to come and work, long-term residency options, and an improved judicial system," says Steffen Hertog, a professor at the London School of Economics who has devoted decades to studying Saudi and other Gulf economies.

If there is a shortage of highly skilled foreign workers, there also is insufficient foreign direct investment. Indeed, FDI has actually declined since 2016 when Vision 2030 was announced. The fact that Saudi's legal system is based on sharia law, rarely understood by foreigners, is one complication. Moreover, certain sectors are off-limits for foreign investment and even in those where FDI is allowed, foreign companies must navigate a complex set of local content and local worker requirements. All this has left foreign investors slow to engage. The kingdom's human rights record, with the risk of reputational damage to a Western company doing business there, has doubtlessly also helped deter foreign investors.

The government has taken a number of initiatives to nudge slow growth in FDI. In 2021 it announced it would exclude international companies from receiving Saudi government contracts unless the company established a headquarters in the kingdom and hired Saudi employees. This clearly was an effort to dislodge international companies from their preferred headquarters in Dubai.

Additionally, the government established an inward investment agency, the Saudi Investment Promotion Authority, and a Ministry of Investment to try to lure more foreign money to the Saudi economy. Despite these moves, foreign investment into the kingdom in 2023 was $19 billion, below the levels of 2022 ($33 billion) and 2021 ($27 billion). And FDI in both those years was inflated by sales of shares in Aramco subsidiaries, which really are hydrocarbon investments, not investment in the non-oil economy. FDI in the first nine months of 2024, according to the Saudi General Authority for Statistics, was $14.5 billion, half the full year target of $29 billion and far off the $100 billion goal for 2030. For historical perspective, the 2023 investment into the kingdom was on a par with that of 2015 before the reforms began. The government's ambitious goal calls for growing FDI to $100 billion by 2030 or 5.7 percent of Saudi GDP, putting the kingdom in the top ten economies in the world for investors. But 2023's FDI was 1.8 percent of GDP, one-third the kingdom's average from 2004 to 2022.[23]

All these things led the government to acknowledge in early 2024 for the first time that it will delay some of its costly giga-projects at the heart of Vision 2030. Finance Minister Mohammed al-Jadaan explained the move by saying more time is needed to "build factories, build even sufficient human resources." Moreover, the government issued a new royal decree intended to further simplify investing in the kingdom by, among other things, replacing a complicated process for securing a foreign investment license with a simple registration and a new provision to treat foreign and domestic investors equally.[24]

At the core, the Saudi economy still is an oil economy. The IMF estimated in 2024 that the kingdom needs oil prices at $96 a barrel to balance its budget if it holds production at 9 million barrels a day. Yet oil prices in 2024 hovered on average at $80 a barrel despite fears of a Mideast war as Israel attacked Hezbollah in Lebanon, and Iran and Israel exchanged direct attacks for the first time. If the kingdom's development spending is included, the government needs to receive $108 per barrel to cover all its expenses, according to Bloomberg Economics.[25] The government has prioritized social change—cinemas, women driving, women working, concerts, sporting events—over economic change. Achieving the former was intended to assist in driving progress on the latter. But more than halfway into Vision 2030 economic reforms, the Saudi economy still relies more on government spending than on increased productivity by private sector workers. "We want to move from a resource-led economy to a productivity-led economy," says Faisal al-Ibrahim, minister of economy and planning.[26]

A further sign that the kingdom is reassessing how long it can rely on oil revenue is Riyadh's decision in early 2024 to at least temporarily pull the plug on plans to increase its oil production capacity to 13 million barrels a day from 12 mbd. The decision seems to make sense, as the kingdom's prolonged efforts to increase prices by holding down production has left it producing only around 9 mbd. Still, prices haven't risen to offset the revenue lost by holding down output. With lower oil revenues, Saudi GDP shrunk −1.1 percent in 2023, the worst in the G-20 other than Argentina, a sharp comedown from its 2022 growth that led the G-20.[27] More ominously, the Saudi Ministry of Finance lowered its 2024 GDP forecast to 0.8 percent from 4.4 percent. Moreover, global oil demand grew less than one million barrels a day in 2024 and is expected to have another low-growth year in 2025 as China's economy continues to falter. And the Saudi budget is in deficit through at least 2027, the government acknowledges. The kingdom is financing those deficits with debt. It sold $12 billion of bonds in January 2024, the largest deal since 2017.[28] Indeed, debt has risen to 27 percent of GDP in 2024 from 1.5 percent a decade earlier.[29] In sum, a yellow warning light is blinking.

In another sign that oil revenues and debt aren't sufficient to finance its plans, the government decided in 2024 to raise $12.3

billion by selling additional shares in its national oil company, Aramco. That sale follows a controversial decision by the Crown Prince in 2019 to take Aramco public to raise $29.4 billion in what remains the world's largest-ever initial public offering. Later he transferred Aramco shares to the Public Investment Fund, raising its combined stake in Aramco to 16 percent, equating to a $327 billion value. More billions from Aramco shares will help the kingdom continue to fund development plans, but at the same time, it erodes government ownership in Aramco and thus government revenues from Aramco's petroleum production, still the major source of revenue for government.

It is too early to declare victory or failure for Vision 2030. To truly diversify the economy off oil, Saudi Arabia will need to reach its goal of growing the private sector's contribution to the kingdom's GDP to 65 percent, up from 40 percent when Vision 2030 was unveiled. More than halfway to 2030, the private sector is contributing 43 percent, well off its 2030 goal. Similarly, the kingdom now is falling short of its goal to grow non-oil exports to 50 percent of GDP from 18.7 percent in 2016.[30] Of course, as minister after minister points out, success for Vision 2030 doesn't require full achievement on every goal but visible progress that continues to earn Saudis' trust in their future beyond Vision 2030—and the confidence and cooperation of foreign talent and investment.

The Crown Prince has sought to frontload spending to create visible change in the kingdom that would persuade initially skeptical Saudis that his plans are viable. There is no question he has created a huge amount of very visible social change, from women driving to ubiquitous entertainment infrastructure including stadiums, hotels, and multiple Disney-like parks. Construction has finally begun on the Line, an out-of-this-world smart city in Neom with no cars and no carbon, as tall as the Empire State Building in New York and stretching 105 miles. But it has been drastically scaled down to a mere 1.5 miles to be complete by 2030 with some 300,000 people living there, not the 1.5 million originally envisioned. Myriad other projects too are increasingly visible and some, like Sindalah, a resort island on the Red Sea with an eighty-six-berth marina, have been completed. If oil prices hold up, Saudi Arabia seems likely to complete most of its grand projects, though not by 2030.

That's a very big if. Oil price volatility has been an historic constant even before the climate change bureaucracy began trying to push the world off the stuff. The good news for Saudi citizens is that government now studies its spending in detail. Having reviewed all its projects and their costs and having projected oil revenues out to 2030, MBS and his team identified a gap between revenues and projected costs. That gap would have to be filled primarily by debt. Excessive government debt could crowd out money for private investors to build the sorts of private sector companies and jobs the economy needs. Hence the decision to stretch out some large government projects beyond 2030 and to raise more funds by selling Aramco shares and government holdings in other companies like Saudi Telecom. All of this is a rigor completely absent during previous Saudi regimes.

Still, Khalid al Sweilem, a sovereign wealth expert and former head of investment for the Saudi Arabian Monetary Authority, says for the kingdom to sustain what he calls "the long push" to develop, it needs to strengthen fiscal policy and participate in emerging mega trends like AI and renewable energy in partnership with key foreign companies. This will boost innovation in the kingdom and create a cutting edge economy, he writes.

Whether the kingdom successfully transits from Vision 2030's "Big Push" to a sustained "Long Push" by truly diversifying sources of public revenue across oil, mining, sales tax, tourism, and financial income on both domestic and foreign assets remains to be seen.[31] Moreover, whether the big projects that are built actually become sound enterprises providing jobs and growth for the economy beyond oil remains an unknown among all the others the Crown Prince is juggling. Yet on that rests his future legacy and the livelihood of his people: Is he a visionary reformer who delivered, or a dreamer who dwindled away the last of his nation's black gold? The Crown Prince remains confident that many of his bets will pay big. His chips continue to ride the roulette wheel that slowly is revealing the future well-being of a nation and the legacy of a ruler.

CHAPTER FIFTEEN

All in the Family

The Al Saud are a shrinking ruling family.

King Abdul Aziz, who founded the modern Saudi kingdom, sired forty-five sons, whose offspring now number at least three hundred sons, grandsons, and great-grandsons and an equal number of princesses.[1] Adding in all the extended branches of Al Saud raises the total family membership to an estimated fifteen thousand males and females of all ages. Yet the future of the monarchy now appears to be in the hands of one man: Prince Mohammed bin Salman, the first of Abdul Aziz's grandsons to lead the kingdom.

During the seven decades since Abdul Aziz's death in 1953, rule passed from one of his sons to another. These brothers, often competitive and at odds, were careful to share power among the many different branches of his family to keep peace. All Al Saud are well aware that family infighting destroyed their rule in the late 1800s, forcing young Abdul Aziz to flee to Kuwait and ultimately to stage a daring predawn raid on Riyadh in 1902 that ushered in a thirty-year civil war that in turn finally restored Al Saud rule in Arabia.

He was so conscious of family cohesion that on his deathbed he called his two eldest sons, Saud and Faisal, who often had clashed, to his side. "Join hands across my body and swear you will work together when I am gone," the old king admonished them.[2] Despite their pledge of assent, Saud was deposed to exile in Greece after a disastrous eleven-year rule that concentrated power primarily among him and his sons. He was replaced by his half brother, Faisal. King Faisal parceled government roles among various half brothers and their sons, a tradition largely continued by successive kings to maintain family support if not always harmony. Indeed, the royal family even developed a pattern of dispersing military might among three powerful princes, one running defense, one the National Guard, and a third the internal security forces, making a palace coup less likely.

No more balancing. Today power—political, economic, and military—is all in the family of King Salman. The eighty-nine-year-old absolute monarch since 2015 is ill and largely leaving day-to-day rule to the sixth of his twelve sons, Crown Prince Mohammed, thirty-nine. Defense is controlled by MBS's full brother, Prince Khalid, thirty-six. And their half brother, Abdul Aziz, sixty-four, fourth son of King Salman, runs the Energy Ministry, still the source of the majority of Saudi Arabia's wealth.

Salman, who ruled Riyadh Province for nearly half a century, became minister of defense in 2011 at the death of his brother who had controlled Saudi defense forces for more than three decades. In 2017, King Salman took control of interior forces when he removed his nephew as crown prince and minister of interior. Only five months later he fired the late King Abdullah's son as head of the National Guard, consolidating those forces under the king and MBS. The military balance among brothers that had helped ensure consensual government among the descendants of Abdul Aziz was over. Gone too was any serious threat to MBS's ascension.

What for decades was a large family juggling competing princely interests to share power now is a single branch determined to hold power. The birth of the Salman dynasty is here. Some of MBS's royal opponents used to express confidence that "we'll get him when King Salman dies." That talk is gone.

Of course, no Saudi prince is king until the Al Saud family swears its *bay'ah*, or allegiance, to him. So succession isn't truly over until King Salman dies and MBS ascends the throne and the Al Saud family provides its pro forma allegiance. It's worth noting that in the long history of nearly three hundred years of Al Saud rule, only three of the fourteen successions have been uncontested. According to Joseph Kéchichian, author of a book on succession in Saudi Arabia, the eleven contested successions included "assassination, civil war, and, in a few cases, bloodless revolution."[3]

Unquestionably, many of Crown Prince Mohammed's uncles, nephews, and cousins resent the ruthless way he and his father have sidelined royal relatives by incarcerating them, confiscating their wealth and placing some, including the king's sole surviving full brother, Prince Ahmed, under house arrest. They may long to contest this succession, but so far there is little evidence they can loosen the Salman line's grip on power.

Thus it's important to take a closer look at this family and especially its most powerful members. But first, here's a scorecard of King Salman's sons by three wives:

Sultana bint Turki Al Sudairi, married Prince Salman 1954, died 2011

1. Fahd	1955	died 2001	businessman
2. Sultan	1956	67 years	astronaut, tourism director
3. Ahmad	1958	died 2002	media executive
4. Abdul Aziz	1960	64 years	Minister of Energy
5. Faisal	1970	53 years	adviser to King Salman

Sarah bint Faisal Al Subai'ai divorced

7. Saud bin Salman	1986	37	businessman

Fahda bint Falah Al Hithlain, married Prince Salman in 1984

6. Mohammed	1985	39	Crown Prince
8. Turki	1987	37	businessman
9. Khalid	1988	36	Minister of Defense
10. Nayef			
11. Bandar			
12. Rakan			

As the chart of progeny suggests, most of King Salman's sons aren't involved in government. But three are in key positions and two others have served. Prince Faisal until recently served as governor of Medina for a decade. Prince Sultan, the king's oldest surviving son and the first Arab astronaut, is chairman of the board of directors of the Saudi Space Commission. He also served as the kingdom's first director of tourism in the mid-2000s.

Brothers

Prince Khalid, thirty-six, is seen as a key ally of Crown Prince Mohammed not just because he holds the important defense portfolio but because he is a trusted full brother of the Crown Prince often called upon for sensitive behind-the-scenes negotiations. Prince Khalid served as deputy defense minister while his brother held the portfolio and was promoted to minister of defense in 2022. Prior to that he was the kingdom's ambassador to the United States from 2017 to 2019.

All his life Prince Khalid wanted to be a fighter pilot. In 2024, at my request, he shows me his childhood bedroom on the second floor of Shati Palace in Jeddah. Toy fighter planes and photos of young Khalid dressed in military uniforms dominate the bookshelves. His father bought the palace in 1988, the year Khalid was born. The room clearly dates from his childhood era. Near his bed is a toy red plastic Lamborghini. Tilt back the car and beneath is an old-fashioned land-line telephone from his youth. In the bottom of his shelves are a Neo Geo game and old movies he used to watch with his brothers on a VCR that he has kept since childhood.

"MBS loved to watch movies," recalls Prince Khalid. "His favorite was *Star Wars*." Even today, long after the VCR, says Prince Khalid, the Crown Prince "always has his Apple TV with him in his room even when he travels. At the end of the day he puts on Apple TV and falls asleep."

Around the circular stairway from Prince Khalid's room is that of his brother, MBS, a large, nondescript bedroom decorated in subdued beige. About the only clue that MBS inhabited this room is a Neo Geo machine on the bookshelf. Their brother Turki's bedroom completes the three childhood rooms upstairs.

These two brothers, who each hold powerful government roles, seem to get along well. Prince Khalid is comfortable around MBS, though very deferential. When I interview the two of them together in 2019, MBS, who at that time was both crown prince and defense minister, did most of the talking. But his younger brother and deputy minister of defense briefed me on the kingdom's war in Yemen.

The prince, a round-faced, easygoing young man, speaks admiringly but also confidently about his brother. While he was the kingdom's ambassador to the United States, he invited me to dinner at his Virginia residence with his wife, a granddaughter of his uncle Mishal bin Abdul Aziz.

He is casually dressed in black trousers and a white linen

jacket. Khalid describes his elder brother as "always ambitious" and a natural leader. As a teenager, he says, MBS began inviting thirty to forty young princes and friends to the desert each weekend to relax and bond. "He's traveled the world but he also knows his own people," Prince Khalid says admiringly.

Asked what leaders MBS admires, Prince Khalid says his grandfather, Abdul Aziz, who founded this latest Saudi state, and Turki bin Abdullah, founder of the second Saudi state in 1824. Turki, an enterprising and ambitious prince, eluded capture by the Ottomans who destroyed the first Saudi state. He then spent two years in hiding before engaging in a round of Al Saud family infighting that left him one of the few survivors able to reign with Ottoman acquiescence. The state he founded lasted until 1891 but Turki's personal rule was short. He was murdered after only eleven years by three assassins working for his second cousin.

Still, MBS's cleverness at the game of politics is often compared to that of Mu'awiyah, Islam's fifth caliph, famous as one of history's great manipulators. Mu'awiyah tricked Islam's fourth caliph, Ali, into allowing his rival to be declared a caliph and thus competitor for leadership of the Muslims.

In brief, Mu'awiyah, the governor of Syria, led his troops against Ali, the revered son-in-law of Prophet Mohammed. When Mu'awiyah's forces began to lose, they hoisted pages of the Quran on their lances, urging that the two armies let Allah decide the rightful leader. Fighting ceased while arbitration was organized. Ali's troops, who mostly believed the rightful caliph must be an heir of the Prophet, grew disgruntled at Ali for allowing challenge to what was rightfully his. At the conclusion of lengthy arbitration, Mu'awiyah's delegate arranged to address the assembled armies last and simply declared Mu'awiyah the caliph. What Mu'awiyah failed to win on the battlefield he secured by guile.[4]

Suddenly Islam, like Catholicism centuries later, had competing religious leaders. Within three years, Ali was murdered at morning prayers by a disgruntled Muslim. Now unchallenged, Mu'awiyah ruled for two decades and founded the Umayyad dynasty that governed the Islamic world for 150 years. Unlike his three predecessors, who all died violently, Caliph Mu'awiyah lived to nearly eighty, passing rule to his dissolute son, who died three years later. It was the first hereditary succession in Islam but surely not the last.

Like all King Salman's sons, Prince Khalid is steeped in Arab and Islamic history. His father divided his time between his two families but when he was with Fahda and her six boys, Prince Khalid says, they ate together and discussed books on Friday nights. Most of those books were history assigned them by their father.

Although only three years older, MBS was something of a second father to his younger brothers. Prince Khalid recalls MBS sitting him down in high school and sternly asking, "What are you going to do with your life?"[5] The answer, of course, was be a fighter pilot.

Prince Khalid earned a degree in aviation science at the King Faisal Aviation Academy in Saudi Arabia before joining the Royal Saudi Air Force. In 2009 he took U.S. Air Force pilot training in Mississippi and later at a U.S. air base in Nevada. He qualified to fly F-15 fighters. In 2014 the prince flew genuine combat missions against Islamic State of Iraq and Syria (ISIS) fighters in Syria as well as missions into Yemen in the kingdom's long war against that neighbor. A back injury ended his flying days and he then worked as an officer at the Ministry of Defense, which he now heads. All of his time living in the U.S. as an air force pilot and ambassador has given him excellent command of English and a knowledge of the country.

These days he fully supports his brother's haste to reform Saudi Arabia by doing hundreds of things all at once. "This generation is ambitious but their standard isn't to match the Gulf but to match the world," he says in our first meeting in 2018.[6] "MBS's view is that the country is too slow rather than his being too fast,"

Prince Khalid says. The Crown Prince, he notes, "is at the center of a storm but he just goes on."[7] Asked what he most admires about his brother, he answers, "He is a good listener and he is decisive."

Between MBS and Khalid is King Salman's eighth son, Turki bin Salman. Prince Turki, thirty-eight, has shunned government for business. According to *Asharq Al-Awsat*, a London-based Arabic newspaper owned by Saudi Research and Media Group (SRMG), Prince Turki is chairman of Tharawat Holding Company. The corporate website describes Tharawat as investing through subsidiaries in real estate construction, education, sport development, food and beverage, telecommunication, and steel. In sum, virtually everything. He also served as chairman of SRMG, a media company with close ties to King Salman's family, from 2013 to 2014.

In addition to Princes Mohammed, Turki, and Khalid, King Salman and Princess Fahda also have three younger boys, Nayef, Bandar, and Rakan, each said to be in his twenties. None appear to have any role in government. Bandar was already an enthusiastic amateur photographer at age twelve when I met him in 2009 at an Arabian horse show outside Riyadh. But typical of the secrecy that surrounds royals who aren't in public service, no one these days will say what the twenty-seven-year-old is doing.

Prince Abdul Aziz, the energy minister, is the kingdom's voice to the world on oil policy. No Saudi minister has ever been more prepared for his job. The prince graduated from King Fahd University of Petroleum and Minerals in the 1980s and has spent his entire professional life focused on oil, mostly at the ministry. Yet he was only given leadership of the ministry in 2019 by his father. "I never thought of being minister," he tells me a month into the job, "as I believed the conventional wisdom that a prince can't have this job." The oil portfolio had been held by a succession of nonroyal technocrats, notably including the late Ahmed "Zaki" Yamani, who held the job for nearly a quarter century, including during the Arab Oil Embargo, which made him a household name in the U.S.

My first encounter with Prince Abdul Aziz was in the mid-1980s when he visited the Council on Foreign Relations in New York with Hisham Nazer, a prominent technocrat then serving as oil minister. The technocratic minister did all the talking; the prince silently observed. The two are said to have had a very contentious relationship while Prince Abdul Aziz served as an adviser to the Oil Ministry. Regardless, the prince makes clear he is happy now to be the top official.

"I am deeply touched by the king and Prince Mohammed's determination to give me this opportunity," the energy minister says. "For my whole life we talked about reducing oil dependence but the Crown Prince had the confidence to just do it."[8]

Prince Abdul Aziz has a reputation for wry wit, which was on display at our 2019 meeting soon after his promotion. When I congratulate him on being the first royal to be energy minister he smilingly observes that his promotion was celebrated in some quarters with "fireworks." Indeed, one week after his becoming energy minister, Iranian drones attacked the kingdom's primary oil-processing facility at Abqaiq, setting the complex ablaze and cutting Saudi oil exports in half. In London at the time of the pre-dawn attack, the minister rushed back to review the devastation with Aramco officials.

Even a month later, the prince is still clearly emotional. He recalls his despair at first viewing the devastation, then leaving his Aramco colleagues to do their work. By morning, he says, he wept "tears of pride" because Aramco engineers had assured him they could restore production in only a few weeks. "For thirty-two years I said Saudi oil was dependable, reliable, secure," he says. "Suddenly this attack comes." He shakes his head recalling the emotional impact.

As minister of energy, Prince Abdul Aziz has earned a reputation for unfailingly putting Saudi interests first. U.S. entreaties no longer get a cooperative hearing as they did so often in the past.

He has worked closely with Russia, another major oil producer, to contain global oil output and keep prices up to help finance the Crown Prince's lavish spending on Vision 2030 development projects. (The cooperation has also helped fund Russia's war against Ukraine, to the displeasure of the U.S.) Prices have hovered in the $80-a-barrel range in recent years, still below the $90–$100 price the kingdom needs to fund its budget at current levels of oil production. As a result, Saudi Arabia has been running budget deficits since 2022, with the 2025 deficit forecast to total $27 billion.[9]

Unlike his workaholic half brother, Crown Prince Mohammed, Prince Abdul Aziz says he stresses work-life balance in his ministry. "People need to see their family, to have a social life. They need to switch off sometimes," he says.

The fourth son of King Salman, Prince Abdul Aziz is a very proud family man. While family is important to all Saudis, speaking publicly of one's wife and children isn't common for royals where family details are closely guarded. Yet this prince in a speech to hundreds of young Saudis in November 2023 voices love of his family. "I have a wife who is in my bones," he says. "I have children who are the dream of my life."[10] When I ask him about social changes in Saudi Arabia in 2023, he immediately talks of his own children as evidence of the younger generation and its opportunities in the new Saudi Arabia. His eldest, a daughter, is working for the Public Investment Fund and wants to study law or business at Harvard, he says. His twin sons are finishing college in the kingdom and one of them also wants to study law in the U.S.

Prince Faisal, the king's fifth son, has had a career mixed between government service and business. He served as chairman of the Saudi Research and Media Group (SRMG), replacing his older brother Ahmed, who died of heart failure in 2002. Faisal left that post shortly before being named governor of Medina in 2013, a job he also held for roughly a decade before being named in 2023 as chairman of the board of directors of the King Abdulaziz

Foundation for Research and Archives, which houses the volumi-
nous papers on King Abdul Aziz, his successors, and the national
history. Prince Faisal, like several of King Salman's other sons
from his first wife, did graduate studies abroad. After earning a
bachelor's degree in political science at King Saud University, he
earned a doctorate from Oxford University in 1999. His thesis was
titled "Iran, Saudi Arabia, and the Gulf: Power Politics in Transition
1968–71." Some Saudi researchers believe MBS now will task Prince
Faisal with finally providing academic freedom in the kingdom to
allow Saudi and non-Saudi researchers unhampered ability to do
research and conduct interviews in and on Saudi Arabia.

During Prince Faisal's time as chairman of SRMG, he is said to
have established a school for training journalists and he also served
as chairman of Jadwa Investment, the kingdom's premier investment and advisory firm, in which he is said to own 7 percent. This
well-educated son is comfortable in both government and business
circles. He is now also an adviser to King Salman.

Prince Sultan bin Salman, sixty-seven, is King Salman's eldest
surviving son. Now largely retired from government, Prince Sultan
chairs the board of directors of the Saudi Space Commission, a
body intended to help the kingdom reach the moon if MBS's vision
materializes. Prince Sultan is famous as the first Saudi—indeed
first Muslim—to travel in space. He was a payload engineer aboard
the U.S. Discovery space mission in 1985. Before going, he went
to visit Sheikh Abdul Aziz bin Abdullah bin Baz, a blind religious
scholar who believed the Earth was flat because that was how it felt
under his feet. Sheikh bin Baz had warned Muslims in a fatwa,
or religious ruling, after U.S. astronauts walked on the moon in
1969 not to believe what infidels wrote without securing proof. After
Prince Sultan returned, he visited the sheikh again to thank him
for his advice on praying and fasting in space. The prince told me
the sheikh asked him many questions and the prince described
the round Earth he looked down upon from his space capsule. "He

didn't ask about the shape of the Earth," the prince recalled. "I think he already knew it was round."

Prince Sultan is thoroughly at home in the world. Having earned a bachelor's degree in communication from the University of Denver and a master's in public policy from Syracuse University, Prince Sultan is the first Saudi official to proudly promote opening the closed kingdom to tourism. He served as director of tourism in the mid-2000s, long before it became a ministry under MBS once he had tethered the religious police. Indeed, when we spoke in 2010 on the twenty-fifth anniversary of Prince Sultan's spaceflight, the religious police were still harassing foreigners unless they adhered to the strict dress and conduct codes of the religious establishment. Even then, Prince Sultan confidently—and in hindsight, correctly—asserted that the new Saudi generation would be open minded. "Yes, technology is being used for terrorism now," he said. "But at the end of the day the new generation will use technology to know each other and they will be comfortable with each other all around the world." Saudis, he said, "need to be able to live in their country and have fun, to love it and enjoy it." That Saudi Arabia, unimaginable to me then, arrived in less than a decade.

While Saudi history tells us that few royal successions are without contention, the impending one from King Salman to MBS may well be a rare exception. That is primarily because MBS is the rare crown prince who already wields most of the kingdom's power. His father, old and ailing, is more a figurehead than a ruler. It is also because MBS, flaws and all, has developed a broader public power base, including Saudi youth and women, who comprise a majority of the population, than other crown princes of Saudi Arabia historically have had. Moreover, opposition power sources like the religious police have been caged, political critics incarcerated, and potential royal rivals sidelined or worse.

Mohammed bin Salman, thirty-nine, has the potential to rule the kingdom for decades, giving him time to solidify his dynasty's hold on power. At present he has three young sons. The eldest, Salman, is only fifteen. The true purpose of a crown prince in Saudi Arabia is to ensure a quick transfer of power. A teenage crown prince wouldn't guarantee seamless government functioning. But MBS has plenty of brothers or cousins he could tap to serve as crown prince if he follows his father as king.

Speculating on royal family politics is a fool's errand. As Rome's Augustus discovered after ruling nearly forty-four years, passing power isn't easy or predictable. He lost half a dozen potential heirs before finally succumbing and passing power to his stepson, Tiberius. Regardless of whom MBS names as his initial crown prince, a Saudi king has the right to fire his crown prince at will. So, as king, MBS could decide to name no heir apparent or to name his brother, Khalid, or someone else. Still, at the time of his choosing, MBS could easily name his son heir apparent and crown prince. So the Salman dynasty seems likely to last.

"Primogeniture is now the system in Saudi Arabia," says Joe Kéchichian, author of an authoritative book, *Succession in Saudi Arabia.* "It's a done deal. It would be very difficult for another branch to come to power for the next several generations."[11]

Still, Kéchichian warns, for MBS to ensure his hold on power beyond an initial six- to twelve-month honeymoon he will have to take care of the demands of key members of the royal family and of the religious establishment.

Undeniably, the cone of power in the Saudi royal family has continued to narrow ever since King Abdul Aziz established this third Saudi state in 1932. Only his sons were allowed to succeed him as kings. Then in the 1970s the late King Faisal further distanced other Al Saud princes from descendants of Abdul Aziz by decreeing that only the latter's direct descendants would be called

"His Royal Highness"; al Saud princes from other branches of the family would simply be titled "His Highness." Now King Abdul Aziz's grandson is seeking to further narrow the pool of princes who will hold power to those in the Salman family—and those to whom he decides to grant power to serve at his pleasure.

To ensure that enough of the Al Saud family supports him, MBS and his father have sought to cement the loyalty of key branches of the extended family by naming them as governors or deputy governors of the kingdom's thirteen provinces. He has also tapped the brightest of some of the descendants not allowed to inherit the throne—those titled His Highness—such as Faisal bin Farhan, who serves as foreign minister. In 2024 the Crown Prince also began holding meetings with princes, scholars, and Saudi citizens, previously having largely eschewed such traditional majlises to devote his time to meetings that would drive his reform agenda. In another nod to tradition, these public gatherings are opened with a reading from the holy Quran.

MBS seems increasingly to see himself as the leader of a more powerful and more concentrated dynasty. Still, it's too early to declare success. Politics in Saudi Arabia are essentially royal family politics, and factionalism, intrigue, and infighting are an inherent aspect of family politics for centuries, requiring constant vigilance by the ruler. Whether the Salman dynasty lasts for generations, as Kéchichian predicts, neither democracy nor dismemberment is a likely scenario for the kingdom. History shows there are always Al Saud princes eager to rule Arabia, and after nearly four centuries it's unlikely the Al Sauds will go the way of the Umayyads or the Ottomans.

The Once and Future King

H ow should the world think about Mohammed bin Salman, his struggles and his flaws, his achievements and his challenges? Is he a transformative historical figure or just another Arab tyrant? Or some of both? Comparing him with other young men in history who amassed and wielded great power can offer some perspective. Also, what hints does history provide about his future leadership?

The Arab world in modern times has produced more than its share of demagogues and charlatans like Egypt's Gamal Abdel Nasser and Libya's Muammar Qaddafi or thugs like Iraq's Saddam Hussein and Syria's Hafiz al-Assad. While MBS clearly is prepared to be brutal if necessary to secure his country's future and his place in it, he is like none of these.

Those close to the Crown Prince say he already sees himself as an historic figure, a leader not only transforming Saudi Arabia but impacting the world with his big dreams and bold intentions. In a world of cosmic problems, from environmental disaster to nuclear holocaust to potentially destructive AI, he wants to be an exemplar of innovative thinking, not incrementalism that he believes characterizes most current leaders.

Historical analogies abound. Already some of his ministers call him Saladin after the legendary twelfth-century sultan of Egypt and Syria who reconquered Jerusalem in 1187, restoring Muslim rule after eighty-eight years of Christian dominance. Others liken the Crown Prince to Ataturk, the founder of modern, secular Turkey in 1923. Both men put modernization at the top of their to-do list and MBS, like Ataturk, seeks to create a national identity apart from religion. "Ataturk wanted to divorce Turkey from the Ottoman Empire and create a Turkish identity," says Charles Freeman, a retired diplomat who served as ambassador to Saudi Arabia in the early 1990s. "MBS is seeking to create a Saudi identity and separate the kingdom from a religious identity."

If the Crown Prince has thought deeply about historic leaders, he doesn't share it. When I ask who has influenced him, he doesn't name a great ruler from the past or his famous grandfather or his father. He implies he is charting an independent path. "I love my father but I am not him," MBS says. "I tell my children, 'Don't be like me; your generation will need new ideas, not mine.'"[1]

Looking for historical parallels is imperfect especially when so many famous leaders were warrior conquerors, rather than reformers. Nevertheless, there are some partial parallels with other men who got power at a young age. Rome's Caesar Augustus, like MBS, inherited power young from his (adoptive) father, had to fight fifteen years to secure it, and went on to rule for nearly forty-four years. Like MBS in Saudi Arabia, Augustus inherited a divided and dispirited nation. He left it a unified empire adorned in monuments.

"I found Rome built of bricks; I leave it clothed in marble," Augustus said seeking to summarize his legacy.[2] MBS inherited a Saudi mired in religious extremism, lethargy, and failed five-year plans. He chained the religious and since then has given the kingdom constant action, confidence, and the grand goals of his Vision 2030. In one of our meetings, I quote Augustus's summary of his legacy and ask the Crown Prince how he would like his own epitaph to read. With only a short pause, he says with seriousness, "I found Saudi in marble and inspired a generation to create more marble."[3] In our meetings he repeatedly says he isn't the only transformational Saudi leader, citing King Saud for ending slavery in 1962 and introducing girls' education (both were done after King Saud was king in name only having been forced to pass power to his crown prince Faisal but not his title), King Faisal for introducing television in 1965, and King Fahd for creating manufacturing, airports, and universities.

Young Augustus forged control of Rome through lies and deception, blood and brutality, even personally gouging out the eyes of an elected magistrate he thought had betrayed him.[4] While pretending to support a republic, he was determined to found his own autocracy. But once firmly in control, Augustus built a nation of peace and prosperity, Pax Romana, that lasted nearly two hundred years after his death. He even allowed free speech, something MBS doesn't. The Crown Prince stands accused of orchestrating the murder of a man he similarly felt betrayed his kingdom and of routinely imprisoning critics. He has the potential life span to rule even longer than Augustus. Whether his new Saudi Arabia will transition into a kinder, gentler one remains to be seen. Given the Crown Prince's many enemies among suppressed Wahhabi opponents—and royal relatives—having the confidence to ease up on repression may continue to prove elusive. Or ultimately deny MBS a long rule.

Like MBS, Peter the Great was a dreamer and decisive doer, never hesitating to take big risks to impose his modernizing reforms on a backward Russia. He transformed a barren swamp on the Baltic Sea into a new city, St. Petersburg, creating a "window to Europe" in 1703 that changed history to this day. Similarly, MBS's $500 billion megacity, the Line, rising in the desert of Neom near the Red Sea, is intended to open a window to Europe by creating a new land bridge from Asia through the Mediterranean to Europe, similarly enhancing Saudi Arabia's centrality in global commerce and geopolitics.

Peter the Great ruled for more than forty years as a bold and sometimes brutal top-down modernizer. He was determined to remake every aspect of his backward society. For starters, he carried a razor to public ceremonies and personally shaved off the beards of important Muscovites to ridicule such unnecessary hair. Like MBS, he reformed religion, subordinating control of the church from a powerful patriarch to a synod of bureaucrats appointed by and controlled by the emperor. Peter also welcomed hordes of talented foreigners to Russia to help advance his modernization plans as MBS seeks to do. (Don't expect to see MBS taking a year off to master a new industry, as when Peter the Great learned shipbuilding, nor sitting down for meals with his foreign workers just as Peter shared beer and gruel with his imported German laborers.)

A more recent young reformer with similarities to MBS is Napoleon Bonaparte. A Corsican by birth, he endured taunts from French students when he moved to France, leaving him, like MBS as a child, determined to excel. While MBS isn't a military leader like Napoleon, some who know the Crown Prince well see parallels between the Saudi prince and the French general. Each amassed power quickly by removing rivals; both gained a deserved reputation for imposing sweeping change on his nation.

Like Peter the Great and Napoleon, MBS has convinced his followers they are taking part in a great cause that will echo through the ages. In the end, of course, Napoleon ran afoul of his own ambitions, making his disastrous march on Moscow and waging one too many wars on Britain. These miscalculations, compounded by unfortunate circumstances, led to his downfall. MBS today is juggling Israel and Iran, two mutual antagonists. He must avoid any miscalculation with either that could ignite war between the two and put at risk all he has developed in the kingdom—and perhaps even his rule.

In his book *Leadership*, Henry Kissinger divides leaders into two categories: Statesmen and Prophets. Statesmen, according to Kissinger, embrace change to preserve their societies. They are ambitious but not revolutionary, he writes, so they manage difficult periods to preserve existing institutions for future generations, as Franklin Roosevelt and Winston Churchill did during World War II. Prophets, Kissinger posits, erase the past and redefine what's possible. "Their goal is to transcend, rather than manage, the status quo."[5]

Certainly, MBS seeks to be a Prophet in Kissinger's parlance. No tradition is sacrosanct. Everything is open to sweeping change. He has tackled removing the cancer of corruption, a task that amounts to surgery on the whole society. He has suppressed religious domination; launched an astronomical building program to change the face of Saudi Arabia; and freed women to pursue any career, including launching one woman to the International Space Station. He is determined to transform his nation and set an example for a world in need of renewal. The world, he says, is like six hundred years ago with the discovery of America. Those who discover the new worlds possible today will dominate for generations to come. He intends to be one of those discovering new frontiers, including the planet Mars. Predicting that by 2050 the U.S., China, Japan, Germany, and India will all be on Mars, he insists Saudi Arabia will be there too. "I have twenty-seven years, a small window to get this done," he tells me.[6]

Lee Kuan Yew, one of the six leaders Kissinger profiles, similarly advocated dreaming big. Like MBS, he believed he was on earth to advance his people and, where possible, the larger world. When he took the helm of Singapore in 1959, at age thirty-six, it was devastated from Japanese occupation and crippled by British colonialism. Nearly four decades later, when he passed leadership to a new prime minister, Singapore was the jewel of Asia and an exemplar to the world of free-market capitalism. Singapore's economy is the most open in the world and one of the least corrupt; year after year its students score at the top on international tests thanks to its superior education. Its per capita income is consistently among the world's top ten, just ahead of the U.S.

"If you are just realistic, you become pedestrian, plebeian, you will fail," Lee said. "Therefore, you must be able to soar above reality and say, 'This is also possible.'"[7] MBS's view precisely.

Lee, like MBS, was an unapologetic authoritarian. Human rights groups, as they do with MBS, chose to focus not on his transformative achievements but his rough handling of critics. For Lee Kuan Yew, the individual was much less important than the good of society—as defined by him. After his retirement, he conceded to the New York Times, "I am not saying everything I did was right but everything I did was for an honorable purpose. I had to do some nasty things, locking fellows up without trial."

Machiavelli endorsed the idea of deception and cruelty in the pursuit of a ruler's goals. A prince, he wrote, must appear to be "merciful, loyal, human, and upright," but if need be he must be prepared to "emulate both the (cunning of a) fox and the (strength of a) lion."[8] In short, a ruler should lie if keeping his word would undermine his interest, and use force if necessary to advance his interest. To sum up, his subjects will respect success regardless how it is achieved.

John Gaddis, author of On Grand Strategy, and who teaches a seminar of the same title at Yale University, studies how leaders through history to today use power. One lesson: they must harness their aspirations to their capabilities because there are limits to what sheer willpower can achieve. He sees a comparison between Napoleon and MBS in their youthful drive to remake their nations. So far, he says, MBS has avoided the miscalculations of Napoleon. The world, Gaddis says, is now undergoing a rising tide of authoritarianism from the Mideast to Latin America and especially in Russia and China. This creates a window of opportunity in the Middle East and globally for MBS to pursue his ambition to dominate his region and be an increasingly powerful player on the world stage.

The world has a stake in MBS's success. He has decapitated fundamentalist Islam's Wahhabi leadership by jailing many to intimidate most. But, if over the next generation he can truly transform Saudi into a beacon of moderate Islam, not extremism, that will impact the whole Islamic world given the kingdom's influential role as custodian of Islam's two holiest sites. And any reduction in extremist Islam and its terror as it seeks to build a caliphate on earth would benefit all nations, especially the U.S., a favorite target of Islamic terrorists. Clearly it's better for the world if MBS's economic reforms succeed than if they fail and the kingdom slowly becomes like Egypt, a poor Arab nation with a large impoverished population. So, for both economic and security reasons, MBS's success would benefit the wider world. Arguably, he is the most ambitious Arab leader since the Muslim conquest of Persia in 637.

Whether MBS, like Lee Kuan Yew, successfully transforms his nation and stands as a model abroad depends on whether he can successfully juggle the myriad challenges he confronts without, like Napoleon, making a fatal miscalculation over the coming years. To an outsider, it isn't clear if any of his close advisers or friends dare to try to dissuade him if they see errors in judgment. Nor is it clear how self-reflective the Crown Prince is. While the world has many naysayers about the Crown Prince and his grand plans, thus far the many colossal projects under construction continue to rise—even if more slowly in recent years—convincing at least his countrymen that Vision 2030 is real. It's worth noting that despite the struggles of the leaders reviewed here, all but Napoleon died peacefully in their beds. Napoleon, of course, died a prisoner on the island of Saint Helena.

Despite all the existing pressures and some clear mistakes in MBS's decade of rule, he shows no evidence of diminished confidence or of dwindling assertiveness. Indeed, as always his guiding philosophy continues to be, in his words, "If you see something to do, do it."[9]

Acknowledgments

My greatest gratitude goes to the hundreds of Saudis who agreed to speak to me over recent years about their history, culture, and religion and about the Crown Prince's new vision for Saudi Arabia. They are too numerous to name and, given the political repression in Saudi Arabia these days, most do not want to be identified.

I also want to thank Crown Prince Mohammed bin Salman, or MBS, the primary subject of this book. He met with me numerous times, often for several uninterrupted hours of conversation. He talked willingly about being reared in the shadows of his father's five elder sons, his early work in government, and the sources of his relentless drive to remake the kingdom his ancestors founded in 1727 and have ruled with two brief interruptions since. Whatever his flaws, in person he is candid, confident, and charismatic. At thirty-nine, he exudes energy, looks an interlocutor straight in the eyes, and evinces power but no regal airs. I also thank Defense Minister Khalid bin Salman for his essential security briefings and for sharing childhood stories of his brother MBS. I thank Dr. Osama Nasser, media adviser at the royal court, for securing my meetings with MBS. And I am grateful to his colleague Haitham Al Rashid, who, over much of my six years of reporting for this book, helped me meet not just cabinet ministers but also young Saudis now serving as tour guides and Uber drivers or working in hotels, restaurants, and spas, performing service jobs so long looked down upon by young Saudis.

With government no longer able to afford to hire any Saudi willing to work, MBS has begun to reshape the expectations of his population.

I also thank the many Saudi women who talked with me about their new opportunities in a kingdom that now has women ambassadors, an astronaut, and CEOs, roles that had been totally forbidden for women during my first three decades of reporting in the kingdom. Princess Reema bint Bandar al Saud, the kingdom's ambassador to Washington, D.C., encountered much opposition from the religious police as the country's first head of women's sports. She graciously helped me meet Saudis and shared her own story.

Above all, I am grateful to the ordinary Saudis who support MBS and also those who voiced privately their reservations about MBS's vision for their country. These days, Saudis are far more reluctant to speak openly than in previous decades when political repression existed but was less prevalent. They won't speak with cell phones in the room; walking outdoors is their preferred interview site.

I also want to thank my colleagues at Harvard's Belfer Center for their willingness to meet periodically to listen to my work and ask questions that helped guide me. Specifically, Megan O'Sullivan, director of the Belfer Center, and Graham Allison, former dean of the John F. Kennedy School of Government, encouraged this project as well as my first book on Saudi Arabia.

Robert Asahina, a gifted editor, greatly helped me focus on the organization of this book. My editor, Sean Desmond, was a wise guide who pushed me to provide the necessary context for first-time readers and yet keep the writing tightly focused on telling the story. I am also grateful to my agent, Michael Carlisle, for his expert support.

I thank my husband, Peter Kann, a Pulitzer Prize–winning journalist who read every word of this book several times, for his encouragement and wise editing advice. And I thank my fifteen-year-old granddaughter, Farrah Lane, for being so intrigued by my fixation on Saudi Arabia that she joined me for a ten-day trip there and loved it, a sign that the kingdom's tourism plans are one of MBS's better bets.

Notes

PROLOGUE | The Race to Rule

1. Dyan Abou Tine, "Saudi Arabia's Tax Revenue Surge Fuels 2023 Budget Growth," *Arab News*, February 18, 2024, https://www.arabnews.com /node/2462131/amp.

CHAPTER ONE | Young Man in a Hurry

1. Author interview with Deputy Crown Prince Mohammed at Irqah Palace, Riyadh, January 26, 2016.

2. Author interview in Miami, August 22, 2023.

3. Author interview with the source, September 4, 2023.

4. Author interview with Minister Majid Al Qasabi, Riyadh, March 2, 2023.

5. Alexi Vassilev, *The History of Saudi Arabia* (New York: New York University Press, 2000), 239.

6. Christine Helms Moss, *The Cohesion of Saudi Arabia* (Baltimore: Johns Hopkins University Press, 1981), 259.

7. "MBS: My Strange Experience of Teaching the Saudi Crown Prince," BBC, December 9, 2018, https://www.bbc.com/news/world-middle-east-46437631.amp.

8. Nada Al Turki, "Saudi Crown Prince Unveils National Gaming and Esports Strategy," *Arab News*, September 15, 2021, https://www.arabnews.com /node/2163196/sport.

9. Author interview with Prince Abdullah bin Bandar, October 2021.

10. Author interview with Prince Khalid at the Saudi embassy in Washington, DC, May 2018.

11. Author interview with Dr. Issam bin Saeed in his Riyadh office, March 14, 2023.

12. Author interview, Issam bin Saeed, March 14, 2023.

13. Author interview with the Crown Prince in Riyadh, March 3, 2023.

14. Author interview with Deputy Crown Prince Mohammed bin Salman in Riyadh, January 16, 2016.

15. Author interview with Prince Khalid at the Saudi embassy in Washington, DC, May 2018.

16. Justin Scheck and Bradley Hope, "I Am the Mastermind: Mohammed bin

Salman's Guide to Getting Rich," *Wall Street Journal*, May 16, 2018, https://www.wsj.com/articles/i-am-the-mastermind-mohammed-bin-salmans-guide-to-getting-rich-1526487353.

17. Author interview with Crown Prince Mohammed bin Salman, Riyadh, March 3, 2023.

CHAPTER TWO | Kinder, Gentler Islam

1. Yaroslav Trofimov, *The Siege of Mecca* (New York: Doubleday, 2007).

2. Yaroslav Trofimov, *The Siege of Mecca*, 239.

3. Yaroslav Trofimov, *The Siege of Mecca*, 225.

4. Alexi Vassiliev, *The History of Arabia* (New York: New York University Press, 2000), 155.

5. Linda Bilmes, "The Financial Legacy of Iraq and Afghanistan: How Wartime Spending Decisions Will Constrain Future National Security Budgets," Harvard Kennedy School Faculty Research Working Paper Series, March 2013, https://www.hks.harvard.edu/publications/financial-legacy-iraq-and-afghanistan-how-wartime-spending-decisions-will-constrain#:~:text=The%20Iraq%20and%20Afghanistan%20conflicts,and%20social%20and%20economic%20costs.

6. Christine Moss Helms, *The Cohesion of Saudi Arabia* (Baltimore: Johns Hopkins University Press, 1981), 92.

7. H. C. Armstrong, *Lord of Arabia* (Riyadh: King Abdul Aziz Foundation, 2005), 151.

8. Rachael Bronson, *Thicker than Oil: America's Uneasy Partnership with Saudi Arabia* (New York: Oxford University Press, 2006), 17.

9. Michael Corbett, "Oil Shock of 1973–74," Federal Reserve Bank of Boston, Federal Reserve History, October 1973–January 1974, https://www.federalreservehistory.org/essays/oil-shock-of-1973-74#:~:text=The%20embargo%20ceased%20U.S.%20oil,a%20barrel%20in%20January%201974.

10. Vivienne Walt, "Saudi Arabia Has the Most Profitable Company in the History of the World, and $3.2 Trillion to Invest by 2030. Who Will Say No to That Tidal Wave of Cash?" *Forbes*, August 1, 2023, https://fortune.com/2023/08/01/saudi-aramco-profitable-oil-company-trillions/amp/.

11. Ryan Vlastelica and Matt Turner, "Saudi Aramco Becomes World's Most Valuable Stock as Apple Drops," Bloomberg, May 11, 2022, https://www.bloomberg.com/news/articles/2022-05-11/saudi-aramco-becomes-world-s-most-valuable-stock-as-apple-drops?sref=2WyzsxDC.

12. Ben Dummett, "Saudi Arabia Aims to Raise Up to $12 Billion in Fresh Aramco Stock Sale," *Wall Street Journal*, May 30, 2024, https://www.wsj

.com/business/energy-oil/saudi-arabia-aims-to-raise-up-to-12-billion-in-fresh
-aramco-stock-sale-8a2387c3?st=zq1qoob9tskxoi5&reflink=article_email_share.

13. Author interview in Riyadh, 2018.

14. David Rundell, *Vision or Mirage: Saudi Arabia at the Crossroads* (London: Tauris, 2021), 132.

15. Author interviews separately with a minister and a deputy minister in March 2009.

16. "Saudis Wishing to Own Homes Left with Limited Options," *Arab News*, April 19, 2011, https://www.arabnews.com/node/374865.

17. John Sfakianakis, "Employment Quandary: Youth Struggle to Find Work Raises Urgency for reform," Bank Saudi Fransi, February 16, 2011, 3.

18. Author interview with Adel Fakieh, Saudi minister of labor, February 5, 2011.

CHAPTER THREE | The Path to Power

1. Tom Friedman, "Saudi Arabia's Arab Spring at Last," *New York Times,* November 23, 2017.

2. "Saudi Foreign Direct Inflows," Trading Economics, https://tradingeconomics
.com/saudi-arabia/foreign-direct-investment#:~:text=Foreign%20Direct
%20Investment%20in%20Saudi%20Arabia%20averaged%203676.55
%20USD%20Million,the%20fourth%20quarter%20of%202017.

3. Karen D. Young, "Saudi Arabia's Problem Isn't Canada Fight but Capital Flight," Bloomberg News, August 17, 2018; https://www.bloomberg.com
/view/articles/2018-08-17/saudi-arabia-s-problem-not-the-canada-fight-but
-capital-flight?sref=2WyzsxDC.

4. Author interview with Prince Talal bin Abdul Aziz at his home in Riyadh, January 9, 2016.

5. Author interview at the minister's office in Riyadh, March 2, 2023.

6. "Haia, Police Officers Face Trial in Fatal Car Chase," *Arab News,* June 3, 2013, https://www.arabnews.com/node/453748/amp.

7. "Saudi Religious Police Members Acquitted in Fatal Car Chase Case," Al Arabia News, June 10, 2014, https://english.alarabiya.net/amp/News/middle
-east/2014/06/10/Haia-men-in-fatal-car-chase-acquitted.

8. "Saudis Tweet Anger at Religious Police Following Car Chase Death," AlArabia News, September 27, 2013, https://english.alarabiya.net
/variety/2013/09/27/Saudis-tweet-anger-at-religious-police-following-car
-chase-death.

9. Author interview with the pollster in Riyadh, January 12, 2018.

10. Ibid.

11. "Saudi Cleric Apologizes for 'Intolerant' Views of Sahwa Movement," *Arab News*, May 7, 2019, https://www.arabnews.com/node/1493956/saudi-arabia.

12. Author interview with a prominent government academic, January 7, 2016.

13. H. C. Armstrong, *Lord of Arabia: Ibn Saud* (New York: Kegan Paul International, 1998), 57–60.

14. David Rundell, *Vision or Mirage: Saudi Arabia at the Crossroads* (London: Tauris, 2021), 69.

15. "Former Saudi Crown Prince Pledges Allegiance to Mohammed bin Salman," YouTube, uploaded by Al Arabiya English, posted June 21, 2017. https://www.youtube.com/watch?v=MEaqocoZVF8.

16. Dr. Abdulrahman al-Hadlag, general director of Ideological Security Directorate, Ministry of Interior, interview by the author, October 10, 2009.

17. Margherita Stancati, Summer Said, and Benoit Faucon, "The Price of Freedom for Saudi Arabia's Richest Man: $6 Billion," *Wall Street Journal*, December 23, 2017, https://www.wsj.com/articles/the-price-of-freedom-for-saudi-arabias-richest-man-6-billion-1513981887.

18. Erik Schatzker, "Prince Alwaleed Reveals Secret Deal Struck to Exit Ritz After 83 Days," Bloomberg, March 20, 2018, https://www.bloomberg.com/news/features/2018-03-20/alwaleed-reveals-secret-deal-struck-to-exit-ritz-after-83-days?sref=2WyzsxDC.

19. Armstrong, *Lord of Arabia*, 96.

CHAPTER FOUR | Early Omens

1. "How Is Saudi Arabia Reacting to Low Oil Prices?" World Bank, July 28, 2016, https://www.worldbank.org/en/country/gcc/publication/economic-brief-july-saudi-arabia-2016#:~:text=To%20emerge%20from%20the%20era,from%20oil%2C%20within%2015%20years.

2. "Saudis Angry at Accusations of Laziness," *Saudi Gazette*, October 25, 2016, https://english.alarabiya.net/en/business/economy/2016/10/25/Saudis-angry-at-accusations-of-laziness-html.

3. Author interview with Mohammed al-Sheikh, March 2023.

4. Interview with Mohammed al-Sheikh.

5. Interview with Mohammed al-Sheikh.

6. Saudi Arabian Monetary Authority, "Gross Domestic Product—Quarterly Growth Rate," www.sama.gov.sa.

7. "Saudi Arabia Restores Perks to State Employees Boosting Markets," Reuters, April 23, 2017, https://www.reuters.com/article/us-saudi

-economy/saudi-arabia-restores-perks-to-state-employees-boosting-markets -idUSKBN17O0NL.

8. "Meet Alwaleed bin Talal Al Saud and His Royal Family; Know Their Gold-Plated Supercars, Palaces, $1.4 Trillion Net Worth and More," Financial Express Leisure, April 11, 2023, https://www.financialexpress.com/lifestyle /meet-alwaleed-bin-talal-al-saud-and-his-royal-family-know-about-their-gold -plated-supercars-palaces-1-4-trillion-net-worth-more/3041651/.

9. "Meet Alwaleed bin Talal Al Saud and His Royal Family."

10. Prableen Bajpal, "An Overview of the Trillion Dollar Economies in the World," Nasdaq, April 22, 2022, https://www.nasdaq.com/articles/an -overview-of-the-trillion-dollar-economies-in-the-world?amp.

11. Saudi Arabia Data, https://data.worldbank.org/country/SA.

12. Oil Reserves by Country, World Population Review, https:// worldpopulationreview.com/country-rankings/oil-reserves-by-country.

13. Saudi Arabia Oil Summary Table, https://www.worldometers.info/oil /saudi-arabia-oil/#:~:text=Oil%20Reserves%20in%20Saudi%20Arabia &text=Saudi%20Arabia%20has%20proven%20reserves,levels%20and %20excluding%20unproven%20reserves.

14. Author interview, January 2018, in Riyadh.

15. "Saudi Arabia Approves the Citizen's Account Policy," Al Arabiya, December 12, 2017, https://english.alarabiya.net/News/gulf/2017/12/12/Saudi-Arabia-to -launch-citizen-payment-program.

16. Abdul Rahman Buzian, "Guide to Citizen's Account Program," Albawaba, June 23, 2023, https://www.albawaba.net/business/guide-saudis-citizen -account-program-1521230.

17. Buzian.

18. Author interview in Jeddah, March 2022.

19. Author interview in Riyadh with Minister Abdullah Swaha, November 3, 2021.

20. "Saudi Arabia Ranks Among Top Countries in Digital Transformation Preparedness," Arab News, March 19, 2023, https://www.arabnews.com /node/2271421/saudi-arabia.

21. Author interview with Princess Reema bint Bandar, Washington, DC, September 2022.

22. Interview with Princess Reema bint Bandar.

23. Mohammed Al Sulami and Rawan Radwan, "Saudi Arabia Approves Physical Education Program in Girls' Schools," Arab News, July 11, 2017, https://www .arabnews.com/node/1127811/amp.

24. "GASTAT Issues Saudi Women's Report 2022," August 13, 2023, https://www.stats.gov.sa/en/news/472.

25. Author interview with Faisal Ibrahim, March 2023 in Riyadh.

26. Author interview with Mohammed al Sheikh, January 2018.

CHAPTER FIVE | Heavy Lies the Head

1. Author interview with Jamal Khashoggi, Khozama Hotel, Riyadh, January 23, 2016.

2. Quran, Sura An-Nisa 4:108.

3. Sahih Bukhari 6178.

4. Bradley Hope and Justin Scheck, *Blood and Oil* (New York: Hachette, 2020), 113.

5. Hope and Scheck, 119.

6. Brakkton Booker, "Saudi Crown Prince on Killing of Jamal Khashoggi: 'It Happened under My Watch,'" NPR, September 26, 2019, https://www.npr.org/2019/09/26/764604566/saudi-crown-prince-on-killing-of-jamal-khashoggi-it-happened-under-my-watch#:~:text=Saudi%20Arabia's%20Crown%20Prince%20Mohammed,Washington%20Post%20journalist%20Jamal%20Khashoggi.

7. Robert Massie, *Peter the Great: His Life and World* (New York: Random House, 1980), 707.

8. Tom Holmberg, "The d'Enghein Affair: Crime or Blunder," Napoleon Series Archive, https://www.napoleon-series.org/research/miscellaneous/c_enghien.html#:~:text=In%20his%20will%2C%20Napoleon%20wrote,in%20the%20same%20way%20again.

9. H. St. John Philby, *Sa'udi Arabia* (Ernest Benn: London, 1955), 313.

10. "Khashoggi Suspect Saud al-Qahtani Seen in Public for the First Time Since Murder," Middle East Eye, June 19, 2023, https://www.middleeasteye.net/news/saudi-arabia-khashoggi-suspect-qahtani-seen-public-first-time.

11. Scott Shane, "The Lessons of Anwar al-Awlaki," *New York Times*, August 27, 2015, https://www.nytimes.com/2015/08/30/magazine/the-lessons-of-anwar-al-awlaki.html?smid=nytcore-ios-share&referringSource=articleShare.

CHAPTER SIX | Women Win

1. Sa'eed ibn ali ibn Wahf al-Qahtani, *Fortification of the Muslim Through Remembrance and Supplication from the Quran and Sunnah*, trans. Ishmael Ibraheem (Riyadh: Ministry of Islamic Affairs, 1998), No. 74, 209.

2. Andrew Pereira, "Can MBS Achieve the Objectives of Vision 2030 Without

the Participation of Women?" Statecraft, May 5, 2021, https://www.statecraft
.co.in/article/can-mbs-achieve-the-objectives-of-vision-2030-without-the
-participation-of-women.

3. "Underground Sport: Saudi Women Shed Veils to Play Basketball," Associated
   Press, May 8, 2008, https://usatoday30.usatoday.com/news/world/2008-05
   -08-saudi-sports_n.htm.

4. Author interview with Sara al-Suhaimi at her home, Riyadh, May 2017.

5. Martin Lings, *Muhammed: His Life Based on the Earliest Sources* (Rochester,
   VT: Inner Traditions, 2006), 35.

6. Lings, 191.

7. Author interview with Sheikh Mutlag, October 2009, Riyadh.

8. Author interview with Mohammed al-Sheikh, June 27, 2018, Riyadh.

9. Author interview with Joharah al-Sheikh and her parents, January 25, 2019,
   Riyadh.

10. Jeffrey Goldberg, "Saudi Crown Prince: Iran's Supreme Leader Makes
    Hitler Look Good," *Atlantic*, April 2, 2018, https://www.theatlantic.com
    /international/archive/2018/04/mohammed-bin-salman-iran-israel/557036/.

11. Author interview at the Khozama Hotel, Riyadh, October 2021.

12. Author meeting on June 30, 2018, with professional Saudi women at Nozumi
    restaurant in Riyadh.

13. Author interview with Rayyanah Barnawi in Riyadh, November 6, 2023.

14. Author interview in Riyadh with Dr. Val Munsami, deputy CEO of Saudi
    Space Agency, November 2023.

15. "Saudi Arabia: Law Enshrines Male Guardianship," Human Rights Watch,
    March 8, 2023, https://www.hrw.org/news/2023/03/08/saudi-arabia-law
    -enshrines-male-guardianship#:~:text=The%20Personal%20Status
    %20Law%20under,a%20male%20guardian%20to%20marry.

16. Julia Buckley, "Saudi Arabia Says It Welcomes LGBTQ visitors," CNN, May 5,
    2023, https://www.cnn.com/travel/article/saudi-arabia-lgbt-tourists/index
    .html.

17. "Saudi Arabia's Private Sector Workers Grow to 11.2m in March," Argaam,
    April 17, 2024, https://www.argaam.com/en/article/articledetail/id/1720173
    #:~:text=The%20total%20number%20of%20workers,the%20National
    %20Labor%20Observatory%20said.

18. "Saudi Arabia's Workforce Strength at 14.6 Million by Q3 2022, 64% Private
    Sector," Argaam, January 30, 2023, https://www.argaam.com/en/article
    /articledetail/id/1618068#:~:text=The%20number%20of%20workers
    %20in,Domestic%20workers%20constituted%20about%2025%25.

19. "Saudi Arabia's Workforce Strength."

20. "Unemployment Among Saudis Declines to 7.7% in Q4," Reuters, March 28, 2024, https://www.reuters.com/world/middle-east/unemployment-among -saudis-declines-77-q4-2024-03-28/.

21. Author interview, Riyadh, March 7, 2023.

CHAPTER SEVEN | Castles in the Sand

1. "Seven Breaks Ground at SAR 1.3 Billion Entertainment Destination in AlMadinah," *Arab News*, July 31, 2023, https://www.arabnews.com /node/2347396/saudi-arabia.

2. "The Line: The Future of Urban Living," Neom, https://www.neom.com /en-us/regions/theline?gclid=CjoKCQjwl8anBhCFARIsAKbbpySUsdjosk9dt 5ibet4qGBXLBPIJrvVaVfAGjAM9ZSudoa-OFFCmkxgaAkjEEALw_wcB.

3. Public Investment Fund, "The Mukaab: A Gateway to Another World," YouTube, February 16, 2023, https://www.youtube.com/watch?v=Dj2jErpwQQk.

4. IBIS World, https://www.ibisworld.com/global/market-size/global-tourism /#:~:text=The%20market%20size%2C%20measured%20by,to%20increase %2013.9%25%20in%202023.

5. "Saudi Arabia Records 93.5 mln Tourists and Total Spending of $49 Billion in 2022," *Saudi Gazette*, February 16, 2023, https://www.zawya.com/en /business/travel-and-tourism/saudi-arabia-records-935mln-tourists-and-total -spending-of-4933bln-in-2022-csk4g3iq?amp=1.

6. Josh Corder, "Saudi Arabia Says Its 100 Million Visitor Goal Is 'No Longer Sufficient,'" Skift, September 27, 2023, https://skift.com/2023/09/27/saudi -arabia-visitor-target-middle-east-newsletter/.

7. "Saudi Arabia: UN experts Alarmed by Imminent Executions Linked to NEOM Project," United Nations, Office of the High Commissioner for Human Rights, May 3, 2023, https://www.ohchr.org/en/press-releases/2023/05/saudi -arabia-un-experts-alarmed-imminent-executions-linked-neom-project.

8. "NEOM and Volocopter: First Electric Air Taxi Flight in Saudi Arabia," Neom, June 21, 2023, https://www.neom.com/en-us/newsroom/neom -volocopter-evtol.

9. Discovery, "'The Line': Saudi Arabia's City of the Future in NEOM," YouTube, June 26, 2023.

10. Discovery.

11. Discovery.

12. Author interview with Jerry Speyer at his New York headquarters, March 4, 2024.

13. Author interview with a senior Saudi government official, June 2017 in New York City.

14. "Amaala Company," World Tourism Organization, https://www.unwto
.org/affiliate-member-organization/597896#:~:text=AMAALA%2C%20located
%20along%20Saudi%20Arabia's,purity%20of%20the%20Red%20Sea.

15. "Saudis' Red Sea Development Is the Size of Belgium Says RSG Boss,"
Arabian Business, August 2, 2023; https://www.arabianbusiness.com/industries
/construction/saudis-red-sea-development-is-the-size-of-belgium-says-
rsg-boss.

16. Rory Jones, "The World's Biggest Construction Project Is a Magnet for
Executives Behaving Badly," Wall Street Journal, September 11, 2024, https://
www.wsj.com/business/the-worlds-biggest-construction-project-is-a-magnet
-for-executives-behaving-badly-9accd37b?st=2v24ghzq3qglije&reflink=article
_email_share.

17. Rory Jones, "The World's Biggest Construction Project Is a Magnet for
Executives Behaving Badly."

18. Rory Jones and Eliot Brown, "CEO of Saudi Arabia's Futuristic City Project
Leaves Abruptly," Wall Street Journal, November 12, 2024, https://www.wsj
.com/world/middle-east/ceo-of-saudi-arabias-futuristic-city-project-leaves
-abruptly-43489eb4?st=LaWn1a&reflink=article_email_share.

19. Author interview, March 2023.

20. Robert Looney, "Saudi Arabia Chases a Mirage," Milken Institute Review,
December 17, 2020.

21. "King Abdullah Financial District," Bin Laden Group, https://www.bcg-uae
.com/projects/king-abdullah-financial-district/.

22. Marwa Rashad, Tom Arnold, and Katie Paul, "Exclusive: Saudi State Finalized
Ownership Transfer of $10 Billion Financial District," Reuters, May 3, 2018,
https://www.reuters.com/article/us-saudi-economy-finance-exclusive/exclusive
-saudi-state-finalized-ownership-transfer-of-10-billion-financial-district
-idUSKBN1I41YK.

23. "Only Three Percent of Projects Finish on Time: Study," Arab News, May 19,
2011, arabnews.com/saudiarabia/article415376.ece?service=print.

24. Ahmed al-Omran and Tom Wilson, "Saudi Arabia Transfers $163 Billion
Stake of Oil Producer Aramco to Its Wealth Fund," Financial Times, March 7,
2024, https://www.ft.com/content/fe8754eb-11ef-4b08-875f-8e1b17c47d01.

25. Julie Steinberg and Stephen Kalin, "Hunt for Critical Minerals Draws World
Powers to Saudi Arabia," Wall Street Journal, July 12, 2024, https://www.wsj
.com/world/middle-east/hunt-for-critical-minerals-draws-world-powers-to
-saudi-arabia-097aca8c.

26. Steinberg and Kalin.

27. Jeremy Mazur, "Texas Is America's Energy Expansion Leader," Texas 2036,
https://texas2036.org/posts/texas-is-americas-energy-expansion

-leader/#:~:text=In%20the%20intervening%20decade%2C%20production,of
%20U.S.%20production%20by%202023.

28. "Texas Energy Sector Goes Beyond Oil and Gas," Texas Economic Development
Corporation, April 4, 2022, https://businessintexas.com/ceo-blog/texass-energy
-sector-goes-beyond-oil-and-gas/#:~:text=By%20one%20account%2C%20the
%20oil,26%25%20of%20natural%20gas%20production.

29. Christopher Slijk and Keith Phillips, "Once Oil Dependent Texas Economy to Keep
Growing as Renewable Energy Expands," Federal Reserve Bank of Dallas, third
quarter 2021, https://www.dallasfed.org/research/swe/2021/swe2103/swe2103b.

30. Saudi Arabia GDP Growth Oil Sector, https://tradingeconomics.com/saudi
-arabia/gdp-growth-oil-sector#:~:text=This%20page%20includes%20a
%20chart,updated%20on%20August%20of%202023.&text=Saudi
%20Arabia%20is%20the%20world,for%2046%20percent%20of%20GDP.

CHAPTER EIGHT | The Sports of Kings

1. "FIFA International Transfer Snapshot Confirms Record-Breaking Figures,"
press release, Inside FIFA, September 8, 2023, https://www.fifa.com/legal
/media-releases/fifa-international-transfer-snapshot-confirms-record
-breaking-figures.

2. Christine Gough, "Total Sports Market Revenue Worldwide, 2022–2027,"
Statista, July 13, 2023, https://www.statista.com/statistics/370560/worldwide
-sports-market-revenue/.

3. Steve Henson, "Move Over Ronaldo, Messi. Jon Rahm Is Highest Paid Athlete
in 2023 after Joining LIV," Los Angeles Times, December 8, 2023, https://www
.latimes.com/sports/story/2023-12-08/jon-rahm-liv-golf-highest-paid-athlete
-pga-tour-merger-saudi-arabia-public-investment-fund.

4. "Crown Prince Says He Doesn't Care About Sports Washing," Fox News,
September 22, 2023, https://www.youtube.com/watch?v=GltwJeWsKaw.

5. Paul MacInnes, "Fifa Is 'Ignoring Human Rights Report' into Saudi Arabia's
2034 World Cup Bid," Guardian, October 11, 2024, https://search.app
/TUmGw3ZEbLJR3qn27.

6. Ewan West, "Rafael Nadal gives brutally honest verdict on Saudi Arabia
criticism and sports washing claims," Tennis 365, October 23, 2024, https://
www.tennis365.com/tennis-news/rafael-nadal-brutally-honest-saudi-arabia
-criticism-sportswashing.

7. "Saudi Cup 2023 Frankie Dettori Eyes $20 Million Prize in World's Richest
Horse Race," Arabian Business, February 24, 2023, https://www
.arabianbusiness.com/lifestyle/lifestyle-sport/saudi-cup-2023-frankie-dettori
-eyes-20m-prize-in-worlds-richest-horse-race#:~:text=Saudi%20Cup
%20horse%20racing%20events,horse%20race%20in%20the%20world.

8. Tim Schmitt, "LIV Golf's Anti-trust Lawsuit Against PGA Tour Handed Severe Blow in Federal Court," *USA Today*, February 17, 2023, https://golfweek.usatoday.com/2023/02/17/liv-golf-news-pga-tour-antitrust-lawsuit-california-court/.

9. Jeff Eisenberg, "It's Not About Sports Washing," Yahoo News, July 24, 2023, https://sports.yahoo.com/its-not-about-sportswashing-045550926.html.

10. Andrew Beaton and Louise Radnofsky, "Steve Cohen, John Henry Group Set to Invest Billions in PGA Tour," *Wall Street Journal*, January 29, 2024, https://www.wsj.com/sports/golf/pga-tour-steve-cohen-john-henry-arthur-blank-liv-golf-f3069958?st=x5g00i7scwlee2g&reflink=article_gmail_share.

11. Andrew Hankinson, "Saudi Arabia's Purchase of Newcastle United Sparks Debate," Air Mail News, October 5, 2024, https://airmail.news/issues/2024-10-5/the-view-from-here.

12. Karim Zidan and Tariq Panja, "Lionel Messi, Saudi Arabia and the Deal That Paid Off for Both Sides," *New York Times*, June 18, 2023, https://www.nytimes.com/2023/06/18/sports/soccer/lionel-messi-saudi-arabia.html?smid=nytcore-ios-share&referringSource=articleShare.

13. Chris Evert and Martina Navratilova, "We Did Not Help Build Women's Tennis for It to Be Exploited by Saudi Arabia," *Washington Post*, January 24, 2024, https://www.washingtonpost.com/opinions/2024/01/24/evert-navratilova-wta-saudi-arabia/?_pml=1.

14. "Kasatkina Concerned About Potential Saudi Investment in WTA," Reuters, July 6, 2023, https://www.reuters.com/sports/tennis/kasatkina-concerned-about-potential-saudi-investment-wta-2023-07-06/.

15. "WTA Returns to China Despite Unresolved Questions About Tennis Star Peng Shuai," PBS, September 24, 2023, https://www.pbs.org/newshour/amp/show/wta-returns-to-china-despite-unresolved-questions-about-tennis-star-peng-shuai.

16. Matthew Martin and Randall Williams, "Saudi Arabia Sporting Expansion Rumbles on with MMA Deal," Bloomberg, August 30, 2023, https://www.bloomberg.com/news/articles/2023-08-30/saudi-arabia-buys-stake-in-professional-martial-arts-league?sref=2WyzsxDC.

17. "His Royal Highness the Crown Prince Announces Savvy Games Group Strategy," Savvy Games Group, September 29, 2022; https://savvygames.com/his-royal-highness-the-crown-prince-announces-savvy-games-group-strategy/.

18. Carla Sertin, "Savvy Games Has $38 Billion to Build a Saudi Gaming Sector; Here's How They Plan to Do It," *Wired*, November 21, 2023, https://wired.me/business/savvy-games-saudi-pif-interview/.

19. Sertin.

20. Bindu Rai, "Gaming Revenues in MEA to Reach $7.2 Billion in 2023; Saudi Arabia Emerges as Key Player," Zawya, https://www.zawya.com/en/business /technology-and-telecom/gaming-revenues-in-mea-to-reach-72bln-in-2023 -saudi-arabia-emerges-as-key-player-ud2s2fxp?amp=1.

21. Annie Pei, "This Esports Giant Draws More Viewers than the Super Bowl and It's Expected to Get Bigger," CNBC, April 14, 2019, https:/www.cnbc .com/2019/04/14/league-of-legends-gets-more-viewers-than-super-bowlwhats -coming-next.html.

22. "Saudi Arabia Launches Esports World Cup," Reuters, October 23, 2023, https://www.reuters.com/sports/saudi-arabia-announces-esports-world-cup -statement-2023-10-23/.

CHAPTER NINE | Six Flags over Saudi Arabia

1. Quran, Sura An-Nisa, verse 77.

2. Author interview, November 8, 2023, Digital City, Riyadh.

3. "Tuwaiq," Wikipedia, accessed January 14, 2024, https://en.m.wikipedia.org /wiki/Tuwaiq.

4. Eric Revell, "Record-Shattering Roller Coaster Simulates Falling from a Cliff with 155 mph Speeds," Fox Business, November 19, 2023, https://www.fox-business.com/lifestyle/record-shattering-roller-coaster-simulates-falling-from-cliff-with-155-mph-speeds.amp.

5. Author interview in Riyadh, April 2024.

CHAPTER TEN | Pied Piper

1. Noor Nugali and Jonathan Gornall, "The Inside Story of Saudi Arabia's Founding Day, Celebrating the Year It All Began," *Arab News*, February 22, 2022, https://www.arabnews.com/node/2029316/saudi-arabia.

2. Nugali and Gornall.

3. Zaina Fattah, "Saudi Developer to Spend $10 Billion on Diriyah Project in 2024," Bloomberg, October 25, 2023, https://www.bloomberg.com/news /articles/2023-10-25/saudi-developer-to-spend-10-billion-on-diriyah-project -in-2024?sref=2WyzsxDC.

4. Culinary Arts Commission, https://culinary.moc.gov.sa/en/about-the -commission.

5. "Founding Day Puts the National History on the Right Track," *Saudi Gazette*, February 22, 2023, https://saudigazette.com.sa/article/630028/SAUDI -ARABIA/Founding-Day-puts-the-nations-history-on-right-track.

6. Kingdom of Saudi Arabia Founding Day Sky Show, https://executivevisions
   .com/event/founding-day-sky-show-celebration.

7. Mariam Nabbout, "MBS Wears Jacket over Thobe and Suddenly Everyone
   Wants One," November 22, 2019, https://stepfeed.com/mbs-wears-jacket
   -over-thobe-and-suddenly-everyone-wants-one-7739.

8. "Demand Goes Through the Roof for Saudi Crown Prince's Al Ula
   Brunello Cucinelli's Zip-Up Gilet," *Arab News*, January 28, 2023; https://
   www.arabnews.com/node/2240446/lifestyle.

9. Author interview, May 2017 in Riyadh.

10. Author interview, October 2017 Riyadh.

11. Abdullah Ansari, "Prophet Saleh and the People of Thamud Story in the
    Quran," Quran for Kids, December 30, 2020, https://quranforkids.com/story
    -of-prophet-saleh/.

12. Author interview, Riyadh, March 13, 2023, via Zoom with Mohammed
    al-Essa in London.

13. Ibn Khaldun, *The Muqaddimah: An Introduction to History* (Princeton, NJ:
    Princeton University Press, 1967), 105–6.

14. David Rundell, *Vision or Mirage: Saudi Arabia at the Crossroads* (London:
    Tauris, 2020), 90.

15. David Hogarth, *The Desert King: The Life of Ibn Saud* (London: William
    Collins, 1965), 118.

16. Hogarth, 90.

17. Author interview in Riyadh with Prince Salman, April 28, 2010.

18. Ilan Zalayat, "Saudi Arabia's New Nationalism: Embracing Jahiliyyah,"
    Dayan, July 27, 2022; https://dayan.org/content/saudi-arabias-new
    -nationalism-embracing-jahiliyyah.

19. Eman Alhussein, "Saudi First: How Hyper-nationalism Is Transforming Saudi
    Arabia," European Council on Foreign Relations, June 19, 2019, 7, https://ecfr.eu
    /publication/saudi_first_how_hyper_nationalism_is_transforming_saudi_arabia/.

20. Alhussein.

21. Alhussein.

22. "Misk Strengthens Global Participation and Youth Dialogue at the 2023
    World Economic Forum, Davos," Misk, January 15, 2023, https://misk.org.sa
    /en/misk-davos-en/.

23. Author attendance at MISK Global Forum, Diriyah, November 15, 2023.

24. Author interview with Jared Kushner at his office in Sunny Isles, FL, August
    2023.

CHAPTER ELEVEN | Venturing Forth into the World

1. Timothy Gardner, Steve Holland, Dmitry Zhdannikov, and Rania El Gamal, "Special Report: Trump Told Saudi: Cut Oil Supply or Lose U.S. Military Support—Sources," Reuters, April 30, 2020, https://www.reuters.com /article/idUSKBN22C1V3/.

2. "Trump Threatened Saudi Crown Prince with Ending U.S. Military Support over Oil Output," New Arab, April 30, 2020, https://www.newarab.com /news/trump-pressured-saudi-threat-weapons-over-oil?amp.

3. Gardner et al., "Special Report."

4. Asharq Al Awsat, "Saudi Summit Eyes Strengthening Partnership with the Caribbean," Aawsat, November 16, 2023, https://english.aawsat.com /gulf/4671716-saudi-summit-eyes-strengthening-partnership-caribbean.

5. Valentyn Ogirenko and Aziz El Yaakoubi, "Russia, Ukraine Announce Major Surprise Prisoner Swap," Reuters, September 22, 2022, https://www.reuters .com/world/europe/russia-releases-10-foreigners-captured-ukraine-after -saudi-mediation-riyadh-2022-09-21/.

6. Daniel Brumberg, "The Russia-Ukraine Jeddah Meeting: A Win for MBS in a Changing Global Order," Arab Center, Washington, DC, August 24, 2023; https://arabcenterdc.org/resource/the-russia-ukraine-jeddah-meeting-a-win -for-mbs-in-a-changing-global-order/.

7. N. T. Wright, *Paul: A Biography* (New York: Harper One, 2018), 63–64.

8. William Cleveland, *History of the Modern Middle East* (Boulder, CO: Westview Press, 2004), 13–14.

9. Hal Brands, ed., *The New Makers of Modern Strategy* (Princeton, NJ: Princeton University Press, 2023), 5.

10. Ben Blanchard, "Saudi Arabia Strikes $10 Billion China Deal, Talks De-radicalization with Xi," Reuters, February 22, 2019, https://www.reuters.com /article/us-asia-saudi-china-idUSKCN1QB15H/.

11. Bruce Riedel, "Saudi Arabia's Relations with China: Functional, but Not Strategic," Brookings Institution, July 20, 2020, https://www.brookings.edu /articles/saudi-arabias-relations-with-china-functional-but-not-strategic/.

12. Riedel.

13. Mutib Al Harbi, Aramco Asia president, "China Is a Land of Opportunities," Aramco China, October 31, 2023, https://china.aramco.com/en/news-media /china-news/2023/exclusive-interview-of-aramco-asia-president-mutib-a-al -harbi#:~:text=%22Our%20cooperation%20with%20China%20has,reporter %20from%20China%20Energy%20News.

14. Ed White in Shanghai, Cheng Leng in Hong Kong, Ahmed Al Omran in Jeddah, and Alex Irwin-Hunt in London, "China's Ties with Saudi Arabia Buoyed by

Green Tech," *Financial Times*, December 3, 2024; https://www.ft.com /content/f0babafc-57e6-434f-9d94-013c312dcof9.

15. "At Riyadh Summit, Saudi Crown Prince Backs Iran, Accuses Israel of Genocide," *Times of Israel*, November 11, 2024, https://www.timesofisrael.com/at-riyadh -summit-saudi-crown-prince-backs-iran-accuses-israel-of-genocide/amp/.

16. *Fareed Zakaria GPS*, CNN, January 21, 2024, https://transcripts.cnn.com /show/fzgps/date/2024-01-21/segment/01.

CHAPTER TWELVE | Persian Peril

1. William L. Cleveland, *History of the Modern Middle East*, 3rd ed. (Boulder, CO: Westview Press, 2004), 13.

2. "Saudi Arabia Participates in International Conference on Combatting Sand Storms Held in Tehran," *Arab News*, September 12, 2023, https://www.arabnews .com/node/2371981/saudi-arabia.

3. Sam Dagher, "Saudi Arabia Offers Iran Investment to Blunt Gaza War," Bloomberg News, November 29, 2023, https://www.bloomberg.com/news /articles/2023-11-29/iran-saudi-proposals-seek-to-deescalate-tensions-amid -israel-hamas-war.

4. "Flashpoints: Iran and Saudi Arabia," *Iran Primer* (blog), U.S. Institute of Peace, September 18, 2019, https://iranprimer.usip.org/blog/2019/sep/18 /flashpoints-iran-and-saudi-arabia.

5. "Iran Calls for 'Puny Satan' Saudi Arabia to Be Stripped of Hajj Duties," Middle East Eye, September 6, 2016, https://www.middleeasteye.net/news /iran-calls-puny-satan-saudi-arabia-be-stripped-hajj-duties.

6. Tom Friedman, "Saudi Arabia's Arab Spring at Last," *New York Times*, November 23, 2017.

7. Friedman.

8. "Iran's Supreme Leader 'the New Hitler' Says Saudi Crown Prince," BBC News, November 24, 2017, https://www.bbc.com/news/world-middle -east-42108986.amp.

9. Ian Black, "Iran-Iraq Remember War That Cost More than a Million Lives," *Guardian*, September 23, 2010, https://amp.theguardian.com/world/2010 /sep/23/iran-iraq-war-anniversary.

10. "Imam Khamenei's Hajj Message-2016," https://english.khamenei.ir /news/4121/Hajj-hijacked-by-oppressors-Muslims-should-reconsider -management.

11. "Rafsanjani Starts 10-Day Visit to Saudi Arabia Today," *Tehran Times*, February 21, 1998, https://www.tehrantimes.com/news/7212/Rafsanjani-Starts-10-Day -Visit-to-Saudi-Arabia-Today.

12. "Timeline of Iran-Saudi Relations," *Iran Primer* (blog), U.S. Institute of Peace, June 6, 2023, https://iranprimer.usip.org/blog/2016/jan/06/timeline-iran-saudi-relations.

13. Faris Al Maari, "Clarifying the Status of Previous Iran-Saudi Agreements," Washington Institute for Near East Policy, March 16, 2023, https://www.washingtoninstitute.org/policy-analysis/clarifying-status-previous-iran-saudi-agreements.

14. Saud al-Zahed, "Hatred of Arabs Deeply Rooted in Persians, Says Iranian Intellectual," Al Arabiya, October 9, 2011, https://english.alarabiya.net/articles/2011%2F10%2F09%2F170927.

15. Oil Revenue Fact Sheet, Energy Information Administration, June 2023, https://www.eia.gov/international/analysis/special-topics/OPEC_Revenues_Fact_Sheet.

16. Iran Inflation Rate August 2023, Trading Economics, https://tradingeconomics.com/iran/inflation-cpi.

17. Author interview with Prince Abdul Aziz bin Salman, Riyadh, October 14, 2019.

18. David Sanger, "Candidate Biden Called Saudi Arabia a 'Pariah.' He Now Has to Deal with It," *New York Times*, February 24, 2021; https://www.nytimes.com/2021/02/24/us/politics/biden-jamal-khashoggi-saudi-arabia.htm.

19. Author interview, September 6, 2023.

20. *Saudi Arabia 2022 International Religious Freedom Report*, U.S. Department of State, 3, https://www.state.gov/wp-content/uploads/2023/05/441219-saudi-arabia-2022-international-religious-freedom-report.pdf.

21. Author interview with prominent Shia in Qatif, 2010.

22. *Saudi Arabia 2022 International Religious Freedom Report*, 9.

23. "Saudi Arabia Is the Mideast Drug Capital," *Foreign Policy*, December 20, 2021, https://foreignpolicy.com/2021/12/20/saudi-arabia-is-the-middle-easts-drug-capital/.

24. Sina Azodi, "A History of Continuity in Iran's Long Nuclear Program," *Iran Source* (blog), Atlantic Council, December 8, 2020, https://www.atlanticcouncil.org/blogs/iransource/a-history-of-continuity-in-irans-long-nuclear-program/.

25. Azodi.

26. "Saudi Crown Prince: If Iran Develops Nuclear Bomb, So Will We," CBS News, March 15, 2018, https://www.cbsnews.com/amp/news/saudi-crown-prince-mohammed-bin-salman-iran-nuclear-bomb-saudi-arabia/.

27. Katherine Malus, "From 'Atoms for Peace' to 'JCPOA': History of Iranian Nuclear Development," Columbia/K=1 Project, Center for Nuclear Studies,

September 9, 2018, https://k1project.columbia.edu/content/atoms-peace
-jcpoa-history-iranian-nuclear-development.

28. Azodi, "A History of Continuity in Iran's Long Nuclear Program."

29. "U.S. Intelligence on Iran's Nuclear Program," *Iran Primer* (blog), U.S.
Institute of Peace, July 11, 2023, https://iranprimer.usip.org/blog/2023/jul/11
/us-intelligence-iran%E2%80%99s-nuclear-program.

30. Laurence Norman and Michael R. Gordon, "Iran Is Better Positioned to
Launch Nuclear Weapons Program, New U.S. Intelligence Assessment
Says," *Wall Street Journal*, August 9, 2024, https://www.wsj.com/world
/middle-east/iran-is-better-positioned-to-launch-nuclear-weapons-program
-new-u-s-intelligence-assessment-says-e39b6c78?st=qmieuoanwarmgns
&reflink=article_email_share.

31. Malus, "From 'Atoms for Peace' to 'JCPOA.'"

32. David Albright, Sarah Burkhead, and Andrea Striker, "Analysis of IAEA's Iran
NPT Safeguard Report May 2024," Institute for Science and International
Security, May 31, 2024, https://isis-online.org/isis-reports/detail/analysis-of
-the-iaeas-iran-npt-safeguards-report-may-2024/.

33. "U.S. Intelligence on Iran's Nuclear Program."

34. Author interview, Prince Abdul Aziz bin Salman's office, Riyadh, October 2019.

35. "Saudi Arabia Plans to Use Domestic Uranium for Nuclear Fuel," Reuters,
January 11, 2023, https://www.reuters.com/business/energy/saudi-arabia
-plans-use-uranium-entire-nuclear-fuel-cycle-minister-says-2023-01-11/.

36. Andrew Hammond, "Saudi Arabia Signs IAEA Protocol as Nuclear Plans
Advance," Arabian Gulf Business Insight, August 9, 2024, https://www
.agbi.com/energy/2024/08/saudi-arabia-signs-iaea-protocol-as-nuclear
-plans-advance/.

CHAPTER THIRTEEN | The Human Element

1. Author interview by phone, June 8, 2024.

2. Freedom Index by Country, https://wisevoter.com/country-rankings/freedom
-index-by-country/.

3. "Saudi Arabia to Penalize Individuals Who Create or Promote Social Media
Content That Disrupts Public Order," *Arab News*, September 2018, https://
www.arabnews.com/node/1367236/amp.

4. "Human Rights and Rule of Law Index—Country Rankings," Global Economy,
2022, https://www.theglobaleconomy.com/rankings/human_rights_rule_law
_index/.

5. "2022 Country Reports on Human Rights Practices: Saudi Arabia," Bureau

of Democracy, Human Rights, and Labor, U.S. Department of State, https://
www.state.gov/reports/2022-country-reports-on-human-rights-practices
/saudi-arabia/#report-toc__exec-summary.

6. "Saudi Arabia: 20-Year Sentence for Tweets," Human Rights Watch, July 9, 2024,
    https://www.hrw.org/news/2024/07/09/saudi-arabia-20-year-sentence-tweets.

7. "Saudi Arabia: 20-Year Sentence for Tweets."

8. Dania Akkad, "Saudi Court Overturns Death Sentence Against Retired
    Teacher over Posts on X," Middle East Eye, August 7, 2024, https://www
    .middleeasteye.net/news/saudi-appeals-court-overturns-death-sentence-over
    -retired-teachers-tweets.

9. Author interview in Riyadh, May 2010.

10. "Cleric Salman al-Awdah 'Held over Qatar Tweet,'" Al Jazeera, January 7,
    2018, https://www.aljazeera.com/amp/news/2018/1/7/cleric-salman-al-awda
    -held-over-qatar-tweet.

11. "After the Expiry of His Sentence, Human Rights Defender Mohammed Al
    Qahtani's Whereabout Are Still Unknown," Front Line Defenders, December 22,
    2022, https://www.frontlinedefenders.org/en/case-after-expiry-his-sentence
    -human-rights-defender-mohammed-al-qahtani%E2%80%99s-whereabouts
    -are-still.

12. "Saudi Arabia: Enforced Disappearance of Mohammed al-Qahtani after
    Completing His Prison Sentence," OMCT World Organization Against
    Torture, November 23, 2022, https://www.omct.org/en/resources/statements
    /saudi-arabia-enforced-disappearance-of-mohammed-al-qahtani-after
    -completing-his-prison-sentence.

13. David Keyes, "Saudi Arabia's Degenerate New Law: Don't Criticize the
    Leaders," Yahoo News, May 16, 2011, https://news.yahoo.com/saudi-arabias
    -degenerate-law-dont-criticize-leaders-234103114.html.

14. "Saudi Arabia Ramps Up Clampdown on Human Rights Activists," Amnesty
    International, June 18, 2012, https://www.amnesty.org/en/latest/news/2012/06
    /saudi-arabia-ramps-up-clampdown-on-human-rights-activists/.

15. "Human Rights Activist Mikhlif Al-Shammari Sentenced to 2 Years in
    Prison," ALQST, January 5, 2015, https://www.alqst.org/en/mikhlif
    -alshammari.

16. Norah O'Donnell, "Saudi Arabia's Heir to the Throne Talks to 60 Minutes,"
    CBS News, March 19, 2018, https://www.cbsnews.com/amp/news/saudi
    -crown-prince-talks-to-60-minutes/.

17. Nazanin Boniadi, "Iranian Women Are Still Fighting," Time, September 14,
    2023, https://time.com/6313431/iran-women-defiant-amini-anniversary/.

18. Ali Shihabi, "The Need for Balance in Judging Saudi Arabia and Its Crown
    Prince," SMT Studies Center, February 9, 2019, https://smtcenter.net/en

/archives/slider/the-need-for-balance-in-judging-saudi-arabia-and-its-crown
-prince.

19. Niccolò Machiavelli, *The Discourses*, Book I, Chapter 58; Matthew Kroenig,
"Machiavelli and the Naissance of Modern Strategy," in *The New Makers of
Modern Strategy* (Princeton, NJ: Princeton University Press, 2023), 109.

20. Machiavelli, *The Discourses*, Book I, Chapter 10; Kroenig, "Machiavelli and
the Naissance of Modern Strategy," 110.

CHAPTER FOURTEEN | Gambling on the Future

1. Author interview with deputy crown prince in Riyadh, January 26, 2016.

2. Marvin Lee, "Saudi Vision 2030: What Are Saudi Arabia's Plans for the Future?" earth.org, September 21, 2021, https://earth.org/saudi-vision-2030.

3. "EIA Slashes US, Global Oil Demand Forecasts for 2025," Reuters, October 8,
2024, https://www.reuters.com/markets/commodities/eia-slashes-us-global
-oil-demand-forecasts-2025-2024-10-08/.

4. Bloomberg, "'Peak Oil' Will Arrive by 2030, IEA Predicts for the First Time,"
Fortune, October 24, 2023; https://fortune.com/2023/10/24/global-oil
-demand-peak-2030-iea-predicts-first-time/#.

5. Yousef Saba and Maha El Dahan, "Saudi Energy Minister Commits to Crude
Capacity Levels and Climate Targets," Reuters, October 29, 2024, https://
www.reuters.com/business/energy/saudi-energy-minister-commits-crude
-capacity-levels-climate-targets-2024-10-29/.

6. Zaynab Khojji, "Saudi Arabia Very Concerned About Climate Change and
Eager to Set Global Standards," *Arab News*, January 17, 2024, https://www
.arabnews.com/node/2443556/amp.

7. "Neom Green Hydrogen Company Completes Financial Close at a Total
Investment of $8.4 Billion in the World's Largest Carbon-Free Green Hydrogen
Plant," Neom, May 22, 2023, https://www.neom.com/en-us/newsroom/neom
-green-hydrogen-investment.

8. "Neom Green Hydrogen Company."

9. Author interview, Riyadh, October 2021.

10. Author interview, Riyadh, October 2021.

11. "Basic Energy Access Lags Amid Renewable Opportunities, New Report
Shows," International Energy Agency, June 6, 2023, https://www.iea.org
/news/basic-energy-access-lags-amid-renewable-opportunities-new-report
-shows.

12. "Some Key Takeaways from the COP28 Climate Summit," UN Environment
Programme, December 20, 2023, https://www.unep.org/news-and-stories
/story/some-key-takeaways-cop28-climate-summit.

13. "New KAUST Report on Climate Change in Saudi Arabia," KAUST, October 12, 2023, 9, https://www.kaust.edu.sa/en/news/new-kaust-report-on-climate-change-in-saudi-arabia#:~:text=The%20report%20highlights%20the%20stark,period%20of%201850%E2%80%931900.

14. Author interview with Minister Al Ibrahim in Riyadh, January 3, 2024.

15. "New KAUST Report on Climate Change in Saudi Arabia," 9.

16. "New KAUST Report," 82.

17. Author interview by phone, October 2023.

18. "Saudi Arabia's Workforce Hits 16.8 M by Q2-End," Argaam, March 11, 2024, https://www.argaam.com/en/article/articledetail/id/1765152.

19. Data provided by the Ministry of Human Resources and Development in March 2023.

20. Marissa Newman, "AI Leaders Gather in Saudi Arabia to Talk Energy," Bloomberg, October 30, 2024, https://www.bloomberg.com/news/newsletters/2024-10-30/ai-leaders-gather-in-saudi-arabia-to-talk-energy?sref=2WyzsxDC.

21. Gayatri Bhaumik, "The Cost of Living in Saudi Arabia," Expatica, January 8, 2024, https://www.expatica.com/sa/moving/about/cost-of-living-in-saudi-arabia-71066/.

22. Bhaumik.

23. Tim Callen, "If You Build It They Will Come: Prospects for Foreign Direct Investment in Saudi Arabia," Arab Gulf States Institute, Washington, DC, June 5, 2024, https://agsiw.org/if-you-build-it-they-will-come-prospects-for-foreign-direct-investment-in-saudi-arabia/.

24. Fareed Rahman, "Saudi Arabia's Series of Law Changes Eases Entry for Investment and Companies," The National, August 21, 2024, https://www.thenationalnews.com/business/economy/2024/08/22/saudi-arabias-new-laws-to-help-attract-more-investment-into-the-country/.

25. Grand Smith and Abeer Abu Omar, "Saudi Arabia Needs Oil Price Near $100, IMF Says," Bloomberg, April 18, 2024, https://www.bloomberg.com/news/articles/2024-04-18/saudi-arabia-needs-oil-price-near-100-amid-opec-cuts-imf-says?sref=2WyzsxDC.

26. Author interview with Minister Al Ibrahim in Riyadh, January 3, 2024.

27. Abeer Abu Omar, "IMF Says Saudi Slump Matched Argentina Among Worst G-20 Laggards," Bloomberg, January 30, 2024, https://www.bloomberg.com/news/articles/2024-01-30/imf-says-saudi-slump-matched-argentina-among-worst-g-20-laggards?embedded-checkout=true.

28. Omar.

29. Eliot Brown, "Saudi Arabia's $54 Billion Haul Still Leaves It Craving Cash," *Wall Street Journal*, June 21, 2024, https://www.wsj.com/world/middle-east/saudi-arabias-54-billion-haul-still-leaves-it-craving-cash-cb5c8b2c.

30. Author interview with Minister Al Ibrahim in Riyadh, January 3, 2024.

31. "Saudi Arabia: From the Big Push to the Long Push: Building Resilience Beyond 2030," Center for Sustainable Development and Global Competitiveness at Stanford University, August 2024, https://sdgc.stanford.edu/.

CHAPTER FIFTEEN | All in the Family

1. Joseph A. Kéchichian, *Succession in Saudi Arabia* (New York: Palgrave, 2001), 31.

2. Robert Lacey, *The Kingdom* (London and New York: Harcourt Brace Jovanovich, 1981), 318.

3. Kéchichian, *Succession in Saudi Arabia*, 15.

4. Lesley Hazelton, *After the Prophet: The Epic Story of the Sunni-Shia Split* (New York: Anchor Books, 2010), 138.

5. Author interview with Prince Khalid at the Saudi embassy in Washington, DC, May 10, 2018.

6. Author interview with Prince Khalid at his office in the Saudi embassy in Washington, DC, May 10, 2018.

7. Author interview with Prince Khalid at his home in McLean, VA, February 19, 2019.

8. Author interview with Prince Abdul Aziz bin Salman in Riyadh, October 2019.

9. "Saudi Arabia Forecasts $21 bln Deficit in 2024," Reuters, December 6, 2023, https://www.reuters.com/world/middle-east/view-saudi-arabia-forecasts-21-bln-deficit-2024-2023-12-06/.

10. Prince Abdul Aziz addressing MISK Foundation Global, Diriyah, November 15, 2023.

11. Author interview with Joseph Kéchichian via FaceTime in Beirut, October 11, 2024.

EPILOGUE | The Once and Future King

1. Author interview with the Crown Prince in Riyadh, March 3, 2023.

2. Suetonius, *The Twelve Caesars*, trans. Robert Graves (London: Penguin, 1957), 59.

3. Author interview with Mohammed bin Salman in Riyadh, March 3, 2023.

4. Matthew Dennison, *The Twelve Caesars: The Dramatic Lives of the Emperors of Rome* (New York: St. Martin's Press, 2012), 45.

5. Henry Kissinger, *Leadership* (New York: Penguin Press, 2022), xxiv.

6. Author interview with the Crown Prince in Riyadh, March 2023.

7. Kissinger, *Leadership*, 319.

8. Hal Brands, *The New Makers of Modern Strategy* (Princeton, NJ: Princeton University Press, 2023), 106.

9. Author interview with the Crown Prince, March 3, 2023.

Index

About the Author

KAREN ELLIOTT HOUSE is a former executive of Dow Jones & Company and publisher of the *Wall Street Journal*. She is also the author of *On Saudi Arabia: Its People, Past, Religion, Fault Lines— and Future*. She lives in Princeton, New Jersey.